FAITH AND INDUSTRIAL REFORMATION

FAITH AND INDUSTRIAL REFORMATION

Basel Mission in Malabar and South Canara

Jaiprakash Raghaviah

GYAN

First Published, 2022

Published by

Gyan Publishing House
5, Ansari Road
Daryaganj, New Delhi-110002
Phone: 9811692060
E-mail: books@gyanbooks.com

Printed at: G. Print Process, Delhi.

Cataloging in Publication Data—DK
Courtesy: D.K. Agencies (P) Ltd. <docinfo@dkagencies.com>

Raghaviah, Jaiprakash, author.
Faith and industrial reformation : Basel Mission in Malabar and South Canara / Jaiprakash Raghaviah.
pages cm
Includes bibliographical references and index.
ISBN 9788121214186 (HB)

1. Evangelische Missionsgesellschaft in Basel. 2. Industrialization—India—Malabar Coast—History. 3. Industrialization—India—South Kanara—History. 4. Malabar Coast (India)—Economic conditions. 5. South Kanara (India)—Economic conditions. I. Title.

LCC BV2365.S9R34 2018 | DDC 330.9548303 23

Dedicated to my sister

Pushpa Raghaviah

1-4-1949

to

30-8-1992

Contents

Foreword 11

Preface 19

Acknowledgement 21

1. Introduction 25

• Chapter scheme of the book • Notes.

2. The Basel Mission: Its Origin and Sense of Self 43

• Calvinism, Basel and enterprise • Towards a view of the world • Praxis of the Basel Mission in India • Dimensions of conversion • Islam and conversion • Caste and Christianity • Notes.

3. Malabar and South Canara - Economy and Society 73

• Malabar district - land and people • Economy of Malabar • Non-agricultural activities • Trade in Malabar • Population of Malabar • Land revenue policy • The land tenure system in Malabar • Towards agrarian unrest • Logan's findings • The Tharawadu as land owner • Other institutional barriers - the caste system • Concluding observations • South Canara - land and people • Land tenures in South Canara • Concentration of land • Conclusion • Commerce and industry in South Canara • Crafts and industries • Growth of the tile industry • Notes.

4. The Trajectory from Craft to Industry 115

• Early Phase • Middle Phase (1852-1881) • Organisation of production • Products of weaving factories • Extension of market • Printing and publishing • Trading activities • Mechanical Establishment • Final Phase (1882-1914) • Financial indicators • Employment and wages • Types of employment • Disciplining of the labour force • Changing attitudes of the British Government towards Basel Mission • First World War and after • Basel Mission Industries -the final questions • Notes.

5. Social Impact of the Basel Mission Industries 161

• Caste and conversion • Social mobility • Female participation in the activities of Basel Mission • The spread of literacy • Dr Hermann Gundert and his work • Contribution of the Basel Mission to Kannada literature • Ferdinand Kittel's contributions to the Kannada language • Basel Mission's contribution to Tulu literature • Medical work of the Basel Mission • Notes.

6. Re-engineering of the Self 193

• Handling of contradictory viewpoints • Love, courtship and marriage • The process of conversion • Binaries of work and leisure • Rites of passage in the re-engineered society • Celebrating the Harvest Festival • Mission Compound and the idea of Christian Village Community • Role of orphanages in re-engineering of the self • Introducing polyphonic music • Summing up • Notes.

7. Economic Impact of the Basel Mission Industries 221

• State of traditional handloom industry in Malabar and South Canara • Chaliya weavers - organisation of production and marketing of products • The impact of Basel Mission textiles on the local handloom production - an assessment • The case of the tile industry • Creation of a new labour force • Market, marketing channels and demand pattern • Transfer of technical knowledge • Accounting and managerial practices • Summing up • Notes.

8. Postscript 251

• Industrial promotion in the Madras Presidency • National Movement and its impact • Spread and localisation of weaving and tile Industries • Tile industry in Malabar • Localisation of the tile industry at Mangalore • Notes.

Bibliography 279

References 287

Index 293

List of Tables

Table 2.1 : Year and place of establishment of centres by the Basel Mission: 1834 to 1914 54

Table 2.2: : Economic and industrial activities of the Basel Mission 56

Table 2.3 : Tabular view of stations and membership of churches of Basel Mission. 57

Table 2.4 : Caste background of the converts of Codacal Parish as on 17-12-1893 59

Table 2.5 : Classification of the population of Malabar and South Canara Districts on the basis of religious groups 62

Table 3.1 : Quantum of imports and exports from Calicut Port: 1901-1905 81

Table 3.2 : Growth of population of Malabar: 1881-1921 82

Table 3.3 : Agricultural population of Malabar: 1893 82

Table 3.4 : Land tenure, occupation and caste hierarchy in Malabar 88

Table 3.5 : Concentration of land in the hands of controlling units 94

Table 3.6 : Trend in population growth - South Canara 99

Table 3.7 : Concentration of land holdings in South Canara 105

Table 3.8 : Imports and exports from the Mangalore Port, 1889-90. 108

Table 3.9 : Names of tile factories employing more than 100 labourers and established on or before the year 1914 111

Table 4.1 : Growth of weaving industry in Malabar and South Canara in chronological order 125

Table 4.2 : Establishment of tile factories: chronological order 136

Table 4.3 : Employment in Industrial and trading activities of the Basel Mission in the Malabar and South Canara districts. 137

Table 4.4 : Comparison of cost structure-weaving and tile industries ... 139
Table 4.5 : Weaving and tile industries: some comparative performance indicators ... 140
Table 4.6 : Employment classified into regular and daily wages ... 141
Table 4.7 : Employment and wages-comparison between tile and weaving industries ... 141
Table 4.8 : Census of employment in the Basel Mission weaving factories as on July 1877 ... 144
Table 4.9 : Balance Sheet of Commonwealth Trust Limited as on May 1919 ... 152
Table 5.1 : Enrollment in schools run by the Basel Mission in the districts of Malabar and South Canara ... 171
Table 5.2 : Enrollment in schools: enrollment by Christian and non- Christian students in the Malabar and South Canara districts ... 172
Table 5.3 : List of some of the books and pamphlets published by the Basel Mission ... 177
Table 7.1 : Technologies demonstrated and adopted - weaving ... 238
Table 7.2 : Technologies demonstrated and adopted - tile industry ... 239
Table 7.3 : Technologies demonstrated and adopted- Others ... 241
Table 8.1 : Activities undertaken for industrial promotion in the Madras Presidency 1915-47 ... 256
Table 8.2 : List of institutions established by the Department of Industries during the period 1915-1947 ... 257
Table 8.3 : Names of some handloom industries in and around Kannur region ... 266

Foreword

Technology, Industry and Faith

Seldom is a missionary society remembered after more than a century for its industrial activities. A Protestant Christian missionary organisation named the Basel Evangelical Missionary Society, known as Basel Mission established in 1816 at Basel in Switzerland and which was active in the south west districts of British India- Malabar and South Canara, between 1834 and 1914, is still remembered for its industrial activities. It is not that they were not known for their evangelical activities. They neatly combined both these activities, in a way that the post Religious Reformation Pietist Movement in Europe had proclaimed. The broad Pietist opinion was that income generation through trade and business was not contrary to Christian tenets. This attitude had all the more significance when Basel Mission sent three of their missionaries to Malabar and South Canara. They and their successors worked in these parts, not only in spreading Christianity but also according to their own theological compulsions through craft based operations, agriculture and modern manufacturing. The author, Jaiprakash Raghaviah has captured this interesting story in this volume.

Narrating the story of a group of Christian missionaries working in the fields of handicrafts, cottage industries, trade and commerce, agricultural operations and industrial activities by itself might have been fascinating. On the other hand, by the second half of the nineteenth century, they amalgamated their Industrial Commission -which was looking after such activities - with a joint stock company with the name Mission Trading Company. Through such an amalgamation, the Mission managed to have an access to the capital markets of Europe. In other words, they were prepared to be big players in the slowly emerging manufacturing sector of India. Following this amalgamation, the Basel Mission invested in a number of big factories in this region, thus becoming practically the biggest industrial group. The Mission appear to have followed the prescriptions given by the Protestant Reformer John Calvin and focused on individual salvation rather than mass conversion, their evangelical activities had a reflective character. Their industrial growth, aided by inflow of capital through various sources was built upon a concept of industrial labour that was far removed from the traditional understanding of labouring groups in Malabar and South Canara. The Basel Mission considered work as worship. In the caste -based land holding hierarchy of this region, Thiyyas and Billavas found the concept of 'free' industrial wage labour more attractive and eventually formed major part of the labour force in the Mission factories. They both were from upper elements of castes considered backward by the existing order. Their positioning in the social order helped introduction of social dynamism.

The missionaries did not mind the industrial caste hierarchies that their own activities created. For them such hierarchies were the result of human enterprise. The Basel Mission's opposition to the caste system was extremely intense. There is clear evidence as Raghaviah points out to the missionaries using their industrial activities including labour recruitment as instruments of social engineering. Though the districts of Malabar and South Canara were geographically and agro- climatically similar, as the author has explained, there were significant differences in the way in which agrarian and social systems have evolved in these two areas. In South Canara, the *mulavargdar* who held proprietary right over land apparently similar to the *janmi* in Malabar could sell their property. Occasionally such property would be auctioned off by the government as part of revenue recovery. Thus, trading capital could enter into this limited land market. Such possibilities might have helped industrial growth and technological adaptation better in South Canara district. In the Malabar district, the Janmom right could not be either sold or auctioned. Meanwhile, in Malabar the 'rewriting' of the so called superior *kanom* tenure officially approved by the British judicial system, prompted people with resource to acquire kanom land and use it to rack rent, thus preventing growth of enterprise and new investment.

Coming from a region between Germany and Switzerland, both late industrialised countries, the Basel Mission does not seem to have entered modern manufacturing as a result of a seriously planned attempt. Starting with coffee cultivation, moving to craft-based activities and trade, the Mission eventually ended up with modern industries. Some of their efforts in this direction ended up in failure. Yet, they were ready to learn from their failures and to move on to new ventures. Their own understanding of their failure in craft-based activities seem to be that that such failures were due to colonial environment which was against the traditional craft based small scale production. Basel Mission weaving establishments were able to produce a range of products (as shown by a list presented by Raghaviah) demand for which might have come mainly from a colonially imposed lifestyle.

Throughout the nineteenth century, the predominant colonial policy in practice was that of free trade with imperial preference. Though free trade was to prevail in the case of all commodities, it had to undergo restrictions whenever a commodity of special interest for the British was involved. This was also a period in which India's traditional manufacturing got diminished in the face of post Industrial Revolution British industry. The non-British Basel Mission industries could survive and prosper using the advantages of free trade and by not being explicitly in competition with the British industrial products. In other words, they could survive in the niche market that they could find. By the twentieth century, intra-European rivalry made its headway and after the outbreak of the First World War, through the operation of an ordinance called Enemy Trading Act of 1916, the operations of the non-British Basel Mission Industries were very severely controlled and in 1920 their industrial assets were transferred to a Private Limited Company called the Commonwealth Trust Limited, incorporated in England. Thus, ended the fascinating story of a non-British, European, inter-denominational Christian evangelical organisation running modern industrial units in a part of the British Empire. The Mission industries which were financially well off at the time of transfer of its assets, may have survived under the British Indian policy of discriminate protection which immediately followed that of free trade with imperial preference. Though protection was not offered to all portions and process of production; but only for selected few, it opened up possibilities for sustenance of non-British industrial production. Similarly, the industrial establishments of the Basel Mission and others who followed the trend had better chances of survival under the period of war-induced demand and industrial promotion which followed the policy of discriminate protection of industries. But Basel Mission industries could not make use of these opportunities.

The industrial activities of the Basel Mission had many social and economic impacts upon the societies in which they functioned. Most noteworthy among them were the deliberate actions they took against the caste system and the caste determined discrimination. Their policy of recruitment of labour in their industrial establishment helped the missionaries to shatter the concept of caste related occupation. The marriages that the Basel missionaries are supposed to have arranged between persons of different caste backgrounds also helped a new synthesis. Even among other missionary organisations which were generally anti-caste, the Basel Mission stood out in this respect. They managed to create groups of converts through the body of industrial workers without any caste identity. Compared to the efforts taken by the Portuguese Catholic missionaries through a religious conference known as the Synod of Diamper (or Udayamperoor Soohanadose) in 1599 with similar intentions, the efforts of Basel Mission were far more successful at least among those whom they worked. In addition, like other missionary groups, the Basel Mission also contributed to the enhancement of women's role in public activities, be it industrial, educational, health care or evangelism. Needless to repeat were astounding contributions that the Basel missionaries made to the languages of Malayalam, Kannada, Tulu and Konkani.

The industrial and commercial activities of the Mission not only supported the social involvements but were the mainstay of the impressive impact that they had. First of all, the industrial activities made Basel Mission in Malabar and South Canara a self sustaining organisation. Secondly, through the industrial employment, the Basel Mission converts could upgrade themselves as operators of modern technology and could be free of social moorings and persuasions. Thirdly, since the Mission chose to work in the areas of weaving and tile making, two areas in which traditional craft production existed earlier, what they did was to introduce increased specialisation of labour , use of external motive power and application of scientific knowledge as in any modern production process. They also operated in a niche market, not in direct competition with the post-Industrial Revolution British industrial production. Thus the Mission Industries might have provided an element of 'protection' from the so-called 'de-industrialisation effect' to traditional crafts.

The idea of, as Raghaviah says 're-engineering of the self,' originated from Calvinist Christian thinking. What we have is a case study of how such a world - view got transformed through evangelical and economic activities in an alien culture and a much different colonial administration. They were certainly able to transmit post-Industrial Revolution technologies to a corner of India where an entirely different world view about social life and its organisation existed. One of the medium that the Basel Mission used was that of industrial activities which was inspired and motivated by the internal logic of capitalism; of investment, surplus generation and further capital accumulation. Values emanating from such logic were not contradictory to the Pietist and Calvinist world-views; which led to their evangelical work. Nevertheless, the logic of industrial activities spearheaded by capitalist compulsions and applied through evangelical activities in re-engineering social relations could not have created possibilities for mass conversions. Even the limited effect that the Basel Mission activities had in Malabar and South Canara, were heavily dependent upon several factors. What seems to have happened in 1914 was that the prevailing political system of the British colonial administration turned hostile toward this kind of an 'experiment'. Hence, it could not be continued. Observers of the take-over by the Commonwealth Trust seem to be of the opinion that the factories that the Trust were running, were in no way continuation of old Basel Mission industries. The moral influences and industrial values promoted by the merchant evangelists from Basel were easily neglected and forgotten.

The religious outlook and theological perceptions planted by the Basel missionaries in Malabar and South Canara survived only in the Protestant Christian communities in these areas. But the technological basis, industrial entrepreneurship and enterprise survived in different parts of the district, as new entrepreneurs took up from where the Basel missionaries had left. There were also policy changes induced by the late colonialism which helped at least in a limited way the indigenous industry. Capitalising on these opportunities, some factories came up in Karnataka and Keralam just before independence. The industrious values and technological aptitude were sustained by the training centres and technical schools started by the missionaries. Between these two British Indian districts, Malabar and South Canara, there were points of difference too as Raghaviah has rightly pointed out. In matter of investment required for setting up industries, South Canara had a definite advantage over that of Malabar. After all, it is well known that South Canara was a district in which five major national banks emerged from the beginning of the twentieth century. It should be remembered that it was into such differing circumstances that the modern technology and industrial entrepreneurship were introduced by the efforts of the Basel Mission.

Jaiprakash Raghviah's interesting study brings forth these and more information, analysis and insights. This is not a case study of an European evangelical society on reasons of missionary objectives, attempting successfully in industrial objectives but not succeeding under hostile attitude taken by the colonial administration. The Basel Mission industries outlived the major disruption created by the First World War. The technologies demonstrated by these industries were copied by local entrepreneurs and this story is told in an interesting manner by Raghaviah. The details of the enterprises undertaken by the Mission are quite fascinating. The different persuasions and attitudes, both social and technical that underplayed these developments are also discussed in an analytical manner. This book would be of immense interest to economic and social historians and social scientists.

P.K Michael Tharakan
Chairperson
Kerala Council for Historical Research
Vyloppilly Samskrithi Bhavan,
Nalanda
Thiruvananthapuram- 695 003

October 24th, 2017

Preface

This book comes as a sequel to my earlier book on the industrial initiatives of the Basel Mission in Malabar and South Canara, published in 1990 by Gyan Publishing House. I was overwhelmed then by the response that I received for my book from the academic community. However, I could not embark on getting the second edition published, as my official assignments kept me busy.

It was perhaps just as well that I waited to bring out this sequel. Several things happened in the meanwhile that helped me do a better job now than I could have done then, and two of them are of vital importance. The first has to do with how my own brain and thoughts developed during the time. Over the years, my insights into, and exposure to the missionary and industrial activities of the Basel Mission have been broadened. My perspectives on the Mission also underwent some changes. Secondly, I had a chance to associate, fraternize and socialize with several prominent personalities, who helped, supported and inspired me to do this write up and I would like to specifically mention those people here.

In my earlier book, I had made a reference to the differences in the nature of the economies of the Malabar and South Canara district, particularly in the area of land tenures. These differences perhaps explain why a capital intensive industry like tile manufacture could get localised in South Canara while a relatively less capital intensive industry like handloom got localised in Malabar. I have since been able to probe these aspects a little deeper.

A second facet that I had not explored in my earlier work related to the social engineering that the Basel Mission appear to have undertaken very deliberately to change the internal disposition of the converts, creation of a new value system and the way of looking at the world. All these were part of the endeavour of the Basel missionaries to create a new 'selfhood' for the converts who had broken away from the cultures to which they had once belonged. In this book, I have added a chapter titled 'Re engineering of the self', that explores these issues.

In my earlier book I did make a reference about the emergence of entrepreneurship in the districts of Malabar and South Canara. I had not investigated these aspects in detail. For example, what were the factors that enabled the Thiyya community in Malabar to become entrepreneurial during the years between the two world wars? What was the source of capital for the Gowda Saraswat and Bunt communities in South Canara to establish tile factories? In this book, I have attempted to address these questions.

I am presenting this book to the readers with a fervent hope that it would throw more light on understanding the industrial development of the Malabar and South Canara districts during the ninteenth century, and the first half of the twentieth century.

Jaiprakash Raghaviah

Acknowledgement

I have received support from a large number of individuals as well as institutions in the process of writing this book. However, it may not be possible for me to acknowledge all of them for reasons of space.

What led me to take up research on the Basel Mission was my getting admission to the M Phil Programme at the Centre for Development Studies, (CDS) Thiruvananthapurm way back in 1979. I wish to first of all express my gratitude to the distinguished economist, late Dr K N Raj who was my first guide for the research for providing me valuable suggestions and guidance. At CDS I received support and guidance from two other faculty members. They are Dr P K Michael Tharakan, who is presently the Chairperson of the Kerala Council for Historical Research and Dr T M Thomas Issac who is at present the Finance Minister of Government of Kerala.

It was with my friend and former Director of School of Management Studies, Cochin University of Science and Technology, Dr K K George that I first discussed the issue of academic work on the Basel Mission. He has continued to be a source of support.

I received help and support from Dr M G S Narayanan, former Professor, Department of History, University of Calicut and later Chairman of the Indian Council of Historical Research for encouraging me to take up this study. Prof K K N Kurup, former Vice Chancellor of the Calicut University and an authority on land relations in

Malabar clarified for me several issues relating to land tenures in the Malabar and South Canara districts.

Rt Rev Dr John Sadananda, and Rt Rev Dr C L Furtado former Bishops of South Karnataka Diocese of the Church of South India and Rev Dr Ratnakar Sadananda, General Secretary to Synod of the Church of South India at Chennai were kind enough to discuss with me various aspects of the work of the Basel Mission in the South Canara District. All of them are scholars in the history and contributions of the Christian missionary societies in India and have intimate knowledge of the activities of the Basel Mission.

In 2010, I made a professional visit to the archives of the Basel Mission in Basel. This visit enabled me to have access to some of the archival records of the Mission, particularly those relating to the Mission Trading Company (*Missions Handlungs Geselleschaft*). Dr Guy Thomas Archivist, Dr Paul Jenkins former Archivist of Basel Mission (now Mission 21), and Ms Claudia Wirthlin, Librarian were helpful in giving me access to the documents. Ms Catherine Stenzl, Research Scholar at the University of London (Birbank) shared with me some of her observations on the Basel Mission. Prof David Washbrook, Professor of History at University of Oxford and a well-known authority on the economic history of South India during the ninteenth century shared with me his insights on the industrial development of South India during the ninteenth century.

Dr S Raju, Director, School of Social Sciences, Mahatma Gandhi University, Kottayam helped me in revising the manuscript. Dr C K Raju, Head of the Department of Computer Science, Jyothi Engineering College, Thrissur went through the manuscript and gave useful suggestions. Dr M Raghavan formerly of the Indian Economic Service read through the draft and gave valuable comments.

Dr P Bhaskaran Nayar, formerly Professor of Linguistics and Communication, Lincoln University, UK went through the draft and helped to sharpen my ideas and improve the language.

There are a few others who are unfortunately not with us today but who helped me in my research. I am indebted to my late father-in-law Mr J L Pavamani, who is a ceramic technologist for my understanding of ceramic technology. Another person who provided valuable inputs is the late Mr William Pandyan, textile technologist. Mr Pavamani and Mr William Pandian had experience in working in the tile and weaving factories of The Commonwealth Trust Ltd, the successor company of the Basel Mission Industries and hence knew very intimately, the technologies used by the Basel Mission Industries. I had fruitful discussions with them on various technical aspects. The librarians of the United Theological College (UTC), Bangalore, Karnataka Theological College, Mangalore, Centre for Development Studies (CDS), Thiruvananthapuram and many other libraries gave me all the support that I needed. I wish to acknowledge particularly the help from Mr Sriram V, Chief Librarian, CDS and his staff, Rev Kuriakose, Librarian of UTC and Bennet Ammanna, Archives Assistant of KTC Mangalore.

My friend Dr Oliver Noone, a medical doctor, deeply interested in history was always a source of inspiration and support in seeing my second book on the Basel Mission published. V Ranjit, Systems Administrator at the Centre for Research and Education for Social Transformation (CREST) gave me support on all computer related matters as well as in formatting the manuscript. Graphic Artists P C Prashanth and Mano Thrissur helped me in conceiving and designing the cover jacket.

My first book on the Basel Mission was published by M/S Gyan Publishing House way back in 1990. I am thankful to Gyan for coming forward to publish this sequel to the first book. My special thanks to Mr Amit Garg, Director, Gyan Publishing House for the same.

I wish to thank each and every one for the support I received from them to publish this work.

Immediate members of my family helped me in several ways in the completion of this book. Here I remember my late mother Mrs Ivy Raghaviah and my late sister Pushpa Raghaviah whose constant inspiration and support were invaluable.

My wife Maleeha maintained an efficient household; patiently bore my frequent absence from home despite bearing the pressures of her own work as a professional journalist, she also went through the manuscript and offered valuable suggestions. Here I also remember my daughters Shalini and Radhika. They have in some sense borne the cost of my academic endeavours. I am thankful to all of them for being with me - all the way.

Jaiprakash Raghaviah

Chapter - 1

Introduction

On October 14, 1834, three German missionaries landed at Calicut after completing a grueling three months voyage that took them all the way from Europe and around the African continent. The sail ship was incidentally named 'Malabar' and the missionaries were Christoff Greiner, Johannes Lehner and Samuel Hebich. These missionaries were sent to India by a Protestant Christian missionary organisation named the Basel Evangelical Missionary Society, a missionary organisation registered in Basel, Switzerland.

This missionary society, the Basel Mission as it was commonly called[1], was established in Basel in Switzerland, in the year 1816. The Basel Mission (BM), started working in the erstwhile Madras Presidency in British India from 1834 onwards. During the period ending with the outbreak of the First World War in 1914, the Mission initiated a number of economic activities. The Mission started with experiments in traditional crafts like weaving and carpentry, later turned to modern crafts like watch and clock making and book-binding. The Mission was also active in the field of agriculture as well as trade. These activities eventually culminated in the establishment of modern industrial units in weaving and tile manufacture in the districts of Malabar and South Canara of the erstwhile Madras

Presidency of the British India. These economic activities were in addition to the very obvious and sizeable religious and social activities that the Mission undertook. Expansion of these industrial activities came to an abrupt end when, following the outbreak of the First World War in 1914, the industrial assets of the Mission were taken over by the British Indian Government under the provisions of the Enemy Trading Act of 1916 and entrusted with a trust named the Commonwealth Trust Ltd, registered in London for the purpose of taking over the industries established by the Basel Mission. At the time of takeover by the British, the Basel Mission had become the biggest industrial entrepreneur in the districts of Malabar and South Canara.

This phenomenon of missionary organisations taking up industrial entrepreneurship, itself is significant enough to engage the attention of any student of history of the region. Many missionary groups which had worked in India had experimented with some economic activities or other. Their intentions included the rehabilitation of converts, some of whom had lost their traditional occupation on account of their conversion to Christianity, increasing the social and economic status of the converts, and propagation of 'Christian values'[2] through instilling industrial discipline.

In Kerala itself, we have the example of functioning of other Protestant missionary groups. Two such groups, the Church Missionary Society (CMS)[3] and the London Missionary Society (LMS) had started their activities in the native state of Tiruvitamkur from the beginning of the ninteenth century.[4] The CMS started working from Kottayam in central Tiruvithamkur from 1816. Initially, the CMS focused in trying to bring the Syrian Christians to their fold. When they started facing resistance from the Syrian Christian community, they shifted their attention to conversion of people from lower castes. The CMS gave emphasis to education and established a large number of schools and one college. It was hoped that the newly educated Christian converts would be able to take up appointments in government service. The CMS was part of the Church of England and due to its peculiar position (Kulakkat, 2002), was often referred as a 'Church within a Church'[5] The LMS had started its work from Nagarcoil in south Tiruvitamkur (at present in the state of Tamil Nadu) from the year 1806. The LMS also had established schools and one college[6] for giving their converts the benefits of modern education. The LMS had initiated some economic activities. The LMS had established an industrial training centre for training converts in leather craft and book binding. The LMS had also trained women converts in lace making, which was practiced as a cottage industry.[7]

The Basel Mission was unique in the sense that it ventured into commercial and economic activities in a planned and deliberate manner and in the process, ended up in establishing large, post- Industrial Revolution type[8] of modern industries in the lines of modern handloom weaving and tile manufacture in the districts of Malabar and South Canara. The Basel Mission considered its industrial activities as religious activities. Moreover, the success and failure of each line of economic activity tended to give rise to newer types of activities. Gradually, it appears that the religious conversion taken up by the Mission, became an instrument through which labour was mobilised for the factories established by them. The market for the products of these industries expanded to cover parts of the British Empire like, Middle East, Ceylon (Sri Lanka), Burma (Myanmar), Malayan Peninsula, Australia and countries in the African continent like Gold Coast (Ghana) and Cameroon.

The industrial orientation of the Basel Mission raises several lines of enquiry. The first question that arises from this scenario relates to the dominant ideology, that is, the theological basis or view of the world which could have prompted the Basel Mission to take up industrial activities as part of their evangelisation. Here, it is pertinent to look into the promptings of the Calvinist ideology which has been linked up with the economic activities of capitalist nature in other contexts and societies.[9]

A second line of enquiry relates to a detailed empirical understanding of the industrial activities as they were planned and executed by the Mission. The two dominant lines of industrial activities which were pioneered by the Mission were weaving and tile making. During the nineteenth century, both these lines of manufacture were practiced as cottage industries in Malabar and South Canara. But, the Basel Mission transformed these lines into modern industries comparable to similar industrial undertakings in the post- Industrial Revolution Europe. There were also significant differences between the structure of handloom and tile industry in terms of capital investment, labour content and the use of external source of power. An understanding of these differences becomes relevant while examining the impact of transfer of technology and spread effect of the technologies demonstrated by the Basel Mission factories. Differences in the structure, as it has been noted, are significant in viewing the spread effect of these industries.

A third line of enquiry relates to the impact the Basel Mission industries had in the economies and societies of the districts of Malabar and South Canara. During the ninteenth century when the Mission started its work in the districts of Malabar and South Canara, these districts were typical feudal agrarian societies. These economies were marginal and almost self-sufficient. Exchange was limited to a few commodities that were not available locally. In both the districts, a trading community consisting of mainly Muslims in the Malabar district and Muslims, Gowda Sarswath Brahmins and Catholic Christians in the South Canara district existed side by side. In the Malabar district, trade flourished from the 12th to the 15th centuries. Trading activity with the Arabian countries declined from the sixteenth century, with the attempt of the Portuguese to control sea trade. Soon after the European powers - Portugal, Netherland, France and England competed and fought with each other for the monopoly of pepper trade. These wars and conflicts ended with the annexation of the districts by the English East India Company (EIC) in 1792, after the defeat of Tipu Sultan in the Battle of Srirangapattanam.[10] After the annexation of the districts, the EIC stopped trading and focused on extraction of agrarian surplus of these districts through tax farming. The districts of Malabar and South Canara started feeling the impact of the colonial exploitation.

The economy and society of the districts of Malabar and South Canara during the ninteenth century is often characterised by the existence of various institutional barriers to economic development (Shea, 1959). Among these, were the rigid caste system carried to extremes by pollution at sight and concentration of ownership of land in the hands of a few joint families or temples, which produced a debilitating impact on individual initiative. In these districts as well as elsewhere in India, the institution of caste was strong[11]. In the social hierarchy of the districts, a person's position vis a vis caste hierarchy was also related to the status in ownership of land. These issues are discussed later in this book. The Basel Mission's evangelical and industrial activities, succeeded in creating a group of converts who did not carry their former caste identities.

The Basel Mission set up factories and successfully demonstrated technologies in tile and modern handloom in an economic and social environment that was characterised by several social and structural barriers. These factories had a role as change agents, demonstrating for the converts that an alternate way of living was possible. Therefore, this discussion relates to understanding the impact the Basel Mission industries had on the economies and societies of Malabar and South Canara. Pre-conditions for economic development did not exist in these districts due to the institutional barriers.

The two lines of manufacture that were pioneered by the Basel Mission - weaving and tile making had existed in the districts of Malabar and South Canara as cottage industries. What the Basel Mission had done was to technically up-grade these industries into mass production using specialisation of labour, superior technology, use of external source of power. Therefore demonstration of new technologies against the backdrop of technologies that were in existence will have an impact. Here, it is argued that during the ninteenth century the spread effects of the industrial activities of the Basel Mission was limited due to the institutional barriers and other factors that we have already mentioned.

It appears that changes started taking place after 1914, when the British colonial administration was forced to change its policies towards industrial development of colonies. The Swadeshi Movement[12], the Freedom Movement as well as some of the industrial promotion activities of the Government of Madras Presidency, played their rather role in promotion of local industries. Technologies were transferred and the period starting with the outbreak of the First World War and ending with India gaining independence, saw the growth of handloom industries and tile industries in the lines demonstrated by Basel Mission. At the time of India gaining Independence in 1947, the main industries in Malabar and South Canara were handloom weaving and tile manufacture, both, in the lines pioneered by the Basel Mission. Here some tentative explanations are given to explain the localisation of tile industries in the Mangalore region in the South Canara district and the weaving industry in Kannur region in the Malabar district.

Chapter scheme of the book

The chapter scheme of this book follows the lines of our enquiry. The overall focus of this book is explained in the present chapter. In Chapter 2, an attempt is made to explore the dominant ideologies, theology and the sense of self of the Basel Mission. Though the Mission had stated that it is not affiliated to any ideology or theology, but, the ideological underpinnings which motivated the Mission to take up industrial entrepreneurship are clearly seen firstly through the various pronouncements of missionaries articulated in different forums and secondly through the praxis of the Mission. It appears that no other Protestant Christian missionary society clearly articulated its orientation on Calvinist theology as much as the Basel Mission had done. Dominance of Calvinist theology and vision is seen in the various statements made by missionaries. The praxis of missionaries reveal the dominant ideologies of the Mission. The importance given to work, thrift, orderliness, circumspection, understanding the importance of time, all these are the qualities demanded of a good Christian, according to Calvinism. Often applicants for conversion to Christianity were sent to the Basel Mission factories to "test the sincerity of their conversion."[13] The underlining logic is that only a good worker can be a good Christian.

In Chapter 3, we take a close look at the two districts of Malabar and South Canara. These districts are contiguous. Geographically and agro climatically and there are several similarities between these districts. Being placed between the Western Ghats and the Arabian Sea, these districts received copious rainfall. Paddy cultivation was the most important economic activity in both districts. There are contrasts as well which are significant to observe. While the Malabar district suffered from famines during the 18th and 19th centuries, the South Canara district was considered as a district that had been free from famines. South Canara was a rice exporting region while Malabar though well endowed for the cultivation of paddy, was a rice importing region. The population intensity of South Canara was much lower than that of Malabar. Linguistically, Malabar was homogenous as Malayalam was the language used most. In South Canara, a number of languages were used. Though Kannada was the language of the largest segment of the population of the South Canara district, a sizeable number of the population spoke Thulu and Konkani. Dialects like Byari were in use among the coastal people in South Canara. The district of South Canara was often referred as 'forest district' in many official records of the British administration.

Caste system existed in South Canara but not to the extent of pollution by sight. Thus, the level of social communication between members of different castes must have been better in South Canara. South Canara as a region has evolved differently. This region was part of the Vijayanagaram Empire and later ruled by Jain kings. Therefore, land tenure patterns of South Canara district have evolved differently. We are looking at the comparisons and contrasts between the two districts as these comparisons and contrasts may explain the subsequent paths of industrial development of these districts. Tile industry requires higher initial capital in comparison with handloom. Yet, the tile industry started developing in the South Canara by the the third quarter of the ninteenth century. Where did this capital come from? It is worth examining whether the land tenure patterns between the two districts can explain the reason for the availability of capital in South Canara.

In Chapter 4, an attempt is made to trace the growth of economic activities of the Basel Mission. The Basel Mission had ventured into agriculture, traditional cottage industry, modern handicrafts (like clock and watch making), trade and finally to large industries. Movement from handicraft to large industry was not linear. The Mission was simultaneously testing feasibility of various lines of economic activities and for this reason, the Mission was constantly innovating and learning from failure. A true spirit of entrepreneurship can be seen evolving within the Mission. Internally also, the Basel Mission was undergoing organisational changes. The industrial orientation of the Mission was getting strengthened. After experimentation in various economic activities, the Mission consolidated two lines of industrial activities - handloom weaving and tile manufacture. It was a critical change in the organisational structure -amalgamation of the Industrial Commission with the Mission Trading Company *(Missions Handlungs Gesellschaft)* that enabled access to the capital markets of Basel which was a centre of banking in Europe. Many of the members of the Home Board of the Basel Mission were themselves prominent bankers. Thus, within a period of 32 years (from 1882-1914) it became possible to establish five large tile factories in the Malabar and South Canara districts. In the process, the Mission became the biggest industrial entrepreneur in the Malabar and South Canara districts during the nineteenth century. In this chapter, the structural differences between handloom weaving and tile making are also examined in terms of intensity of capital and labour content. In this chapter we also examine some other aspects of the of industrial activity of the Mission, like recruiting and disciplining of labour force, extension of market and its managerial and financial structure that facilitated rather rapid rate of expansion of industrial activities.

Factories, schools, college and even hospitals established by the Basel Mission were agents of social change. These institutions established by the Mission, by their very nature challenged the caste system prevailing in the districts. In the factories workers from different caste backgrounds worked side by side. Women entered the public sphere as factory workers, teachers and office-workers, nurses and helpers. In the schools established by the Mission, there was no caste based segregation. In fact, the caste identities were never looked into and any type of segregation was not tolerated. In the hospital and clinics established by the Mission, people from varied background shared the common facilities. In Chapter 5, we look into the social impact that the Mission had on the traditional societies of Malabar and South Canara. Issues like caste and conversion, spread of literacy, social mobility and female participation in the activities of the Mission are looked into. Through their educational and industrial activities, the Mission had created a technically oriented labour force. This labour force had basic formal education. They had also acquired a fair level of competence in dealing with modern technologies. This group certainly commanded a greater reserve price. The Basel Mission was undertaking social engineering by offering opportunities for people from all segments of society to acquire education, participate in industrial labour and acquire social mobility. But, due to the prevailing social situation, members of some castes like the Thiyya caste in Malabar and their equivalent Billava caste in South Canara could make better use of the opportunities offered by the Basel Mission.

Chapter 6 titled 'Re-engineering of the Self,' is an attempt to take a look at the internal processes the new community of converts to Christianity might have gone through. Along with conversion, the belief systems as well as the way converts looked at the world changes drastically. Considering that these aspects of the intangible culture of the communities that the converts came from have evolved over centuries, this process of re-engineering of the identities of converts is looked into. Missionary institutions like schools, orphanages, factories and even the life of new converts in Mission Compounds are part of creation of a disciplining g society in the Fucouldian[14] sense. Even creation of new names for converts, are part of this internal process because in the traditional societies, caste is known through one's name. The newly created society also required rites of passage. Creation of a new Industrial Man, in the western sense is what is attempted by the Mission. This chapter does not make ethical judgment on some of the practices; leave that judgment for future scholars to look into. Thus, Chapter 5 and Chapter 6 are inter-related, looking at the social reality from two different angles.

Chapter 7 examines the economic impact of the Basel Mission industries. As it was stated earlier, the two lines of manufactures pioneered by the Mission, weaving and tile manufacture existed in Malabar and South Canara as cottage industries. Therefore it is pertinent to examine the impact the industrial activities of Basel Mission had on traditional weaving and tile making. The very obvious question is, did the products of the Basel Mission industries take away part of the market of traditional handloom and weaving industries? Did some of the technologies get transferred? If so, which technologies? Who were the conduits of technology transfer and what factors limited the transfer of technology? Did the industrial activities of the Basel Mission succeed in expanding the market for handloom products as well as the modern tile industry? And finally, were the Basel Mission industries responding to the felt needs of society in which they were functioning are the questions examined in this chapter.

The expansion of the industrial activities of the Basel Mission came to an abrupt end in 1914, with the outbreak of the First World War. But during the war and after the war, these industries continued to function, continuing to demonstrate the technologies introduced by the Basel Mission. But the environment around had undergone drastic changes. The economic policies of the British colonial government had undergone some change, giving a limited encouragement to industrial development. The Swadeshi Movement was focusing on boycott of foreign products and import substitution. In Chapter 8, entitled "A Postscript" an attempt is made to trace the subsequent trajectories of the industrial expansion of the two districts of Malabar and the South Canara with a focus on the two lines of industries established by the Basel Mission and transferred to Commonwealth Trust in 1920. As it is argued here, there was a gradual decline in the performance of the industries established by the Mission since it came under the Commonwealth Trust. In this chapter we also trace the growth and of the two lines of manufacture, handloom weaving and tile making. It is known that from the beginning of the twentieth century handloom industry as demonstrated by the Basel Mission was getting localised in the present Kannur region of Malabar where the Basel Mission had established first weaving factory in 1852.The industries that started coming up in the Kannur region were small factories with 20-30 looms though a few of these like C Aaron and Sons grew into large enterprise. We argue that several factors played their role for such a localisation like the extension of railway line to Kannur in 1908, Industrial Exhibition conducted at Kannur in 1908, and the outbreak of the First World War. Obviously entrepreneurship had evolved in these regions. But who were the entrepreneurs? From which social backgrounds did these entrepreneurs come from? We offer some tentative explanations that can be studied further. Tile industry got localised in the South Canara district to the extent that even now, roofing tiles are referred as Mangalore tiles. Since establishment of tile units requires a higher level of capital, it may be appropriate to enquire as to the source of capital, entrepreneurship and marketing network that sustained these tile units.

Our final arguments are that at the time of establishment of industries by the Basel Mission in the Malabar and South Canara, there were considerable structural barriers in these districts to industrial development. Most of the structural barriers continued well into the twentieth century. It appears that it was the industrial development that started taking place from the first decade of the twenteenth century that started breaking some of the structural barriers.[15] The change in colonial policies implemented under compulsion arising out of world wars as well as India's warming up towards independence, further facilitated this process.

Notes

1. The name of the missionary society has undergone changes as reflected in the Annual Reports of the Mission. For example:

   German Evangelical Society - 1844

   Basel Evangelical Missionary Society-1866

   Basel German Evangelical Society - 1869

   All the above reports are hereafter referred as RBM (Reports of the Basel Mission). Example: RBM 1846.
2. As the Basel Mission understood it, 'Christian values' meant seeing work as worship, diligence in performing duties allotted to an individual, understanding the value of time, circumspection, truthfulness in all dealings. Discussed in detail in the next chapter.
3. The origin of the CMS can be traced back to the eclectic society founded in 1783 by a group of evangelical clergy and laity in England. It acquired its present names in 1812. The CMS was a voluntary organisation within the Church of England but it did not separate itself from the Anglican Church. The CMS started working in Tiruvithamkur (Travancore) from 1816.
4. The London Missionary Society was established in London at the end of the eighteenth century. This society was not affiliated to the Church of England and functioned independently. The LMS sent its first missionary, Ringeltaube, to Travancore in 1806. For a detailed account of the activities of the CMS and LMS see: Augur, C A, opp.cit.
5. For a detailed account of the growth and conflicts within the CMS in India, see: Kulakkat J.,Augustine, opp.cit.
6. The college established by the LMS was Scot Christian College, Nagarcoil.
7. The Basel Mission also trained girls in the orphanage at Chombal the art of lace making. Generally, it was the missionary wives who imparted the above training. Later, these women practiced lace making as cottage industry. Articles made of lace, like table covers and napkins were sold in Europe

during missionary festivals. The BM did not develop lace-making further. The weaving factories established by the BM had embroidery department which employed women. For the LMS, lace making was a cottage industry.

8. Post Industrialisation type factories are defined by the specialisation of labour and use of external source of power as motive force and extension of market.
9. John Calvin was the most important theologian of Protestant Christianity. The theology of Calvinism is discussed in the next chapter.
10. After the defeat of Tipu Sultan in the third Anglo-Mysore war in 1792, Tipu was forced to broker peace with the East India company's Cornwallis. By the Treaty of Srirangaptanam concluded on March 19, 1792, Tipu surrendered half of his territory, including Malabar and Canara to the EIC. These included the territories that were ruled by chieftaincies under local rajas. These chieftaincies were amalgamated to form two districts, Malabar and Canara and were affiliated to the Bombay Presidency. The Malabar district was transferred to the Madras Presidency in 1800. In 1862, the Canara district was divided into North and South Canara. South Canara was affiliated to the Madras Presidency and North Canara continued to be part of the Bombay Presidency.
11. Caste system takes its origin from the Hindu concept of *Varnashrama Dharma* according to which human race is divided into four castes. The castes determine the profession. The *brahmins,* (priestly class) were deemed to perform religious and intellectual professions. The *kshatriya* caste were warriors, the *vaishya* caste traders and the *shudra* caste in service of the above three castes. In the districts of Malabar and South Canara the exact composition of the Hindu society was not in the above order. For example, in Malabar, the vaishya caste (trading caste) did not exist. Their place was taken by the Muslims. In the South Canara district, it was Muslims, Gouda Sarswath Brahmins and Roman Catholic Christian community who did trading. Yet, it will be appropriate to state that the caste hierarchy in general was related to the position of ownership or possession of land.
12. Swadeshi Movement was a protest movement started first in the Presidency of Bengal when, in 1903, the British Indian Government decided to bifurcate Bengal into East Bengal and West Bengal. The British partitioned Bengal as the Presidency was increasingly coming under nationalist surges. The

Swadeshi Movement acquired different shades and contours like the boycott of foreign goods. Later, such activities became part of the agenda of Freedom Movement.

13. This observation is made by missionary Frohnmeyer in a paper entitled 'Industrial Mission', presented by him at the Decennial Missionary Conference at Bombay, in 1882. (Frohnmeyer 1882)
14. Explained as an endnote in Chapter 2.
15. To give example, the tile and weaving factories employed people from different caste background. The work in the factories do not permit polluting distances. There was certainly a move from the caste consciousness to class consciousness.

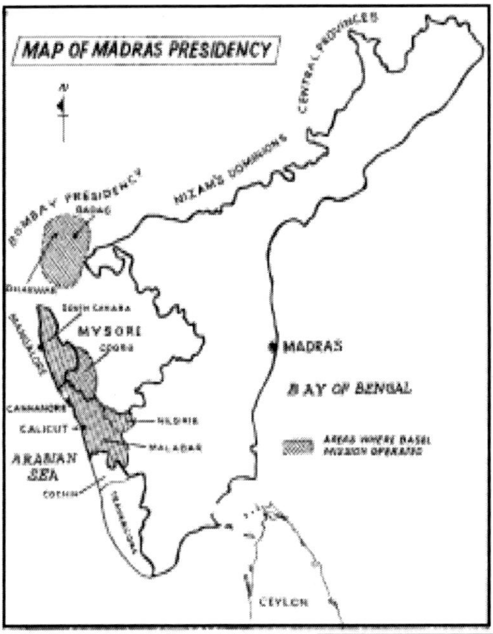

Map of the Madras Presidency-1859

Some of the first missionaries, (L to R), Hermann Gundert, Samuel Hebich and Herrmann Moegling.

Chapter - 2

The Basel Mission: Its Origin and Sense of Self

During the nineteenth century, a number of Protestant Christian missionary organisations were formed in Europe. They generally followed the paths of colonial expansion and established centres of activity in various European colonies. The Basel Mission was one such missionary organisation. But, it was unique in its approach towards industrial activities to the extent that such industrial activities were considered as part of missionary activity. This raises several questions regarding the dominant ideology or perception of the world which prompted the Mission to develop such an approach. An understanding of the social origins of the Mission may be appropriate here.

Basically all Protestant Christian missionary organisations in Europe derived their inspiration from the Pietist Movement[1] which had flourished in Europe during the seventeenth and eighteenth centuries. The emphasis of the Pietist Movement was on (i) personal salvation through acceptance of Christianity and (ii) Christian restructuring of the world. The concept of Christian restructuring of the world emanated from the understanding that the European civilisation as superior because of its knowledge of Christ. Information about distant countries brought about by colonialism further strengthened the belief that these societies of 'heathens living in darkness' needed to be civilised on the basis of Christian understanding. Certainly, such an approach has something to do with universal ecumane or creation of Christendom. The Pietist Movement was first centred in the University of Halle in Germany.[2]It spread eventually to other centres of learning like the University of Basel. The influence of the Pietist Movement became very strong in the Swiss city of Basel. This city is situated at the borders of France and Germany, and the trade route in Europe. By the eighteenth century, forward trading and banking flourished here, supported by a system of unified currencies.[3]

As it is argued that Pietism was the most dominant influence in the formation of the Basel Mission, it may be appropriate to explore Pietism in some detail. Pietism emerged in Europe during the 18th and 19th centuries. Well after the Religious Reformation of Europe,[4] various strands of Pietism came into existence in Europe. Some branches were meditative in content. At the other end of the spectrum were the social activists. One such Pietist organisation called Moravian Mission *(Unitas Fractrum)* which was started by Count Nikolaus Ludwig Zinzendorf, had attempted setting up an independent village community called the Herrenhut, for the re- settlement of refugees from Russia. The Herrenhut was located in the estate of Count Zinzendorf at Saxony, in Germany. This community took up production of all articles that were required for their livelihood within their village and thus became self sufficient (Dankar, 1971). Later, a branch of the Moravian Mission, which was started in Labrador in Canada, subsisted on the income it generated by trading with the Eskimos. This was during the middle of the eighteenth century (Dankar, 1971). The economic activities of the Moravians were successful and the Mission generated funds for its evangelical activities from the trading it conducted at Labrador in Canada and other places in the Americas. The essential message which thus evolved was that income generation through business was not contrary to Christian tenets.

From the beginning of the eighteenth century, Basel became a centre of the Pietist Movement. A Pietist Society called *Deutsche Christums Gesellschaft* (German Christian Society) was founded in the Wurttemberg province in Germany during the eighteenth century. A branch of this society was established in Basel in 1780. Members of this society used to congregate for weekly prayer meetings. In these meetings they used to read and discuss reports of missionaries working in different parts of the world. It was due to the initiative of some of the members of this society that the Basel Mission was formed.

According to historical sources, there were some historical circumstances that were behind the formation of the Basel Mission. Napolean's army had besieged the city of Basel and threatened it with destruction. At that time a few influencial citzens of Basel which included a pastor, a Professor of Philosophy in the University of Basel and a banker met at St.Martin's Church located in the city centre of Basel and took a pledge that if the city was saved from destruction, they would establish an institution for training missionaries. In this event, the French commander who had besieged Basel did not destroy the city. Napoleon himself as is well known, was defeated at Waterloo in 1815. A missionary society called Evangelical Missionary Society of Basel was established in 1816 with a prominant clergyman of Basel, Nichlaus Von Brunn as the President, and Rev. Christian Gottlieb Blumhardt was the first Inspector, or Director. Board members of the society included prominant businessmen and bankers of Basel.The Basel Mission Seminary was established on 26th of August 1816. The background of the founders revealed a unique combination of theology, philosophy and business acumen.

Later as it is seen, in its idelogy and praxis, the Basel Mission appear to have endeavoured to combine the three aspects.

Another significant influence on the Protestant Churches of Europe in general and hence also on the Basel Mission was the theology of John Calvin.[5] Calvin lived during the sixteenth century and is considered as the chief theologian of Protestantism. As R H Tawny observes "The influence of Calvinism was not simple, but complex, and extended beyond the churches which could properly be called as Calvinist" (Tawny, 1975, p. 121). As it is observed here that Calvinism has had a profound impact on the ideology and praxis of the Basel Mission, it may be appropriate to explore the theology of Calvin. It was Max Weber who first attempted to relate the influence that Calvinist ethics had on the emergence of capitalist enterprises in Europe. Weber argued that Calvinist ethics was instrumental in supplying the moral energy and drive for the capitalist enterprise in Europe during the eighteenth and nineteenth centuries (Weber, 1976). In view of the fact that we are mainly focusing on the relationship between the theological orientation of the Basel Mission and the setting up of capitalist enterprises by the Mission, the basic precept of Calvinist ethics has to be explored in detail. We will follow the line of reasoning of Weber in this case.

Calvinism, Basel and enterprise

The basic understanding of Calvinism is that the whole world of economic order is one not alien to the life of the spirit. World existed for the glorification of God and for that alone. But God requires social achievements, because He wills that the social life is organised according to His commandments. At the centre of Calvinist ideology is the doctrine of predestination. This doctrine states that only a small portion of men are chosen for eternal grace by the superior wisdom of God. The chosen Christian is in the world only to increase God's glory by fulfilling God's commandments to the best of his ability.[6]

Here, it may be appropriate to understand how Calvinism viewed the external manifestations of a person pre-destined for salvation. The manifestation according to Calvinism was revealed through a person's capacity to do good and honest work. By this, Calvin meant collective labour, like the work in a factory or an organisation. Calvin saw labour not as individual action, but as part of the social system leading to social achievements. Calvin saw labour as something good in itself and destined for man after God's expulsion of Adam and Eve (the first man and woman according to the Bible) from the Garden of Eden.[7] The person who is predestined for salvation is revealed as the 'man of calling' or an individual dedicated to a profession. Calvinism emphasised the rational organisation of labour. By this, it is meant "...routinised, calculated administration with continuous functioning enterprise" (Weber, 1976, p. 3).

It was sociologist and historian Max Weber who first explored the relationship between Protestant Christian ethics as it was explained by Calvin to the evolution of capitalist enterprises in Europe during the eighteen and nineteenth centuries. "In its extreme inhumanity," comments Weber, "this doctrine must above all have had one consequence for the life of a generation which surrendered to its magnificent consistency......a feeling of unprecedented inner loneliness" (Weber, 1976, p. 104). This was because a Christian believer does not know whether he is predestined for salvation or not and so has to reassure himself by constant good work. Weber believed that it is from this inner torment, that the spirit of capitalism was born.

Thus, Calvinism is associated with an outlook of a very specific kind. Calvinism did not consider acquisition of wealth as bad, or a sin, but considered that indulgence in wealth and all unearned income was sin. Calvin's approach to receiving interest on capital lent is also significant here. Throughout the Medieval Ages, there was objection to receiving of interest on money lent as lending money for interest was proscribed in the Old Testament of the Bible and considered as 'sin of avarice'. Calvin, while administering the Canton of Geneva did not object to lending money on payment of interest but he limited the rate of interest for such moneys lent and punished the money lenders who charged exorbitant rates of interest.

While discussing Calvinism, Weber frequently used the term 'this worldly asceticism' and juxtaposed it against 'other worldly asceticism'. Other worldly asceticism is complete renouncement of this world and its pleasures. As against this, this worldly asceticism demanded from the believer neither the celibacy of monks nor poverty, but elimination of enjoyment of all unearned income. According to Weber, this worldly asceticism, "substituted the spiritual aristocracy of the monks outside and above the world by the spiritual aristocracy of the saints" (Weber, 1976, p. 104). (Here, the term 'saint' is used to describe the predestined souls.) As Weber saw it, the typical representative of this worldly asceticism, was the man of vocation and its unique result of it was the rational organisation of social relationships. Factories and similar institutions where people join hands and work together in synchrony with machines represent a rational organisation of social relationships.

The historical background under which Calvinist theology emerged is also significant. In Europe, feudalism was gradually collapsing and capitalist enterprises were emerging. Values like capacity for honest and hard work, use of wealth without indulgence, judicious use of time and labour conceived as a unified part of action were values that are supportive of capitalist enterprise.

Weber's exposition of Calvinism was a source of polemic during his life time. The debate continues even now. Here, it is not intended to follow the entire course of arguments that arose out of the publication of Weber's thesis. The intention here is to note some of the most important criticisms that are raised against Weber on this topic. Important among the criticisms of Weber's thesis are:

- Weber mistakes the nature of casual connection between Puritanism and modern capitalism.
- Countries have experienced rapid economic development without possessing anything akin to the Protestant Ethic.
- Weber's assertion of connection between Puritanism and modern capitalism is based on unsatisfactory empirical evidence.[8]

Even when such criticisms are taken into account, at least a sporadic link between the Protestant Ethic and the rise of capitalism remains intact in its generalisations. Here we are trying to argue on the basis of evidences that the link is found to be more than casual, at least in the case of the Basel Mission. The Basel Mission had not identified itself with any particular sect within Protestantism. At one stage the Mission even stated: "It is not intended to give the minds of future missionaries the stamp of Luther, Calvin or Zwingli; but to endear Christ in their heart and establish His truth" (RBM, 1846, p. 5). But a very close link between Calvinist ideas and the praxis of the Basel Mission when it started its industrial activities can be seen in various pronouncements of the Mission. For example, in one of the reports of the Industrial Commission it is noted that "Even acquisition of working capacity and loyalty has a missionising influence on human nature" (RBM, 1854, p. 7). The importance attached to industrial labour is further emphasised by the daily routine in factories established by the Mission. Work in factories started and ended with worship. The prayer was led either by the factory manager or by a senior *maistry* (supervisor). The applicants for conversion were usually sent to the Mission factories to test the seriousness of their intention for conversion. As the Basel Missionary Frohnmeyer states rather unabashedly: "I consider it to be one of the great advantages of these (industrial) institutions that they can offer an opportunity to *test the sincerity of probationers*" (Frohnmeyer, 1893, p. 11) (emphasis mine). The underlying notion is that a good Christian would be a good worker and *vice versa.* In the parishes established by the Basel Mission, such a perception gave rise to curious situations. The maistry of the Mission factory was usually elected as the 'Elder'[9] of the church. This had the implication of the supervisor being presented as a model worker and hence a good Christian. This approach to employment enabled the Mission authorities to have an indirect means of controlling labour by the use of a model worker.

The whole bundle of western Christian virtues which the missionaries wanted to impart was expressed by the Mission was expressed as under:

> Loyalty in word and deed, loyalty in fulfilling duties to oneself and others, awareness of the value of time, circumspection and looking forward, understanding and acquisition of what is new and changing are found so seldom in heathens, for he sees nothing of them, and hears nothing of them, and an entire generation may be needed till those more external Christian achievements may emerge as quite visible and effective fruits of first conversion. (Report of the Industrial Commission, 1854, p. 11)

It is thus possible to see three different influences which eventually can be called specific characters of the Basel Mission. The first was the influence of Pietism, the second the historical context under which the city of Basel was influenced by Calvinism and the third was the geographical location of Basel with its trade, commerce and intellectual enlightenment.

Towards a view of the world

The Basel Mission was established with the only objective of training missionaries for other missionary organisations. Some of the first missionaries trained by the Mission College served in other missionary organisations including the London Missionary Society (LMS) and the Church Missionary Society (CMS), both of which had started working in other parts of Kerala (Yesudas, 1975) from the beginning of the nineteenth century. The Basel Mission did not consider taking up industrial activities when it started its work in India. The missionaries who were sent to different parts of the world were asked to study the language and the traditions of the people with whom they would work in order to understand them better. Further, the missionaries were also asked to teach the native converts field or garden work to enable them to make an independent living. The missionaries were also expected to develop a deep affection and love for the people for whom they worked. At this stage, the Mission did not appear to have any intentions to initiate industrial activities on its own.

This perspective underwent a change after the Mission started receiving converts in larger numbers. Many converts had lost their traditional occupation and became dependent upon the Mission for sheer survival. The missionaries started attempting several craft -related activities which they were familiar, with a hope to settle the converts in some gainful occupation. The system of organisation for managing the industrial and other economic activities of the Mission started getting formalised gradually. The Mission was having an Industrial Commission in its Home Board in an informal way, from 1844. In 1852, this Industrial Commission was made a formal entity with its own treasury. This period 1852-1882, has been categorised as the Middle Phase of industrial activities of the Basel Mission in India (refer, Chapter 4). With the setting up of the Industrial Commission, planned industrial, trading and other economic activities became part of the overall strategy of the Mission. The influence of Calvinist ideology and German ethos to work started having a determining influence on the work of the Mission. The idea of pray and work gave way to the notion that praying is working and working is praying. As a consequence, the industrial and other economic activities which the Mission started came to be considered not just a support for the Mission but as a mission itself and very often as the 'crown and centre' of the activities of the Mission.

The Basel Mission was unique in its perspective of considering economic and industrial activities as essentially religious activity. Such an approach naturally attracted criticism. In various missionary conferences the Basel Mission was often ridiculed as 'Towel Mission' because, the Mission had come to be known to the outside world more for the towels and other handloom articles that its factories had manufactured than its religious activities. (Frohnmeyer, 1893) The Basel missionaries had to frequently defend their stand relating to industrial activities during the missionary conferences.

Praxis of the Basel Mission in India

In the year 1833, the Charter Act that gave monopoly to the East India Company (EIC) for trading in India came up for renewal by the British Parliament. At this time, a demand was made in the Parliament to allow non-British Missionary organisations to work in British colonies. This amendment was passed by the British Parliament. It is this enactment that enabled the Basel Mission to send missionaries to India, which was then a colony of Britain. (Kulakkat, 2002) By that time, the Basel Mission had already sent missionaries to Russia, and a few other places. Following the renewal of the Charter Act in 1833, a decision was made by the Basel Mission to send its own missionaries to the western coast of India. At that time two British missionary societies had already started working in the central and southern parts of Kerala respectively. These were the Church Missionary Society (CMS) and the London Missionary Society (LMS), both based in London. There was an agreement among missionary societies to demarcate their areas of work in order to avoid duplication of activities in the same area. Therefore, the decision was made by the Basel Mission to start working in the districts of Malabar and South Canara. Both these were coastal districts, contiguous and located on the western coast of India. These districts were newly formed; having been wrested by the East India Company from Tipu Sultan after the defeat of Tipu in the Battle of Sreerangapattanam in 1792.[10] The first three missionaries sent by the Basel Mission landed at Calicut on the 14th October 1834. They proceeded to Mangalore, South Canara to start their activities. The welcome and support the missionaries received from the District Collector of Mangalore was the reason for Mangalore being chosen as the first centre of evangelical activity by the Mission.

From the year 1834, when the first Mission station was established at Mangalore to 1907 when the last station was established at Manjeri in Malabar, a total of 24 Mission centres were established. Out of these, some centres like Guledgud, Betgeri, Bijapur, Dharwar and Hubli were located in the South Mahratta and North Canara districts of the erstwhile Bombay Presidency. The stations at Anantapur and Mercara were in Coorg, which was an independent principality under the British. Centres like Kotagiri and Kalhatti were in the Nilgiri District of the Madras Presidency. The missionaries used to go to Ketty Valley in the Nilgiris for rest and recuperation. Kalhatti and Kotagiri were close to Ketty valley and the missionaries also preferred to take up evangelisation among the Thoda[11] tribe there. The following table gives a picture of the expansion of activities of the Mission over the period 1834 to 1914.In this table classification of districts are as it was in 1834, the year the Basel Mission started its work in India.

Table 2.1: Year and place of establishment of centres by the Basel Mission: 1834 to 1914

Year	*Place*	*District*	*Presidency**
1834	Mangalore	Canara	Madras
1837	Mulki	Canara	Madras
1837	Dharwar	Canara	Bombay
1837	Hubli	Canara	Bombay
1839	Guledgud	Canara	Bombay
1841	Cannanore	Malabar	Madras
1841	Tellicherry	Malabar	Madras
1842	Calicut	Malabar	Madras
1846	Ketty Valley	Nilgiris	Madras
1849	Chombala	Malabar	Madras
1853	Betgeri	South Mahratta	Bombay
1854	Honnavar	Canara	Madras
1855	Bijapur	South Mahratta	Bombay
1856	Anantapur	Coorg	Principality
1857	Codacal	Malabar	Madras
1858	Palakkad	Malabar	Madras
1867	Kotagiri	Nilgiris	Madras
1870	Mercara	Coorg	Principality
1872	Karkala	Canara	Madras
1876	Kundapura	Canara	Madras
1886	Vaniyamkulam	Malabar	Madras
1886	Kasaragod	Canara	Madras
1900	Puthur	Canara	Madras
1907	Manjeri	Malabar	Madras
Not known	Udipi	Canara	Madras
Not known	Basrur	Canara	Madras
Not known	Kalhatti	Nilgiri	Madras

(Source: Taken from various RBMs.)

* *As on 1.1.1914*

Had sub stations at Elathur and Quilandy

@Had sub stations at Parapperi

The Basel Mission took up several activities in their centres of work. These are industrial, educational, medical and literary and journalistic. Our focus here is on the industrial activities of the mission. This is discussed in Chapter 4 and 7. The educational, literary and medical activities which are equally significant are discussed in Chapter 5, though not in great detail while discussing the social impact of the Basel Mission.

There are a few things that are common about the establishment of Basel Mission station. All stations that were established had a church, size of which depended upon the size of the congregation. Another facet is that at all stations at least one school was established. In very small stations it was primary school, while in bigger stations (depending upon the membership) there were high schools. Thus, at Calicut, Palghat (now Palakkad), Tellicherry (now Thalasseri), Codacal and Vadakara, there were either middle or high schools. In South Canara, high schools were established in Mangalore, Udipi and Mulki. In Calicut, Udupi and Betgeri, the Mission established hospitals. The Mission started hospital at Calicut (started in 1892 in a very small scale and converted to a full -fledged hospital in 1908) and a Leprosy Hospital at Chevayur, in 1903. The Mission also had established dispensaries at Codacal (1894) and Vaniyamkulam (1896)

This book explores the industrial activities of the Mission; particularly the establishment of large Industrial units that were confined only to Malabar and South Canara and South Canara Districts. The following table details the centres of economic activities of the Mission, which includes industrial, trading, agricultural activities.

The geographical spread of the industrial activities reveals that these activities were concentrated at locations with transport facilities. Both Calicut and Mangalore were coastal cities with a vibrant sea trade. Places like Codacal, Palghat have access to the river Bharathapuzha. Palghat is also a railway junction. By the year 1882, railway line was laid from Chennai to Calicut. Availability of transport may be the reason for the establishment of large industries in coastal cities.

Table 2.2: Economic and industrial activities of the Basel Mission

Place	*District*	*Type of economic activity*
Mangalore	South Canara	Tile factories, at Jeppo and Kudroli and Malpe (near Udipi). Weaving factory, hosiery factory mechanical engineering establishment, press, book binding establishment, trading branch, agriculture.
Mulki	South Canara	Weaving (a branch of Mangalore factory)
Hubli	North Canara	Carpentry training
Cannanore	Malabar	One handloom and one power loom weaving factory
Tellicherry	Malabar	Weaving unit
Calicut	Malabar	Two tile factories, one weaving factory with a branch at Codacal. Dye House at Quilandy, near Calicut, trading branch.
Chombala	Malabar	Embroidery training, lace making, a branch of the Kannur weaving establishment.
Anantapur	Coorg	Trading in coffee, a coffee plantation at Anadpur, a coffee curing unit.
Codacal	Malabar	Tile factory, weaving unit (branch of Calicut) agriculture and agricultural school.
Palakkad	Malabar	Tile factory
Mercara	Coorg	Trading branch.

Dimensions of conversion

The basic objective of the Basel Mission was the spread of the Christian religion. The following table gives the dimensions of conversion. The table relates to the year 1914 which is the final year of reference of this study.

Table 2.3 Tabular view of stations and Membership of churches of Basel Mission.

District/Names of Stations	Membership of congregations
South Canara	
Mangalore	2630
Mulki	1152
Udupi	2270
Karkal	432
Basrur	163
Kasaragod	256
Puthur	79
Honnavar	110
Total	**7092**
Coorg Principality	
Mercara	130
Anandpur	219
Total	**349**
South Mahratta	
Dharwar	282
Hubli	665
Gadag/Betgari	672
Guledgud	665
Bijapur	156
Total	**2430**
Malabar	
Kannur	1615
Tellicherry	649
Chombala	549
Calicut	2735
Manjeri	121
Codacal	1225
Vaniyamkulam	241
Palakkad	430
Total	**7565**
Nilgiris	
Ketty Valley	**751**
Kalhatti	**121**
Kotagiri	**424**
Total	**1296**
Grand Total	**18732**

(Source: RBM1914)

Taken in terms of sheer numbers, as on 1914, the entire membership of churches established by Basel Mission did not cross twenty thousand persons. There are reasons for this. Calvinist theology lays emphasis on individual salvation; which would counter the possibility of mass conversion. Many observers have highlighted the fact that there have not been many instances of mass conversions by the Basel Mission. Conversion was a long process. At times, persons wanting to be converted were sent to work in the Mission factories to test their sincerity as probationers. As the missionaries understood, a good Christian had to be a good worker or a good worker had to be a good Christian. This shows that, perhaps, one of the earliest instances of the constitution of the individual as subjects started with such endeavours of the Basel Mission; both discursive and non-discursive processes might have played roles in the making of individuals as working or labouring subjects as much as believing or Bible reading subjects.

The Basel missionaries demanded that every convert be made literate and competent to read the Bible. The Basel Mission established primary schools attached to their churches or Mission Stations. As a result, literacy level was very high among the converts. Establishment of primary schools in every parish also *ipso facto* served another purpose of supplying a labour force of a superior quality for the industrial undertakings started by the Mission.

Conversion from one religion to another is a transition that touches the very root of the existence of human beings. Conversion of an individual affects both, his or her kinship ties as well as rights to property. Conversion throws the convert into unprecedented vulnerability and loneliness. At the same time conversion is a profound inner experience. The convert re -defines his or her value base and develops a new way of looking at life.

As far as the Basel Mission was concerned a few aspects relating to conversion emerge. Conversion was usually the result of intense self- reflection. This process is described as case studies, in various Annual Reports of the Mission. There are very few instances of mass conversion. Mass conversion need not destroy kinship ties, but individual instances might result in breaking such ties.

As in the case of any social transition, there are push and pull factors that lead a person to move out of his or her religion and accept a new faith. Push factors could be the dissatisfaction which one felt with one's own religion, and a search for something different. Another is the social oppression that a convert might have experienced in his or her former life. Pull factors could be the sense of redemption from sins that Christianity offered, possibility for an alternate life style, yearning for education, and mobility to a job that cut across caste boundaries proscribed in a traditional society. Therefore, an effort is made to understand the caste background of the converts as it is seen in the records of the Basel Mission from the limited studies that exist in this regard. Rudolph Fischer who examined the former caste backgrounds of the converts from the baptism records of the Codacal parish in Malabar gives the following data. Codacal Parish was the second biggest parish of the Basel Mission in Malabar and stood next only to Calicut.

Table 2.4: Caste background of members of the Codacal Parish as on 17-12-1893

Caste	*Number*	*Percentage to total*
Nayar	22	4.9
Chetti	13	2.9
Thiyya	206	45.5
Carpenter	11	2.4
Goldsmith	8	1.8
Veettuvan	1	–
Cheruman	128	28.4

(*Cont'd...*)

Vannan	33	7.3
Kaniyan	15	3.3
Unspecified 16	3.5	
Total	453	100.0

Source: Rudolph Fischer: *Die Basler Missionindustrie in Indien 1850-1913: Recruitering Und Diszplienung der Arbeiterschaft* (German) Verlag RehieW, Zurich, p. 112.

The above table is to be interpreted with caution. The caste pattern of conversion differs among the various congregations established by the Basel Mission. This is because the distribution of population along caste lines varied from region to region. As it is seen in the above table relating to Codacal parish, 45 per cent of the converts came from the thiyya caste. In the Malabar district taken as a whole, the share of thiyya population was roughly 30 per cent. The next biggest representation was of the Cheruma castes. The share of members from the Cherumman caste was 28.4 per cent. These two castes together constituted 73.9 per cent of the converts. The remaining members of the congregation came mainly from castes whose traditional profession was various types of services. In the population as a whole their numbers were small. The representation of converts from the relatively upper castes like the *nayars*[12] was only 4.9 per cent.

The largest share of converts from the South Canara District came from the Billava caste,[13] equivalent of the Thiyya caste in Malabar. Like the thiyya caste in Malabar, the traditional occupation of the Billava caste was tapping of toddy (a fermented drink derived from the coconut tree), and mending of coconut trees. Following conversion to Christianity, there arose problems. A landlord could deny a Thiyya or Billava convert the opportunity to tap toddy or mend coconut trees in his land. This leads us to the discussion on loss of occupation of converts which was the most important reason that made the missionaries seek alternate avenues for employment.

As Table 2.4 shows, in the Codacal parish, the Cheruma caste constituted about a quarter of the converts. Cherumans were virtually agricultural slaves who were tied to the land of the landlords. In earlier days, they were bought or sold along with the land and could be even mortgaged. They constituted one of the lowest castes, considered polluting and subjected to very inhuman conditions in life. There was still another caste called *nayadis*. This caste remained outside the caste system. They were not allowed to be seen and hence had to remain away from the gaze of the public. As a contemporary observer notes about the impact of conversion on *nayadis*; "Acceptance of Christianity besides conferring boons upon these races also considerably enhances their freedom of movement from place to place which is otherwise beset with great obstacles" (Panikkar, 1983 (1900), p. 175). However, for the members of these castes, realisation of such freedom automatically necessitated seeking alternate employment from their traditional occupations. For the missionaries, industrial employment of their converts was a necessary step in their Christian concept of emancipation.

Sufficient information is not available as to how conversion would have affected the service conditions of barbers, washermen, astrologers, temple shamans, etc. At least in the case of some of them, the missionaries themselves objected to the pursuing of their traditional trade in view of the missionaries' perception of these activities. The traditional medicinal practices which had a combination of application of medicines and chanting of *mantras* were referred by missionaries as 'witch doctoring' (Frohnmeyer, 1893). The missionaries considered some of the rituals performed in a state of trance as 'devil dancing.[14] Missionaries certainly objected to the continuance of these traditional practices which the missionaries called unchristian.

It is clear that most of the converts came from the lower sections of society. In material terms they had a few things to gain. With conversion to Christianity, the convert moves out of the social obstacles that surrounded him or her. In an environment in which the caste structure demanded keeping polluting distances, the convert had the freedom to move about which improved his or her social communication. A convert had access to education and through education access to employment either in the Basel Mission factories or in other sectors such as the government departments.

Islam and conversion

Islam has a history of more than a thousand years in Malabar. Islam came to Malabar along with trade. Islam, like Christianity is a proselytising religion. According to the census data relating to 1881, treated as the first reliable census, the population of Malabar and South Canara districts are classified on the basis of religious groups as under:

Table 2.5: Classification of the population of Malabar and South Canara Districts

Religion	***Population***	
	Malabar	***South Canara***
Hindus	16,92,817	797430
	(70.82)	(83.11)
Muslims	653130	93652
	(27.32)	(9.76)
Christians	43196	58215
	(1.80)	(6.07)
Others	1332	10217
	(.06)	(1.06)
Total	**2390475**	**959514**
	(100.)	**(100.0)**

(*Source:* Imperial Census of1881,Operations and Results in the Presidency of Madras, Government Press.Madras,1883, Chapter IV, pp. 37, 39 44.)

Muslims constituted 27.32 per cent of the population in Malabar and 9.76 per cent of the population in South Canara. Yet, these Muslims did not form any significant proportion of converts to Christianity. Some of the towns like Manjeri and Kasaragod in which Basel Mission had opened stations were centres of Muslim population. Yet, other than making some general references to a few instances of conversion, missionary sources do not mention about large scale conversion from among the Muslims. Making a general reference about this issue one Report states:

> The lower classes of Mappilas (Muslims) are extremely ignorant, rude and fanatical...It cannot be said that there is no opposition to the gospel among the Hindus, but on the whole the work among the Hindus is much easier, and affords much greater satisfaction than the work among Mappilas. (Basel Mission, 1906, p. 81)

This requires a deeper analysis. First, unlike Hinduism, Islam is an organised religion which makes conversion difficult. But this is only one of the reasons. The more significant reasons relate to some agrarian problems, particularly the implication of British tax farming policies. British interpretation of the land tenure patterns that existed in Malabar resulted in loss of fixity of tenure for the actual cultivators who were tenants at will. These issues are discussed in detail Chapter 3. A substantial number of such tenants were Mappila Muslims. The ever increasing burden of taxation was also passed on to these tenants. This situation gave rise to agrarian unrest and outbreaks during the last quarter of the nineteenth century (Panikkar K. N., 1990). It is quite possible that the Muslims equated the Basel missionaries to a wing of the British administration.

The census of 1871 and 1881 period, noted that nearly 50,000 non Muslims had embraced Islam during this period. Such large scale conversion was sought as a means of escape from the oppression of the rigid caste system. That Islam could offer some organised resistance against caste oppression must have been a factor which led to large scale conversion to Islam. In contrast, the total number of population in the parishes of Basel Mission churches established in Malabar was 19,762 (Basel Missiion, 1914). It is not surprising that a Christian Missionary Conference in 1882 observed that "the Mappilas (Malabar Muslims) are increasing so rapidly especially from the lower levels of Hindu society as to render it possible that in a few years the whole of the lower race of the West Coast may become Mohammedan" (Miller, 1976, p. 121).

Despite the limitations that have been mentioned here, the Basel Mission did attract a small number of converts from Islam. Such conversion was usually followed by violent reactions from the Muslim community. The general approach followed by the Mission in such cases was to send the convert to other missionary organisations, particularly the Church Missionary Society in Kottayam or some other place. The convert usually returned to Malabar after a gap of twenty or twenty five years (Shiri 2009, pp. 164-178).

The evangelical activities of the Basel Mission seem to have brought about a curious type of revival among the Mappila community. A report of the Mission notes: "A curious kind of revival is perceptible among the Moplas in Tannur. Collections are being made to the benefit of Mohammedanism." (RBM 1901, p. 86).

Caste and Christianity

Some of the Protestant missionary groups that worked in Kerala had taken an ambivalent attitude towards caste. For example, the Church Missionary Society which had started working in Central Kerala with Kottayam as the base initially converted a large number of persons from the lower castes and communities. The upper caste converts did not have anything to do with the lower caste converts and the lower caste converts had to establish their own churches (Firth.C.B., 1960).

Converts to the Basel Mission came mainly from lower classes. In Kerala, there was polluting distances between lower castes but these castes were a heterogeneous group. As stated earlier the two major social groups that formed the bulk of converts are thiyya and cheruma communities. In the traditional society, a cheruman had to keep a distance of 16 feet from the thiyyan who was considered above in the caste hierarchy. Similarly a member of the Thiyya caste had to maintain a distance of 16 feet from a Nayar. During the nineteenth century within the Protestant churches there was discussion on the compatibility of caste and Christianity.[15] It was only during the third half of the century that within the Protestant churches there was an agreement that caste was not compatible with Christianity. The Basel missionaries opposed the caste system as part of their overall opposition to caste hierarchies. Though they themselves accepted hierarchies of a commercial and industrial society, such inequalities could be explained as a result of human endeavour. Hierarchies created by the value system unalterable by action attracted opposition from these missionaries.

The missionaries also found that their predominantly lower caste converts were condemned to life of low social esteem even after adopting Christianity. Therefore, the missionaries went all out to create conditions for the converts to achieve some economic prosperity and through that enhanced social esteem. One of the best avenues available to them was through the commercial and industrial enterprises established by the Basel Mission. Apart from achieving social mobility, industrial labour had the added advantage of lessening the social stratification among the converts themselves. The general atmosphere of the Mission industries where the converts from the higher castes and lower castes worked side by side helped eradicate caste prejudices. The Basel missionaries are supposed to have taken interest in arranging marriages between converts with different caste background.[16] Missionaries held the key for employment and livelihood of converts. The missionaries were thus empowered to implement their general approach towards caste. As far as the converts were concerned, they had to find partners from among the small flock of new Christians. Referring to the issue of caste Report of the Basel Mission for the year 1914 stated: "From the beginning of our work in India to the present day, we have never allowed this monster(caste) to raise its head in our churches and our strict loyalty in this respect has been crowned with success." (RBM 1914, p. 22)

The Basel Mission was started as a non-denominational missionary organisation. Officially the Mission did not align itself to any theology or dogma within the frame of Protestant faith. This enabled the Mission to receive support from a wide variety of churches and congregations.

But, when examined carefully, it is possible to identify the factors that shaped the theology of the Mission. First was the location of the city of Basel on an important trade route in Europe, which enabled banking and forward trading to flourish. The Canton of Basel was one with fewest restrictions for trade. Close to Basel was the South German province of Wurttemberg from which the majority of missionaries came. This district was a centre of Pietist Movement which demanded a return to essential Christianity. It also exclaimed the Christian restructuring of the world. Missionary groups like Moravian Mission that was started in this district demonstrated that the missionary enterprise could be self supporting. It also demonstrated its belief that commerce and trade was not contrary to Christianity. Thus the trading and commerce could be a means for the Christian restructuring of the world. The backbone of the society of Wurttumberg was the small tradesmen like the carpenter, weaver, and small trader. This class remained relatively independent. Apart from their trade, they did have a piece of land in which they could cultivate something and ensure some food security. They were also a bit free from the oppression of church councils. It was predominantly members from this class that that came forward to serve the Basel Mission as missionaries. As Basel was a centre of Swiss banking, there were bankers who were interested in financing commerce and business in far and distant lands. Some of these businessmen had also served as members of the Home Board of the Mission. The decision to establish a mission was made by a Professor of Philosophy, a banker and a pastor indicating the convergence of interest of different groups in the society of Basel. Thus, while most of the missionaries sent by the Mission came from the class of artisans, many members of the Home Board of the Mission were leading bankers and businessmen of Basel. For example, one of the first Presidents of the Mission, Karl Sarasin was a leading banker in Switzerland.

And finally it was the ideology of Calvinism that united the interests of businessmen and evangelists and the small and independent group of artisans and traders. Calvinism was a theology of 'this worldly asceticism' and was not against commerce and business. All these facets had an influence on the shaping of the sense of self of the Basel Mission and its view of the world.

Yet, the entry of Basel Mission to industrial activity was something not foreseen at the time when it sent its first missionaries to India. Entry of the Mission into the world of commerce and industry happened by default, triggered by the loss of employment the converts faced on account of their conversion. It appears that gradually, the spirit of entrepreneurship and the capitalist ethics developed its own logic of expansion. Over a span of seventy years, that is, from 1844 to 1914, the Basel Mission emerged as the biggest industrial entrepreneur in the districts of Malabar and South Canara.

Notes

1. A movement in Protestantism seeking a return to vital evangelical Christianity as over against the intellectualism and formalism of the seventeenth Century Protestant Orthodoxy (is known as Pietist Movement)....Pietism spread through Germany, Scandinavia and Switzerland. "The new spirituality which it engendered found expression in Francke's philanthropic institutions, the establishment of Protestant foreign Missions, etc." (Virgilius Ferm: *An Encyclopedia of Relilgion,* The Philosophical Library, New York: 1945. p. 585)
2. The Pietist Movement originated in the University of Halle and was founded by Spencer, Francke and Christian Thomasius. Firm,Vergilius. Opp.cit
3. Benjamin Haggot Beckhart notes that a number of banks arose in Basel during the ninteenth century on philanthropic motive. See: Beckhart., opp.cit. The system of unified currencies refers to a system of exchange parity based on gold standard. This system that existed in Europe for some time during the ninteenth century, facilitated trading between European countries. See: Shepard B. Clough, (1959). *The Economic Development of Western Civilisation.* New York: Mc Graw Hill.
4. Reformation Movement was started in Germany by Martin Luther (1587-1600) who rebelled against what he considered as perversions that had crept into the Catholic Church. John Calvin and Ulrich Zwingli were the leaders of Reformation Movement in Switzerland.
5. John Calvin (1509-1564) lived in Geneva, Switzerland. He was a leader of Reformation Movement and preached ethics as established in the concept that the ability to live according to the Christian law is an evidence of predestination for salvation. His leading works are "Sleep of the Soul" (1534) and "Institutes" (1536). (Chadwik, 1965)
6. "The doctrine of predestination is implied in the doctrine of salvation by divine grace alone. It is affirmed that man cannot save himself by reliance upon powers (also religious potentialities) inherent in him but that he is only redeemed by the initiative of the gracious merciful God; it must also be

said that his eternal destiny is determined by God." (Firm, opp.cit, p. 603)

7. See: Book of Genesis, Chapter 3.
8. It was argued that Weber made his observations looking at a small geographical region in Germany and generalised the results.
9. In churches established by the Basel Mission, the 'Elder' is a member of laity who is elected by the congregation. The elder was placed in a position almost an equal to the priest.
10. Following his defeat in the Third Anglo-Mysore War, Tipu Sultan was forced to enter into peace treaty with the East India Company's Cornwallis. By this Treaty of Srirangapatanam concluded on March 19, 1792, Tipu surrendered half of his territory including the districts of Malabar and Canara to the EIC. Initially, both the districts were placed under the Bombay presidency. In 1800, Malabar district was transferred to the Madras Presidency. In 1862, the Canara district placed under the Bombay Presidency was divided into North and South Canara and the South Canara district was transferred to the Madras Presidency.
11. This tribal community lives in the Nilgiris district. This is one of the few communities that practices polyandry.
12. Issues relating to castes and their traditional occupations are discussed in Chapter 3.
13. For a detailed discussion on this subject, see: David, D. Mohan. (1985) Caste background of Basel Mission Christians. Shiri Godwin (Ed), opp.cit
14. Here, two different types of ritual performances are to be noted. One is done by a temple shamen or oracle who is referred as *velichappadu*. Here, God speaks through *velichappadu*. Another ritual performance is referred as *theyyam*. In this case, a distinguished ancestor speaks to the community through the theyyam.
15. For a detailed discussion on this topic see; Forrester, B.Duncan. (1980). *Caste And Christianity*. London: Kurgon Press.
16. Told to the author by elder members of Basel Mission congregations.

Map of Europe

Some of the missionaries who served in Malabar and South Canara

A missionary visiting a family

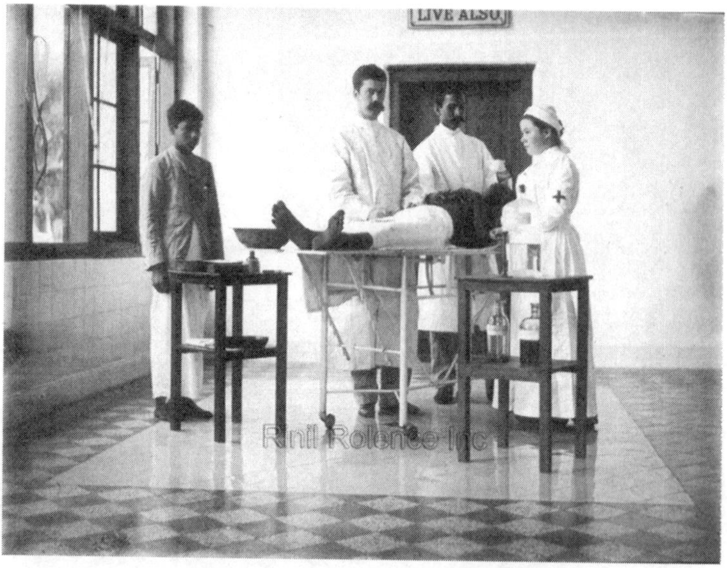

A surgical procedure in progress at the Mission Hospital in Calicut

Chapter - 3

Malabar and South Canara - Economy and Society

The two districts - Malabar and South Canara are located at the south western coast of India. These districts are contiguous and share similar geographical and agro - climatic features. Ancient seafarers referred to the entire western coast of India as Malabar Coast. According to the prevailing legend,[1] the sage Parashurama raised this land from the sea by throwing his axe into the Arabian Sea. He did this to atone for his sin of killing Brahmins (Members of the priestly class). Parashurama rehabilitated Brahmins in the land which he had raised from the sea and called this land *Keralam.* According to this legend, geographical area of Keralam extended from Gokarnam near Goa at the western coast of India to Kanyakumari (Cape Comorin), the southern- most tip of India. The districts of Malabar and South Canara that are the focus of this study are located in this broad region. These districts were sandwiched between the Arabian Sea and the Western Ghats. South of Malabar was the territories of the kingdoms of Cochin and Thiruvithamkoor (Travancore).

Yet, there are contrasts between the two districts, which are worth noting. The South Canara district is smaller than the Malabar district. According to the census of 1891 area of the South Canara district was 3902 sq miles (10,109 sq kms) and the population was 10,56,081. Density of population per sq km was 104. The area of Malabar district was 5583 sq miles (14,467 sq kms) and population in 1891 was 26,52,565. The density of population per sq km of land in the Malabar district was 176. British administrators often referred to South Canara district as a 'forest district' perhaps, due to the abundance of forests there. Yet, interestingly, during the same period, the South Canara district was a rice exporting region, while Malabar was a rice importing region.

The language spoken in the Malabar district as well as the rest of Kerala is Malayalam. In the South Canara district, a number of languages are in use. Though Kannada is the most important language as well as official language of the present Karnataka State, many other languages and dialects are spoken here. A sizable part of the population speak the Thulu language, a language which does not have a script of its own. Another significant number of the populations in the district speak the Konkani language. This language is used in the coast north of Mangalore. Muslim populations residing in South Canara speak Urdu, which is a mixture of Hindi and Persian languages. Marathi language is spoken by the descendents of Marathi immigrants living in South Canara. The people living at the coast speak a dialect called 'Byari' which is a mixture of Malayalam, Kannada and Thulu.

The Malabar and South Canara districts remained, as various principalities under various chieftains. These districts were formed by the English East India Company (EIC) in 1792 after the defeat of Tipu Sultan in the Third Anglo Mysore War. Both, the districts were affiliated first to the Bombay Presidency. In the year 1800 the Malabar district was transferred to Madras Presidency. The region that the British administrators referred as 'Canara' was a part of Bombay Presidency till 1862 when the district of Canara was divided into North Canara and South Canara.

The North Canara district continued to be part of the Bombay Presidency while the South Canara district was transferred to the Madras Presidency. Headquarter of the Malabar District was Calicut (also called as Kozhikode) and that of South Canara was Mangalore (now Mangaluru).

Malabar district - land and people

The entire western coast of India was referred to as Malabar Coast by ancient seafarers. According to Logan, Arab navigators and seafarers referred to the region by various names, such as *Malibar, Manibar, Mulibar, Malabaria* and *Melibaria.* (Logan, Malabar Manuel Vol. 1, 1887 (2000), p. 1) For centuries, traders and travelers from the different parts of the world navigated through the Red Sea, the Arabian Sea and the Indian Ocean and reached this coast for trading. The city of Calicut was known to the whole word from the middle of the fourteenth century, for its emporium trade (Narayanan, 2006).

In order to contextualize this study, we need to touch upon the history of this region. Malabar was part of the Chera Kingdom with its headquarter at Mahodayapuram, believed to be the present Kodungallur.[2] The last of the Chera king is supposed to have relinquished his throne during the twelfth century[3] and after accepting Islam, he is supposed to have gone to Arabia. The whole of present Kerala was a then loosely knit body of fiefdoms.[4] The Malabar district was formed in 1792 by the British by the amalgamation of about 30 fiefdoms big and small in the northern part of Kerala. These fiefdoms had earlier accepted the suzerainty of either King Zamorin or Kolathiri. The King Zamorin ruled from Calicut and the headquarter of King Kolathiri was Kannur.

The Malabar District, thus formed, extended from the north to south along the coast, a distance of about 150 miles lying between N lat 10°15' and 12° 18' and E Long 75°14 and 76° 56'. The coast line of Malabar proper stretched from North, (north-west) to south (south - east) and the distance of inland from the coast vary from 20 miles to 150 miles. Geographic boundaries of Malabar to the north was the district of South Canara, south the Native State of Cochin, in the east Coorg, Mysore, Nigiris and Coimbatore and the west, the Arabian Sea. The district can be seen vertically divided into three agro - climatic regions. The foothills of the Western Ghats form the *malanad,* (hill country), the *edanad* (the middle country) is a region sandwiched between the *malanad* and the coast and the *theerapradesham* is the coast. A few areas were later added to the district. These were a two sq. miles area, Fort Cochin surrounded by the erstwhile Cochin State and Anjengo in the Travancore State. Out of the Lakshadweep islands, four islands (Kalpeni, Kavaratti, Androth and Agathi) and the island of Minicoy were brought under the jurisdiction of Malabar. These islands were earlier under the possession of a small sea- faring kingdom called Arakkal located at Cannanore. There are extensive ravines, dense forests, and cultivable valleys, plains of paddy fields, rivers, backwaters and canals. There are 21 rivers, big and small that originate in Western Ghats and drain into the Arabian Sea. There are three rivers that are tributaries of river Kaveri that originate from the Western Ghats and flow all the way into the Bay of Bengal. The three rivers are the Kabini, Bhavani and Rampur.

The recorded mean average rainfall in the district during the ninteenth century was 104 inches (256 centimeters). During the same period, Mean Average Rainfall in Punjab was 20 inches(50.1 cms) and in Western India, it was 27inches(68.6 cms). In Eastern India it was 48 to 92inches (121.9 to 233.6cms) and in South India as a whole, it is 33to 52 inches (83.8 to 132.1cms). Malabar district received one of the highest levels of rainfall in the country.

Malabar has two types of surface soil.

1. Laterite soil in hilly areas.
2. Alluvial soil in low lying areas.

The laterite soil is mostly found in hill areas and is suitable for the cultivation of plantation crops like coconut, areca nut, rubber, condiments and spies. In low lying areas, the laterite soil is suitable for cultivation of paddy. The alluvial soil found here can be divided into 'coastal alluvial soil' and 'non coastal alluvial soil'. Out of these, the non coastal alluvial soil is highly suitable for the cultivation of paddy.

Economy of Malabar

During the nineteenth century, the economy of Malabar district was primarily agrarian and paddy was the most important food crop. The fertile valleys of Malabar were well suited for the cultivation of paddy. Paddy was raised three crops a year. The other food crops that were cultivated were ragi, millets and horse gram. A number of garden crops were produced in the district. These included fruit crops like mango and jack fruit and various types of tubers. The Wayanad region, which is part of Western Ghats, was centre of production of cash crops like coffee, tea, pepper, ginger, cardamom and cloves. It was for the monopoly of pepper trade that rivalry took place among European powers from the fifteenth century. By the middle of the nineteenth century, a major change started taking place in the agricultural production pattern in the Wayanad hills. English companies like M/S Pierce Leslie and Co, Aspinwall and Co, William Goodacre, Stanes Maylor and Co, Alstons and Co and English and Scottish Company had started establishing tea, coffee and cardamom plantations here. Some of these companies had branches in Cochin, Alleppy (present Alapuzha) and Mangalore (now Mangaluru). Parts of the forest area in Wayanad were converted into plantations.

There is a certain aspect of the geography of Malabar and its main city, Calicut that brought the region into the centre of world trade. Malabar is located roughly half way from Europe to China. Products from two opposite geographic regions - the Middle East as well as China were brought to Calicut for trading. Different trading communities like Arabs, Bohra Muslims, Gujaratis, Katchies and Gowda Sarswat Brahmins settled here and different languages were spoken. When Vasco de Gama landed at Calicut in 1498, there a few persons in Calicut, who knew the Catalonian language, and could, translate this language spoken by Gama. Trade in Malabar did not have significant linkages with hinterland. Some exceptions did exist. Malabar timber was in great demand for ship building. Teak wood from Nilambur was felled and flowed down the river Chaliyar to Beypore, a few miles from Calicut. From here, timber was exported. Timber was also used for the traditional ship building industry localised at Beypore. This place has been a centre of traditional ship building for more than 1000 years and wooden ships and country crafts up to 1000 dwt are still built here.

Non-agricultural activities

The non-agricultural activities in Malabar were mainly coir rope- making, oil -pressing, processing of dry fish, weaving, and animal husbandry. Out of the above, coir making was an activity that had forward linkages as coir was in great demand by the shipping industry. Coir ropes were used for maritime trade as these ropes do not get spoilt through continuous exposure to salt water. Manufacture of coir rope was undertaken through a manual process. Later, during the second half of the ninteenth century, European companies like M/S Pierce Leslie and Co, Aspinwal and Co and Volkart Brothers started coir factories in which production was partly mechanised. Oil pressing was done using animal power. It was during the 1920s that oil engines started being used for oil pressing.

Weaving was a traditional activity in Malabar and was undertaken by a caste called *chaliyas*. They used primitive pit looms. There were settlements of weavers in every Taluk in Malabar. Weaving in Malabar was mainly for self-consumption and not for export. Malabar was not a cotton producing district. Cotton yarn was obtained from the neighbouring Coimbatore area. There was a service sector in the district comprising of carpenters, iron smiths, brass metal workers, makers of gold ornaments. Their numbers were small. Moreover these craftsmen were settled in the villages and *desoms* (smaller administrative units) and their services were mainly confined to their respective areas.

There was a vibrant wood industry in Malabar. From the beginning of the ninteenth century saw mills came up on the banks of Kallai river. Timber was first manually sized and exported. From the beginning of the twenteenth century, these timber factories started using at first steam engines and later oil engines. Electricity came to Malabar only from 1930.

Trade in Malabar

It was from the ninth century, that the city of Calicut (Kozhikode) started acquiring ascendance for trading activities (Narayanan, 2006). Arab traders mainly controlled the trade from here. From the twelfth century, the Chinese traders also started making a presence in Calicut. Portuguese navigator, Vasco de Gama landed at Calicut in 1498 opening the sea route from Europe to India, by circumnavigating the African continent. From the fifteenth century onwards, the European powers started appearing in the scene. The Portuguese were followed by the Dutch, who were followed by the English and the French. The rivalry between European powers for the control of spices trade of Malabar is a well-known part of history. (Dasgupta, 1967) By the beginning of the nineteenth century, a major change started taking place in the trading pattern. Till the end of the eigtheenth century the centre of English trading was the Tellicherry Fort, established by the EIC in the year 1700 (Logan, 1887 (1989)). The EIC was competing with other trading companies like the French East India Company, the Dutch East India Company and The Danish East India Company all of which had established their 'factories' (processing centres) in different parts of the district. There was continuous competition and rivalry between these companies. But after the annexation of Malabar, the EIC stopped its trading activities and focused on tax farming or extraction of agricultural surplus of the region. For this purpose, the Company started making comprehensive settlement of land revenue.

From the second quarter of the nineteenth century, the actual trading activities were left for the English and other European private or joint- stock companies that had established their branches in Calicut. Companies like M/S Pierce Leslie and Co. did varied activities linking trade to production. The company established factories for the processing of cashew and also for manufacture of coir, and fish guano (fertilizer). The Company also owned tea and coffee plantations and was involved with travel business and owned a few ships for the purpose (Langely, 1962).

The economy of Malabar at the beginning of the nineteenth century was, a marginal economy that consumed almost everything that it produced. Exchange was limited to a few products that were not readily available there. Being a net rice importing region, rice was imported from South Canara, Bengal and much later from Burma (present Myanmar). The data relating to import and export from Calicut Port is a highly reliable source on the composition of trading activities that went through Calicut Port. Following table gives the value of imports and exports from Calicut port during the period 1901-1905.

Table 3.1: Quantum of imports and exports from Calicut Port: 1901-1905

(Amount in Rupees)

Year	*Imports*	*Exports*
1900-1901	4,46,486	17,855
1901-1902	5,72,939	1,738
1902-1903	4,31,272	1,943
1903-1904	6,60,715	13,064
1904-1905	10,41,761	3,602

Source: Annual Volume of the Sea-Borne Trade and Navigation of the Madras Presidency and its Chief Port and each of the Subordinate ports for the years 1900-1905. Madras: Government Press.

As it is obvious from the above table, imports far exceeded exports from Calicut in terms of value. Exports mainly consisted of commodities like coffee, pepper, arrowroot powder, dry ginger, cardamoms, cinnamon coir rope and fish guano. Imports consisted of grain and pulse flour, hardware, agricultural implements, instruments, boilers matches, twists and yarns, kerosene, beam, pillar and girders, metal and ores, etc. Coir and fish guano appear to be the only industrial product that was exported.

Population of Malabar

The first official census of Malabar was undertaken in 1871. However, it is the next decennial census taken during the year 1881 that is treated as more reliable. The 1881 census enumerated detailed break-ups of population with average family-size and occupational categories. The total population of Malabar, according to 1881 census was 2.36 million comprising 1.17 million males and 1.19 million females. The average family size in the district was 5.8. The children under 6 years of age constituted 15 per cent of the population in Malabar. The following table gives decennial growth of population from 1881 to 1921.

Table 3.2: Growth of population of Malabar: 1881-1921

Census year	*Population*	*Percentage increase over previous census*
1881	23,65,035	
1891	26,52,565	12.1
1901	27,90,281	5.2
1911	30,15,119	8.1
1921	30,98,871	2.8

Source: Statistical Atlos of Malabar. (1892). Madras: Government Press. p. 7.

As it is seen here, decennial growth rate has been irregular. This could be due to the famines that took place. The years 1900 and 1918 were famine years. (Raghavan, State failure and human miseries:A study with special focus on famines in British Malabar, 2016) For the year 1881 total population was 2.36 million. According to the Statistical Atlas of Malabar (Government of India, 1882), the population dependent upon agriculture was 1.64 million. This works out to 69 per cent. Statistical Atlas classifies agricultural population as under:

Table 3.3: Agricultural population of Malabar: 1893

Group	*Number*	*Percentage to total population*	*Percentage to total agricultural population*
Landlords	1,57,425	5.9	9.6
Tenants	6,84,452	25.8	41.5
Farm labourers	624,631	23.6	37.9
General labour	159,521	6.0	9.7
Care cattle	13,634	0.5	0.8
Other agricultural pursuits	8434	0.3	0.5
Total	**16,48,095**	**62.1**	**100.00**

Source:Staatistical Atlas of Malabar, (1892). Madras: Government Press. p. 7.

The above publication of the government makes some important observations about the land ownership in the Malabar district.

> In no other districts in the Presidency except Vishakapatanam and South Canara does so large a proportion cultivate land for others and in no district whatever is so large a proportion of the people who are entirely dependent on agriculture without any ownership in the soil. Of the agricultural class 89.94 per cent are either tenants or regular farm labourers whilst in not other district these group exceed 51 per cent. (Statistical Atlas of Malabar, 1882, p. 7)

These observations will become pertinent while discussing the state of land tenures in this chapter.

Land revenue policy of the British administration

The objective of annexation of Malabar by the English East India Company (EIC) as a territory was extraction of the agrarian surplus through taxation. For this purpose, it became necessary to identify the owner of land. This was the problem the British faced whenever they annexed a new territory. Multifarious systems of ownership and possession existed in India. As a rule, there are three claimants for the agrarian surplus. These claimants are the state, the land owner and the tenant. The British had inherited the legacy of the Mughal Empire and therefore the attempts made by the British were basically altering the Mughal pattern of revenue administration for their benefit. Some of such changes made by the British resulted in disastrous consequences. Basically three types of revenue administration had existed during the time of Mughals. These were the *zamindari, mahalwari* and the *ryotwari*.

The zamindari system is also called as the Permanent Settlement. This system was initially introduced in Bengal and was extended to almost the whole of north India excepting Avadh and Agra. Under the Mughal governance, the zamindar was an intermediary *through whom* revenue was collected. He received a percentage of the revenue collected as his services charges. But under the British, the zamindar became the owner *from whom* the revenue was collected. The owner was given powers to extract revenue due from each piece of land under them. Under the British rule, the zamindari became a marketable right. People with money could bid for it and often it was the rich traders who became zamindars. The EIC also had a political objective in implementing the zamindari system. Through such a system, the then Governor General, Lord Cornwalis was attempting to enlist loyalty of a powerful group of people - the zamindars, whom they could look for support in times of political and social unrest. The zamindari system on the other hand resulted in creating a group of parasitic landlords who squeezed the peasantry to the maximum. Thus, the zamindari system was instrumental in increasing the immiseration of the peasantry.

The mahalwari system of land revenue existed under the Mughals as well as the Marathas. According to this system, land holdings in a village or a group of villages, constituted a *mahal* or an estate and was owned and operated by the entire people within the area. The assessment of land and settlement of revenue was fixed for the estate as a whole. The individual's share in the land revenue was determined in proportion to the land holding that he possessed. The person who was responsible for managing the collection of revenue was known as Patil, which was a position hereditarily given to them by the Mughal rulers. Under this system also, the condition of actual cultivators became pathetic due to excess demand, arrears in revenue and mounting debt burden.

By its very concept, the ryotwari system of revenue collection aimed at removing the intermediary between the state and the cultivator of land. It is a settlement between the State and the ryot (cultivator). It presupposes "the state itself as the supreme land lord, and the individual peasants as landowners who obtained title by paying annual cash rent, or revenue assessment to the government" (Ludden, 1985). The ryotwari system was first implemented in the erstwhile Barmahal district (present Salem district) and later extended by the EIC to the other districts of the Madras Presidency. In Malabar, initially the EIC attempted a system of settlement of revenue with local Rajas. According to this settlement, 80 per cent of the total revenue collected was to be given to the government and the remaining 20 per cent to be retained by the local Rajas as permanent *malikhana* or perpetual pension to be retained by them for the services rendered to the EIC. This could be successfully implemented only in a few cases. One case was that of the King Zamorin who was based at Calicut. The ryotwari system became prevalent in due course in major part of today's Tamil Nadu, Andhra Pradesh, Karnataka, Kerala, Maharashtra, large areas of Madhya Pradesh and Assam and the princely states of Jaipur and Jodhpur in Rajasthan.

In the Madras Presidency, the ryotwari system was introduced by Governor Thomas Munro, who in his earlier stint as an official in the government of Madras Presidency had lived for some years in the Presidency and closely studied the land tenure patterns. Most of the officials who were involved with the implementation of the system were trained by Thomas Munro, during his earlier stint at the Presidency. After Munro left the scene, situation changed. One major change was that the rate of assessment of revenue was made inversely proportional to the size of holding. Thus ryots who had large tracts of land paid relatively lower tax than ryots with smaller tracts of land under their ownership. Another change related to the method of collection and recovery of dues. District Collectors were permitted to sell the defaulter's land without getting permission from the Board of Revenue or the court of judicature. Lastly, to prevent any untoward things to happen, including an injunction from the court of law, all defaulters could be imprisoned before being ousted from their lands. (Dykes, 1858).

The land tenure system in Malabar

Here, it may be appropriate to begin with an understanding of the land tenure system that existed in Malabar before the annexation of the region by the English EIC in 1792. In Malabar as well as in the rest of Kerala, ownership and possession of the land were separate. All land belonged to either the temples or to joint families of Nambudiri Brahmins. According to historians, during the 100 years Chera - Chola wars,[5] there was turmoil and consequent insecurity for life and property. It became convenient for individual owners of land to write off their property in favour of temples (Varghese, 1970). All land in Kerala thus became gradually owned either by the temples or by the Nambudiri Brahmins joint families who were earlier trustees of the temples. There is an interesting history behind this.

Migration of Nambudiri Brahmins to Kerala and South Canara are supposed to have taken place during the period 3rd to 8th century. It was the Nambudiri brahmins who brought the Sanskritised Hindu religion to Malabar and South Canara. They established temples of which, they were the trustees. The land that was assigned to temples was called *devaswam* (belonging to God). The tenants of these lands had to make certain obligatory payments to the temples, particularly during the festival seasons. The tenure under which the temples held these lands was known as *janmom* and in its original form meant an interest in the soil. Gradually some lands became assigned to the temples were appropriated by the trustees called *uralars* who were Nambudiri Brahmins. This land was known as *brahmaswam*. Thus, all lands in Kerala were either devaswam or brahmaswam. The tenure of ownership of this land janmom was a perpetual and inalienable ownership. At the same time the janmom ownership was different from the absolute ownership of land. A Janmi could not sell his land. Janmom right could not be sold or purchased in the market. A janmi could mortgage his land but that charge remained perpetually attached to the land and became passed on to the individuals to whom the janmi preferred to give as lease or mortgage called Kanom.

In the Malabar, generally the janmis did not directly cultivate his land. He could not do it without crossing the polluting distances between them and the actual labourers who were from the Pulaya and Cheruma castes. Actual cultivation, directly or indirectly was undertaken by the holder of the right called *kanom* which could be described as a usufructory mortgage. Holder of kanom tenure deposited some money with the janmi for which he was paid an interest. Apart from this, the *kanakkar* gave his *pattom* or a share of his crop at an agreed rate, after each harvest. The kanakkars either directly took up cultivation with the help of agrestic slaves if the size of the holding was small. If the holding was large, the land was sub-let to *verumpattakkar,* who were tenants- at- will. Tax to the government was paid either by the janmi or by the kanakkar as per mutual agreement. This was done according to the customary practice known as *kana-janma maryada.* There were no written contracts.

As per the existing custom, as long as the holders of kanom and verumpattom tenure paid their dues, they could not be evicted from the soil. Therefore, security of tenure existed, providing a safety net for the holders of inferior tenancies.

The position that each community occupied in the agrarian hierarchical order corresponded to its position in relation with land holding which was also connected to his position in the prevailing caste hierarchy.

Schematically we could relate caste and agrarian hierarchy in the Malabar district at the advent of British in the following format. This is only an abstraction of a more complex reality.

Table 3.4: Land tenure, occupation and caste hierarchy in Malabar

Occupation	*Tenure*	*caste*
Priests, rulers and administrative officials	Janmom	Brahmins, Rajas, aris tocratic Nayars
Militia in charge of law and order, petty officials	Kanom (superior lease rights)	Nayars and Nambiars
Petty producers, traders artisans, dry land labour	Verumpattom (inferior lease rights)	Non-aristocratic Nayars, Thiyyas, Christians and Muslims
Wet-land labour	Agricultural labour	Pulayas, Cherumas, Holeyas in South Canara

Source: T.M. Thomas Issac and P.K.Michael Tharakan, "Sree Narayana Movement in Travancore 1888-1939,A Study of Social Basis and Idological Reproduction," Working Paper No. 214, Centre For Development Studies, Trivandrum. 1986. p. 5.

It was stated earlier that the holders of janmom tenure were either the temples (referred as *devaswam)* or or Nambuthiri Brahmin joint families *(brahmaswam)*. Over the period some aristocratic Nayar families also acquired this title.[6]

When it was evolved, the tenure janmom did not mean absolute ownership of land. At best it meant an interest in the soil. Very few janmies cultivated their own lands which was very vast. The actual cultivation was done by holders of kanom tenure. These kanakkars were usually Nayar tharawadus or their equivalent Nambiar tharawadus in north Malabar. The kanakkars also cultivated land directly only in very few cases. Actual cultivation was mostly undertaken by holders of pattom tenure. These sub-tenants or tenants-at-will were usually from the Thiyya,

Muslim or Christian communities. Agricultural labourers were from the Pulaya and Cheruma who were treated as part of the soil and hence bought and sold along with the land.

The interpretation of the existing tenurial practice by the British administration substantially altered the balance of relationship between the holders of the three tenures mentioned here. The British administrators interpreted janmom tenure as absolute ownership comparable to *dominium* in the Roman law. According to the Roman law, the term *dominium* involved multiple rights like the right to enjoy the fruits, right to sell, the right to gift, right to bequeath, right to alienate and even the right to renounce ownership. The tenure title janmom did not include all the above rights. It could not be sold, for example. The British further interpreted kanom as usefructory mortgage and verum pattom as tenancy-at-will.

The ryotwari system of land revenue involved settlement of revenue with the ryot directly. The issue was in identifying the ryot from the plethora of holders of different land tenures. Here the EIC faced some difficulty. Finally after much consideration, the government of Madras Presidency decided that the janmi was the 'owner' of the land. The possession of land was mostly in the hands of kanakkar. In its interpretation of the existing tenurial practice of land ownership in Malabar, the British conferred janmom as the absolute ownership of land. The British government interpreted the tenure kanom as a perpetual lease and sometimes as a usufructory mortgage and verumpattom or pattom as tenancy-at-will.

Traditionally, there existed a system of renewal of contract between the holders of janmom and kanom tenures. This was called by several names. For example in some places, it was called as *polichezhuthu.* This was traditionally required as some of the contracting parties might have expired over time and fresh contract would be necessary. There was no specific period of interval for conducting a polichezhuthu. By traditional custom, such a renewal of contract did not mean enhancement of pattom or rent by the janmi. By custom, a kanakkaran who paid his pattom would not be removd. The most crucial judgments regarding polichezhuthu was made by Justice Thomas Strange. He opined that polichezhuthu could be conducted after 12 years of lease. This decision was confirmed by the Sadre Court in Madras in 1856.[7] The judgment was silent about the terms of polichezhuthu, for example, whether the rent could be enhanced or not. With this judgment, the janmies gave up the pretention of protectors of the holders of lower tenancies. They started evicting the existing kanakkars and overleasing the land to a new kanakkaran through a system of overlease called *melcharthu.* In effect, melcharthu was given to the person who offered highest kanom price. Thus, a market for kanom tenure emerged. Some of the existing kanakkars, fearing eviction, started borrowing money from money lenders to retain their kanom. Those who succeeded in successfully competing for kanom made up their investment by squeezing money from verumpattakkar. The traditional balance in the agrarian systems in Malabar was lost once for all, along with the security of tenure that it offered. Eviction suits started increasing in the court. Gradually, the district of Malabar become one of the most rack rented districts in the Madras Presidency.

Here, it may also be appropriate to discuss some aspects of the implementation of the ryotwari system of taxation in the Malabar district. The EIC officials had left out certain items that Mysore rulers included in the calculation of the net value on which the revenue was fixed. The excluded items comprised of bullock charges, and the cost of transportation of inputs and outputs in and out of the villages. They also included payments that ryots made to carpenters, blacksmiths and other rural artisans. According to Logan, when the Mysore rulers had estimated the net produce for assessment, as much as the 20 per cent of the gross output produced in each field remained within the village. This 'farm retention' in kind was a major source of insurance against food deficiency in times of famine.[8] This was not allowed under the regime of tax farming by the EIC.

Secondly, under the land revenue system implemented by the British administration, the land revenue was revised upwards every year by using tactics that did not require any official announcement. Very often, land under cultivation was over estimated. The Famine Code of 1883 as adopted by Madras Presidency had provisions to suspend revenue collection during times of bad harvest. The Famine Code further specified that prompt enquiries should be made and relief granted. This direction was rarely Implemented. (Raghavan, 2016). It appears that in most cases cost of damage was higher than the value of remissions. When arrears payable to the ryot was also added, the revenue demand became burdensome. Further, the British authorities demanded that the land revenuebe paid in cash at the end of every harvest. This was the time when the prices of agricultural commodities were low. Thus the actual producer tended to lose.

Penalty was imposed on the ryot for the uncultivated lands at the rate of 6 annas[9] an acre. The revenue authorities made several miscellaneous demands. These included fees collected for lands cultivated for which official *patta* (title) was not given, earnings made by cultivators through production or transactions in honey, wax, brick kilns in the fields, cultivation of jungle lands and backyards of residences without permission, quit- rent on bungalows and gardens etc. All these demands made on the janmies or kanakkars as the case may be, was eventually passed on to the tenant- at - will who did the actual cultivation. The position of tenant was thus very often worse than that of agricultural labourer.

Towards agrarian unrest

The situation was gradually becoming more and more volatile. From 1836 onwards there were peasant uprisings. These uprisings were more prominent in Ernad taluk where the tenants-at-will were mainly Muslims. From 1836 onwards there were as much as 35 uprisings mainly in Ernad taluk (Panikkar, 1990). The British government initially considered these as purely law and order problems to be dealt with an iron hand. When there was no respite, the government deputed William Logan, the then Collector to study the causes of these riots from economic and other angles. Consequently Logan was relieved from his duties. He travelled extensively through the district and spent time meeting people from different walks of life. He submitted a detailed report to the British government.

Logan's findings

Logan, after making a year- long enquiry submitted his report in the year 1882. (Logan, Report on tenancy in Malabar, 1882) He found that it was the tenant farmers - particularly those cultivating paddy, that were most affected by the British policy of land taxation. A large number of these tenants were Muslims. It was due to historical circumstances that the owners of the land were Hindus and tenants were Muslims and the social unrest and rebellions were generally targeted against the Hindus. Logan noted that in many occasions, Muslim tenants had risen against Muslim money lenders as well.

Logan's recommendations were that small farmers who are tenant farmers should be given security of tenure. He defined small farmer as one who is cultivating a piece of land not more than 15 acres of miscellaneous type of land or 5 acres of wet land. Such farmers should be given security of tenure as long as he does not sub-let his land. Logan also felt the need to protect some of the interests of the land owners or janmies. He felt that if a janmi planned to improve his agricultural activities, for that reasonable purpose, he should be allowed to take back a portion of land that he had given as kanom. Logan felt that the janmi should be able to recover rent arrears from his tenant. Government did not accept the report submitted by William Logan and Logan himself was transferred out of the Malabar district. Consequently Logan took premature retirement from the government service and returned to his native place, Scotland. The points brought out by Logan after his study stands as a classic analysis of the agrarian condition that was prevailing in the Malabar district during the nineteenth century.

The Tharawadu as land owner

As stated earlier, the unit of land holding in Malabar was the joint family or tharawadu. Ownership of land was concentrated in the hands of tharawadus. A noted writer on the agrarian transition in Malabar, TC Varghese made this pertinent observation on the nature of concentration of lands in the hands of Tharawadus.

> The population of Malabar in 1861 is estimated to have been about 1.71 million, of which possibly two thirds were dependent on land. Out of the 1.15 million comprising agricultural population, the Janmies (ie the land owners) numbered only 24,714; of them 829 were classified as principal farmers and 250 were religious institutions. All the Janmies together account for less than two per cent of the agricultural population. To these Janmies constituting an insignificant minority of agricultural population belonged practically every right and interest connected with land in Malabar. (Varghese, 1970, p. 29)

In such unevenly distributed land ownership system, the actual cultivators, whether they were kanakkars or verumpattakars did not enjoy fixity of tenure. This worked back as a disincentive for accumulation. The tenants being burdened with rent appropriation did not go in for such re-investment in agricultural production. This worked as a preventive for the initial spread of market for industrial goods.

The following table gives a picture of the nature of concentration of land in the hands of the controlling unit - the tharawadus.

Table 3.5: Concentration of land in the hands of controlling units

Nature of land holdings	*Number of controlling units*		*Total*
	North Malabar	*South Malabar*	
Dewaswams	12	34	46
Nambudiri Houses	44	86	130
Moosad's Houses	-	8	8
Nedungadi Houses	17	41	58
Nayar Tharawadus	63	60	123
Total	**136**	**229**	**365**

(Source: Varghese, T.C. (1970) Agrarian Change and Economic Consequences. New Delhi: Allied Publishers)

As seen above, all rights relating to the land in Malabar were vested in the hands of 319 tharawadus and 46 temples. During the nineteenth century, these joint families were indivisible. In 1813, the Provincial Court of Western Division, Calicut decided that the Marumakkathayam law did not admit division of family property and that decision was confirmed by the Sadar Court in its judgment, A.S 28 of 1814. (Kurup).

These tharawads were managed by their heads called karavanans. Prosperity of the tharawads depended upon the efficiency of its head. In case, a karavanan was incompetent or a spendthrift, it was not easy to remove him. Robert Wigram, a noted authority on the prevailing civil laws in Malabar noted:

> In Malabar and Canara where the property is indissoluble, the members of the family may be said rather to have rights out of property rather than rights to the property. The head of

> family is entitled to its entire possession and is absolute in its management. The junior members have only right to maintenance and residence. They cannot call for an account except as incident to the prayer for the removal of the manager for misconduct or claim any specific sphere of income nor even require that their maintenance of fair outlay should be in proportion to their income. An absolute discretion in this respect is vested in the manager. (Wigram, 1900, p. 236)

Robert Wigram further illustrates the position of joint families thus:

> There are cases which go to the length of saying that a spendthrift and incompetent person may be excluded from the post of manager. But it is difficult to see how such matters could be settled otherwise than by suit for Karanavan's removal. (Wigram, 1900)

During the nineteenth century, many such joint families had grown into unwieldy size with concomitant evils. Such families discouraged enterprise while they offered security and subsistence to its members. Along with this, there was a tendency to spend large sums of money on social functions like marriages and puberty related ceremonies and such other things purely for upholding their social status. At the same time, tharwadus had a number of men who had no gainful employment and only lived out of the income of the tharawadu. An enterprising member in a tharawadu had little opportunity to have some capital for starting any economic activity on his own.

The system of land relations and social organisation of joint families offered considerable disincentives to agricultural development and therefore, commercialisation in agriculture. Throughout the nineteenth century, land utilisation in Malabar was poor. For example, during the first quarter of the nineteenth century, the total cultivable area in Malabar was 5 million acres, out of which only .58 million acres were cultivated.[10]

Other institutional barriers - the caste system

It was observed earlier that, in Malabar and South Canara, agrarian hierarchical order closely followed the caste hierarchy. This apparent coincidence between agrarian and social hierarchy mutually reinforced each other by making it doubly difficult for persons belonging to the bottom rungs to change the structural determinants.

The caste system that evolved in Kerala had acquired an extra ferocity and inflexibility which was not present in other parts of the country. It was carried to grotesque limits of untouchability and unseeability[11] and had developed into a system of extreme social discrimination. In such a situation, the relatively lower castes who formed the majority of the population would have found it difficult to acquire sophisticated technological skills; and even if they managed to have these, to find investment funds to set up new industries.

Concluding observations

The district of Malabar was geographically blessed with bountiful rainfall and favourable climatic conditions. The district, with Calicut as its main port had a history of trade. It had a cosmopolitan character. This trade however was not connected with the hinterland. The economy was a subsistence economy. After annexation of this district, the English EIC focused on tax farming. The re interpretation of the existing land tenure system by the British while converting the district into a ryotwari settlement area as well as many other interventions made by the British, immiserised the actual cultivators of the soil. Malabar faced famines many times during the 19th and 20th centuries. The district had other structural barriers to economic development. These were the caste system and concentration of ownership of land in a few joint families. Thus the Malabar district of nineteenth century presents a picture of contrasts - immense natural wealth posited against social and institutional barriers to development. All this happened in the background of British colonial policies, interest of which was to extract agrarian surplus to the maximum.

South Canara - land and people

The district of South Canara is contiguous to the Malabar district. The district is located at 13°.00 degrees North and 75.°40 degrees East. This district covered an area of 3902 sq miles (10,109 sq kms) and the population was 10,56, 081 as per the 1891 census. Density of population is 104 persons per sq.km. Northern boundary of the district was the North Canara district. Eastern boundary is the Western Ghats, southern boundary was the Malabar district and the western boundary was the Arabian Sea. Till recently, the South Canara district though truncated[12], existed as Dakshina Kannada district of the Karnataka State. At present the former Dakshina Kannada district is divided into Udipi and Mangalore districts.

The geographical area covered under the British South Canara consists of the Mangalore and Udipi districts of the present Karnataka state as well as Kasaragod district of the present Kerala State. At the time of reorganisation of states in India in 1956, the South Canara district was administratively divided into Seven taluks (smaller administrative regions, each under its own headquarter). These taluks were Coondapore, Udipi, Mangalore, Karkala, Belthangady,Puthur, and Kasaragod. Earlier, Amindweep, (the northern most island of Lakshadweep, located in Arabian Sea about 200 km to the west) was also under the administration of the South Canara district.

The South Canara district came into existence after the defeat of Tipu in the 4th Anglo Mysore War in 1799. The region described above, as well as the present North Canara district of the Karnataka state, were annexed by the English EIC and made into one district called Canara and was attached to the Bombay Presidency. In the year 1800, the Malabar district was separated from the Bombay Presidency and attached to the Madras Presidency, but the district of Canara continued to be part of the Bombay Presidency. In 1862, the southern division of the Canara District was transferred to the Madras Presidency and this district was called South Canara. Thus, from 1862 onwards, the South Canara district became part of the Madras Presidency.

The Gazateer of South Canara district describes the district as under:

> South Canara is essentially a forest district. The slopes of the Western Ghats from north to south clothed with dense forest of magnificent timber and the forest growths, stimulated by the heavy rainfall approach within a few miles of the coast. (Sturrock, 1906)

The district has plains up to 30 km inside the coast and changes to an undulating hilly terrain sharply towards the east in the Western Ghats. Soil is laterite with high aluminum content. The district has copious rainfall. The mean average rainfall during the nineteenth century was 159 inches (403.8 cms). The rivers Netravati, Kumaradhara, Gurupura, Shambhavi and Nandini which originate in the Western Ghats flows through the district and drain in the Arabian Sea.

The first reliable census of the district was conducted in 1871. The population of the district from the year 1871 to 1911 is given as under:

Table 3.6: Trend in population growth - South Canara

Year	*Population*	*Percentage growth over previous decade*
1871	9,18,362	
1881	9,59,514	4.5
1891	10,56,081	10.1
1901	11,34,713	10.7

Source: Census Reports, Government of India.

As it is seen here, the growth of population was steady unlike the district of Malabar which was affected by frequent famines. As the Madras District Manuals, South Canara notes, "Famine is in consequence unknown in the district" (Stuart, 1895, p. 223). As seen here, the population was gradually increasing during the above period.

As on 1901, 81 per cent of the population was Hindus, 11 per cent was Muslims and 7 per cent was Christians. The main communities in the South Canara district are Billavas, Bunts and Brahmins. Other communities are Mogaveera, Mahar and Koraga. Kannada is the official language of the district. It is the language of communication for 23 per cent of the population. Tulu language is spoken by 44 per cent of the population and Konkani by 19 per cent. (Sturrock, 1906) The Billava community and sections of the Bunt community uses Tulu language. Konkani is used by the Brahmin communities. There are three types of Brahmins communities residing in the South Canara district. These are the Shivalli, Sarswat and Havyaka groups. Konkani language is spoken by all the three communities. About one per cent of the populations who live mostly in the coastal area speak a dialect called Byari.

South Canara formed part of Vijayanagara empire till its collapse in 1565.[13] After the collapse of the Vijayanagara empire, local kings and chieftains appeared in the scene. It was this weakened conglomeration of fiefdoms and kingdoms that came under attack and annexation by Tipu Sultan. Thus, the South Canara region, though contiguous to Malabar, had evolved under different influences and had a character quite distinct from that of Malabar district.

Land tenures in South Canara

As it was the case with the Malabar district, the EIC intended to implement a revenue settlement that was 'fixed' 'and 'permanent'. In table 3.4, we have shown the comparative picture of the Malabar and South Canara district in terms of ownership of land. In the Malabar district, the janmi was defined as the owner while in the South Canara district, it was the *mulawargdar.* As its objective was that the state is brought into direct contact with the owner of land and collects its revenue through its own servants without the intervention on an intermediate agent. There is a parallel between the mulevargdar in South Canara and janmi in Malabar. In the South Canara district, all land was owned by either mulevargdars or by temples. Both the tenures janmom and mulawarg were similar in many respects. But there were differences. For example:

> The Malabar land holder who was known as Janmi claimed his land as a hereditary possession and enjoyed absolute proprietary right. The forest and waste land comprised in his patta were not assessed by the colonial government. A Wargdar in Kasaragod although he was a Janmi was quite inferior in status. His land was classified as "Sarkar" (belonging to the government) and he had to obtain permit from the authority to quarry stones. The revenue realised from his land was quite higher than the revenue realised from the same category of land in Malabar. He had to pay revenue for forest and waste land. (Kurup K., 2000, p. 10)

There were big land owning Nair families like Kodoth, religious institutions like the Sri Anantheshwar temple and political authorities like the Raja of Nileshwaram holding the Warg title for the land they possessed. There were also Brahmins (Gowda Sarswat, Shivalli and Havyek) who were holders of the wargdar title for lands. Interestingly, there were some Roman Catholic Christian families (who were converts from Brahmins) who held wargdar title. Most of the cultivable land belonged to the wargdar families.

Mulawargdars rented their lands to holders of inferior title called mulagani. The land rented to each person was known as *gani* and the person to whom it was rented was called mulaganidar. These tenants were mostly from the Bunt community. A good many of these tenants cultivated their land directly with the help of labourers from the Holeya community. The *Bunt* community, who were mostly mulaganidars are described as hard working farmers. They worked along with the Holeya labourers indicating that concepts of polluting distance that was held in Malabar district were not practiced in the South Canara district (Sturrock, 1896). Bunt families were matrilineal and followed the *aliya santhana* line of succession.[14] In leasing of land the quantity of grain was fixed on mutual consent of mulawargadar and mulaganidar and it was not expressed as a share of the produce. Unlike the kanom tenure that became a marketable one in due course, there was a permanency about mulagani tenure. It was a permanent right in the soil that could be passed on to the successor. The system of renewal of contract that existed in the Malabar district was not necessary here. On the other hand the mulagani right could be mortgaged but not sold.

Mulaganidars cultivated their land directly with the help of Holeya labourers or sub-leased this land into smaller tracts called *chalagenis.* As it was In the case of mulaganidars, the chalaganidars though tenants-at-will, could not be evicted or removed from their soil as long as they paid their rent. Some of the chalaganidars even claimed mulaganie rights if they had remained in the possession of land for a long time. As reported by administrators, this was done only in cases where extensive improvement or new cultivation undertaken by them. Midway between mulagani and chalaganai was *vaidagani* which was a lease for a specific length of time.

In Table 3.4, the tenures janmom in Malabar, and mulawarg in south Canara apparently looked the same. Similarly the tenure kanom in Malabar and mulagani in South Canara were placed together, and verumpattom in Malabar was placed along with chalagani. When examined closely, there are differences. For example, a wargdar and janmi are not synonymous. They differed much in the legal incidents. The janmi in the Malabar district was considered absolute proprietor of the soil. In the case of the South Canara district, the Government was the absolute proprietor of land. The wargdar had to pay land revenue to the government for the forests and wastelands that were in his possession. He had also to make payments for quarrying in his own land. But a janmi could undertake transaction without making any payment to the government. The janmi, when in distress, could not sell his jenmom. He could borrow money on the security of his land, which he pledged to his creditor for the liquidation of the interest on the debt and by a series of deeds he could gradually raise the full price of his estate in the shape of a loan, on this kind of mortgage. The debt thus occurred was considered fastened to the soil. A janmi could make second charges on the security of his land, but, the debt remained with the land and could never be separated from the land. Whoever was in actual possession was responsible for payments.

In South Canara, the settlement of the land tax was made with the wargdars. But, observers like K.K.N. Kurup have observed that the level of tax settled by the government was higher in the case of South Canara compared with the Malabar district. (Kurup K., 2000, pp. 22, 23)

Now, let us attempt to conceptualise the differences between the land tenures in the Malabar and South Canara districts as these differences have a determining influence in the agricultural output of the district. As mentioned earlier, the Janmi in Malabar district enjoyed a greater absolute power over the land when compared with mulawargdar. At the same time in the South Canara district the incidence of ryotwari settlement was higher in comparison with the Malabar district (Kurup K., 2000). This created almost a crisis situation in the South Canara district. Many wargdars were not able to pay the tax to government. In such cases, land belonging to the wargdars were confiscated and sold by the Government for recovery of tax dues. These lands were sold in auction. Land sales increased and some estates were sold for as low price as equivalent to one year's land tax. The buyers of these lands appear to have been either people from the Brahmin community, (particularly the Gowda Saraswat Brahmins) or Roman Catholic Christians who were from the Gowda Saraswat Brahmin lineage or Muslim traders. Both the communities, the GSBs and Muslims were traders and it was part of the trading capital that got invested in land. A new class of Brahmin, and Muslim and Christian wargdars emerged in the South Canara district altering the land ownership profile of the district. As it will be seen in the last chapter, such a change has had important consequences when the pattern of industrial development of the South Canara district. Such a change of profile in the ownership of land did not take place in the Malabar district. What happened in the Malabar district is another story.

In Table 3.4, the *kanakkar* in the Malabar district has been classified along with the mulawargdar in the South Canara district. Kanom is a usufructory mortgage in its pure and simple form. In South Canara the position of mulaganidar went by lineage like from father to son. This was not the case with the Malabar district. Renewal of contract was done through a process called polichezhuthu about which a mention has already been made. According to the traditional custom as long as a *kanakkar* paid his dues to the Janmi, the contract could be renewed in the same terms. The most important difference came with the passing of a judgement by Justice Holloway. According to this judgment, the period of conducting renewal of contract was specified as 12 years and the Janmi was given freedom to enhance the rent (pattom) with every renewal of contract. (Kurup K., 2000, p. 31) The number of eviction suits increased and as it was noted earlier in this chapter.

The objective of the British intervention in the land tenures of India was to make land a marketable property. In Bengal under the Permanent Settlement, the zamindar who was earlier an intermediary for collecting land tax was made owner on whom the responsibility of collection was entrusted. It was wealthy traders who had trading capital that purchased the zamindari and later made demands on lower levels of peasantry. In the case of the South Canara district, the tax burden on mulawargdars were raised to such a level that they had to sell the land in order to pay the dues to the government. Otherwise, the government sold the land confiscated from the mulawaradars and sold in auction. In most such cases, the purchasers of these lands were traders. In the case of the Malabar district, it was the kanom tenure that became a marketable one with the intervention of the British administration. Since the numbers of kanakkars were many, a market emerged for the kanom tenure. The district of Malabar became one of the most rack-rented districts as the British administrators themselves admitted. On the whole, the South Canara district appear to have possessed a greater security of tenure. This might be the reason for the greater agricultural productivity of South Canara district. It appears that the South Canara district offered greater potential for capital accumulation. We shall examine the consequences of such a situation in the last chapter.

Concentration of land

An indication to the land holding pattern is the pattas given as revenue settlement. J.Sturrock, in his Gazateer of South Canara gives a picture of distribution of land.

Table 3.7: Concentration of land holdings in South Canara

Assessment value of Pattas (holdings)	*Number*	*Percentages*
Pattas under revenue assessment of Rs.10	21347	46.9
Between 10-50	10944	24.0
Between Rs. 30-50	5584	12.3
Between Rs 50-100	4901	10.8
Between Rs. 100-250	2212	4.9
Between Rs. 250-500	377	0.8
Between Rs.500-1000	98	0.2
Rs.1000 and above	21	0.1
Total	**45,534**	**100.0**

Source: J. Sturrock. (1896). *Manual of South Canara.* Mangalore: Government Press.

The above shows a highly skewed distribution of land holding. For example there were 21 patta holders who held it for the value of Rs. 1000 and above and 98 holders for the category Rs. 500-Rs 1000. These land monopoly institutions were upper caste Hindu religious groups, Brahmin, Jain and Nair communities and temples. As Prof. Kurup observes:

> The land revenue regulations of the colonial system facilitated the depressed castes and other religious groups like Muslims to invest their merchant or primitive capital in land and function as landlords. This process has been strengthened by the end of the nineteenth century and the land survey and settlement of 1903 recorded the titles of many Muslim families as land monopolists in different villages of South Canara. (Kurup K., 2000, p. 25)

The interesting observations or hypothesis that we suggest is that some of these communities were equally willing to move from land holding to industry.

Conclusion

The locales of enquiry of this book are the districts of Malabar and South Canara of the Madras Presidency of British India. These districts are contiguous, being located at the western coast of India. Geographically and agro-climatically, these districts are similar. But, there are considerable differences as these districts have evolved differently. An insight into the comparisons and contrasts will be appropriate here and these may explain the respective paths of industrial development of these districts.

In terms of land area as well the size of the population, the Malabar district is almost double as that of the South Canara district. But, unlike the Malabar district, the South Canara district is multi-lingual.

Though, the land area of the South Canara district is smaller that of the Malabar district, the South Canara district was a rice exporting region, while the Malabar district was a rice importing region. The reason for this differential performance may have to be enquired. It appears that an examination of the systems of land tenures might throw some insights. The land tenure systems as well as the changes made by the British India Government have already been discussed in this chapter. In both the above district, there was a three tier system regarding ownership and possession. Settlement of revenue was made with the janmi in the Malabar district and its equivalent, mulawargdar in the South Canara district. Though these tenures look apparently similar at the first sight, there are considerable differences between these two. The mulawargdar of South Canara is not as much an absolute owner of land as the janmi in the Malabar district. In the South Canara district, the *sarcar* or the state was the absolute owner. The mulawargdar had to obtain permission and pay tax to the government even for quarrying the land under his possession.

As observers like K K N Kurup has shown, the incidence of taxation was higher on mulawargdar compared to the janmi in Malabar. Often, the mulawargdar had to sell his property for paying tax to government and in many cases the lands were taken over and auctioned by the government. Those who purchased these lands were from the Muslim and Christian communities and it was often the trading capital that was diverted to investment in land. A janmi in the Malabar district could not sell away his land. He could mortgage it and raise capital, but the mortgage remained on the land whoever was in possession of the land was liable for the mortgage.

The most important difference in the tenures in respect to the above two districts were on the kanom tenure in the Malabar and its equivalent in the South Canara district. In Malabar as well as in South Canara this tenure was considered as a usufructory mortgage. In the South Canara district, it was a perpetual mortgage and offered a security of tenure to the mulaganidar as well as chalaganidar. The mulawargdar certainly passed on the extra tax burden on lower tenancies, but that did not upset the security of tenure. In the Malabar district the British government decided that the period of re writing the kanom contract was 12 years and that the kanakkar could be changed even if he had paid his pattom to the janmi. This resulted in rack renting and kanom became a marketable tenure. People with resources competed for the kanom tenure. Those who succeeded in getting the tenure through bid, attempted to squeeze the amount from the tenants- at-will. This created immiserisation of peasantry in Malabar. This might also explain the high incidence of famines in Malabar. There was a deep agrarian problem in the Malabar district which expressed itself through many uprisings. The South Canara district was remarkably free from such a situation and was famine free during the nineteenth century. Capital accumulation in the district must also have been higher. Impact of this situation will be again discussed in the last chapter.

Commerce and industry in South Canara

The South Canara region was well-known for trading for more than a thousand years. Trading was the profession of more than one community, each community seem to have specialised in some particular articles. These trading communities were the Kuchies, Gujaratis, Konkanis, Bohras, and Catholic Christians. The South Canara district was a rice exporting region and rice was the most important item of food in south India, Rice was exported to the Malabar district as well as to Arabian countries like Oman and also to coastal towns like Dar-es-Salam in Africa. The South Canara district was not much of a pepper producing region though agro-climatically the region was suited for pepper production. The reason could have been that pepper export got concentrated in Tellicherry in Malabar, much earlier.

From the beginning of the nineteenth century, coffee plantations started being established extensively in the Coorg region by the British companies. Coorg was a Princely State under the British. Coffee was exported through the Mangalore port. The following table gives a picture of important items and value of imports and exports from the Mangalore port. In this table only items above the value of Rs.1,00,000 are included.

Table 3.8: Imports and exports from the Mangalore Port, 1889-90.

Imports		***Exports***	
Item	***Value (Rs)***	***Name of item***	***Value (Rs)***
Twists and yarn	1,13,357	Books and printed matter,	42,415
Piece goods	10,66,418	Bricks and tiles	3,94,293
Copra (dried coconut)	1,08,393	Coffee	51,46,658

(Cont'd...)

Copper and copperware	2,07,315	Manufactures of cotton	62,736
Kerosene	1,58,320	Twist and yarn	12,912
Coconut	1,13,358	Piece goods	85,822

Source: Madras District Manuals, South Canara. Vol II. Government Press. Madras. (1895). p. 156.

The most important of import was cotton piece goods. The next most important item of import in terms of value was copper and copperware. There was a large group of coppersmiths in South Canara who had emigrated from Goa. They were Catholic Christians. Though the South Canara district was suitable coconut cultivation, coconut apparently was not cultivated in commercial basis, which explains import of coconut and copra (dried coconut). The most important item of export was coffee. One item 'piece goods' appear on both sides. The piece goods that were imported are different from those exported. Imported piece goods were mainly for common ware while exported piece goods were mainly specialised weaving products produced by the Basel Mission industries which had established the first modern weaving factory in Mangalore in 1851.

Crafts and industries

Various crafts were practiced in South Canara district as small-scale industries. Their products included coir matting, oil - pressing, manufacture of jaggery (brown sugar), making of agricultural implements, wood carving, basket manufacture, book-binding, pottery and weaving. According to the Gazateer (Stuart, 1895, p. 143) there were 7877 potters in the district. These potters were from the Kumbhara community. These potters manufactured ceramic pottery, mainly utensils and some of them also manufactured traditional tiles using their potter's wheel.

The district had a total of 13,020 weavers in the year 1895. (Stuart, 1895, p. 145)The two important weaving castes in the South Canara district were the Jadas and Sales (equivalent of Chaliyas in Malabar). Their products included silk, cotton, jute, flax and coir. We do not have a picture of the exact number of cotton weavers in the district. We do not have a picture of the organisation of production of traditional weaving and the marketing patterns of the cotton weaving community. Apparently, yarn was imported from Bombay. Piece goods were also imported from Bombay. There must have been competition for their products from the imports of Manchester cloth. The Manual however made a simple comment; "It may be concluded with a fair amount of confidence that weavers have not been driven to other occupations as is so often alleged by the competition of Manchester goods" (Stuart, 1895, p. 145). A comment like the above would certainly call for a detailed understanding of the situation. In the Manual and other government reports relating to the Malabar district it is clearly stated that the chaliya weavers of Malabar have suffered greatly due to the large scale import of machine made textiles from Manchester. What constitutes the difference in the situation in South Canara? Only a detailed study can throw light on the issue.

Growth of the tile industry

As it is stated earlier, in this chapter, the manufacture of roofing tiles was undertaken by the kumbhar community as a cottage industry and in a limited scale. But at the same time, modern tile industry as it was demonstrated by the Basel Mission got localised in Mangalore and other parts of the South Canara district within a very short time. There were big and small factories. As early as 1868, A Albuquerque Pai had started a factory at Jeppo, located very close to the Basel Mission tile factory. This factory was bigger than the Basel Mission factory in terms of output. The Gazateer also reports about very small tile factories like the Vyasachari and Company at the taluk headquarter Coondapoor which employs 7 workers uses an oil engine (Stuart, 1895, p. 144). According to the Gazsteer, This factory used an 8 hp oil engine. The Manuel notes the name of the following factories in South Canara that employs more than 100 workers. Most of these tile factories were located on either sides of the Netravati river or other rivers in the district.

Table 3.9: Names of tile factories employing more than 100 labourers and established on or before the year 1914

Name of the factory	*Year of establishment*
Basel Mission Tile Factory	1865
A Albuquerque and Sons	1868
Rego Tile Works	1871
Premier Tile Works	1882
Highland Tile Works	1887
M. Rebello and Sons Tile Works	1880
Battery Tile Works	1896
Premier Tile Works	1902
Sudarshan Tile Works	1914

Source: Karnataka State Gazateers. South Canara District (1973). Bangalore: Government Press.

We thus come to the conclusion that, while the tile industry got localised in the South Canara district within a very short time after the first tile factory was established by the Basel Mission in 1865 in Mangalore, tile factories of varying dimensions and varying levels of mechanisation and technical sophistication got established in the district within a very short time. The questions that need to be understood is about the sources of capital, the social origins of the entrepreneurship and the extension of market for the new tile industries that came up in the South Canara district. These issues will be discussed in the last chapter of this book.

Notes

1. The oft cited source for this legend is *Keralapazhama* which is part of oral tradition. Hermann Gundert published this work after examining oral sources.
2. The Chera kingdom flourished in Kerala from 9th and 10th centuries,AD. Original capital was Karur in the present Tamil Nadu. Later capital is believed to be Mahodayapruam.

3. There are different views on the actual year of relinquishment of the throne by Cheraman Perumal. Historian MGS Narayanan identifies the year as 1124 AD.
4. Tiruvitamkur kingdom emerged as a stable kingdom under king Marthanda Varma in mid eighteenth century.
5. The Chera-Chola war is supposed to have taken place from 990AD to 1105 AD. Chera conquest reached up to Mahodayapuram, which was the capital of the Chera kings. Finally Chera king Ramavarma Kulashekharan is supposed to have put an end to the Chola rule.
6. At the time of occupation by Tipu Sultan, some land owning Nambuthiri families fled Malabar and took refuge in Tiruvithamkoor (Travancore). Many of these families did not return to Malabar and gradually the holders of kanom tenure of the lands owned by the above janmies were deemed to be considered as janmies.
7. For a detailed write up on the land relations in Malabar see: Kurup, K.K.N.(1981). *William Loagn: Malaborile Karshika Bandhangalil Oru Patanam* (Malayalam).(William Logan: A Study in the Agrarian Relations in Malabar). Thiruvananthapuram: State Institute of Languages, Kerala.
8. For details see: Raghavan. Opp.cit
9. Under the British currency and coinage system 16 annas made one rupee.
10. This observation was made by Ward and Connor in *A Descriptive Memoir of Malabar*, 1826,Madras, 1906 as quoted by Varghese T.C,opp.cit p27
11. There were casts like the Nayadis who were not expected to be seen in public. They had to hide themselves from the public and travel only during night times.
12. After the reorganisation of states on linguistic basis in 1956, the Kasaragod taluk which was part of the South Canara district was transferred to the newly formed Kerala State.
13. The year of collapse of Vijaya Nagar empire is 1565 when in the Battle of Thalikkot, Vijayanagaram king was defeated by Deccan Sultanate.
14. A matrilineal system of inheritance practiced by the Thuluva community in the coastal districts of Karnataka.

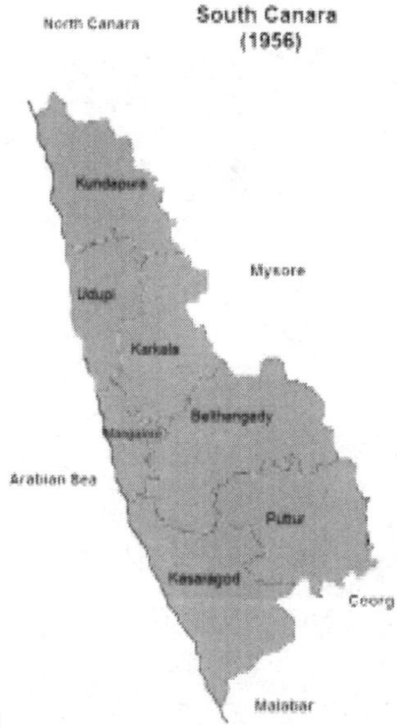

South Canara District- Administrative divisions

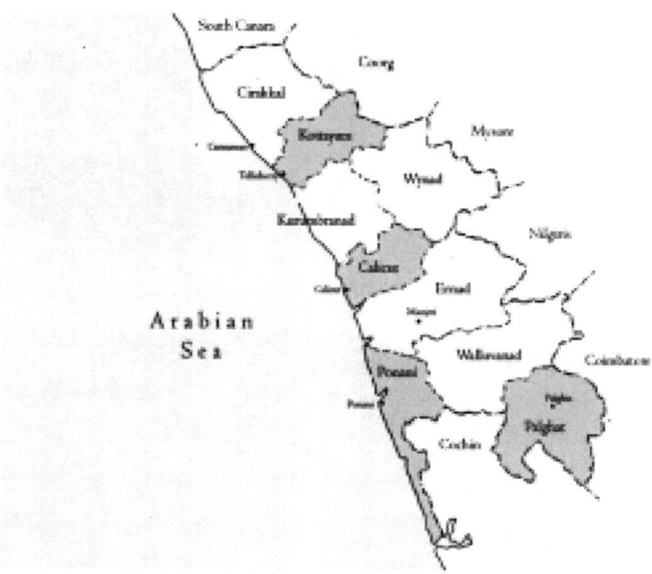

Malabar District - administrative divisions

A Tharawadu

Rural scene in Malabar

Chapter - 4

The Trajectory from Craft to Industry

In spite of the positive orientation that the Basel Mission had about economic activities, the entry of the Mission into industrial and other economic activities were neither planned nor deliberate. The first missionaries who were sent to India by the Mission did not have much knowledge of modern industries. Moreover, during the first half of the nineteenth century, Germany and Switzerland were not industrialised nations yet. It may be more appropriate to state that a series of circumstances made Basel Mission to enter into economic activities and these activities culminated in the establishment of modern industries in Malabar and South Canara.

When the whole process of industrial activity that Basel Mission embarked upon is looked at in hindsight, three distinct phases can be seen. The nature and background of the whole process spontaneously divide the process into three distinct phases. These phases chronologically are:

Phase	Years
Early Phase	1834-1852
Middle Phase	1852-1882
Final Phase	1882-1914

Early Phase

It is logical to think that the early phase began with the beginning of missionary work in Malabar and South Canara. Missionaries started several economic activities on their own initiative, based on their background and orientation. By 1846, that is, within twelve years of starting of the missionary work In India, an Industrial Commission was established in a very informal way within the headquarters of the Mission in Basel. The objective of the Commission was to give direction to the economic and income earning activities initiated by the missionaries on their own initiative to provide a gainful occupation for the converts. This Commission did not have a separate treasury until 1852 when this Commission was reconstituted with a separate treasury. This event was an important nodal point in the organisation of mission's industrial activities. The year 1852 therefore can rightly be seen as the end of the early phase and the beginning of the Middle Phase.

The earliest economic ventures of Basel Mission were in the field of agriculture. Basel missionary, Samuel Hebich attempted to set up a coffee plantation at Balmatta Hill, which was the centre of Basel Mission activities in Mangalore. Balmatta Hill is situated at the heart of the present Mangalore town. Balmatta Hill was acquired by the Mission from the District Collector. This was the period when coffee plantations were being established by the British capital at the nearby Coorg region,[1] nothing more is heard of this venture. One of the first Brahmin converts of South Canara, Ananda Rao Kauntinya had started a coffee plantation at Anantapur, a place near Mercara named after him. He had also converted many of the workers of his plantation, to Christianity. Here, the Mission established a coffee curing unit and attempted to sell coffee in the international market. This attempt was not successful. The reason attributed was "competition of almost European dimensions."[2] As it would be seen later in this chapter, a company called Mission Trading Company which was connected with the Mission had already been involved with trading in coffee. During this same period, missionaries made attempts to manufacture a type of brown sugar called jaggery, out of toddy. As we have seen earlier, the majority of converts had come from the Billava Caste[3] and the traditional occupation of Billava caste was coconut climbing, toddy tapping and mending of coconut trees. The attempt to manufacture jaggery out of toddy proved uneconomical and so it was abandoned. The stated reason that was attributed was the high cost of firewood as fuel.

Following the failure of the above experiments, missionaries attempted to encourage the converts to take up agriculture, as a means of sustenance. With such an objective, in 1852, the missionaries purchased 2620 acres of paddy fields in places like Bolma, Mulki, Uchilla, Gudde, Kadiki and Udipi- all near Mangalore. These lands were leased out to the converts for cultivation. This venture was not successful. The Annual Report of the Basel Mission for the year 1882, rather ruefully evaluated this experiment.

> A great number of fields have however never been used in this wise and were in the course of years more and more recognised as an encumbrance to mission work as the management caused much labour and vexation. (RBM, 1882. p. 10)

The reasons for failure in rehabilitating the converts in agriculture may have to be understood. South Canara was agro- climatically suitable for paddy cultivation and hence this district was a flourishing paddy growing area. The converts also badly needed a means for sustenance. Yet, it appears that this experiment was not successful. Reports of the Mission states that many of the converts who were allotted paddy fields on a nominal rent did not succeed in transforming themselves to agriculturists. One reason must have been that most of the converts were from the Billava caste and may not have had the required knowledge of wet-land farming. We have very little knowledge about the organisation of production of paddy in these Mission-leased lands. For example, how was the cost of cultivation met? Was there a crop-sharing arrangement between the Mission and the lessees? Who provided the technical expertise needed for the cultivation of paddy? All that is known is that the Mission was charging a nominal rent from the members to whom land was allotted. Here, the Mission was assuming the role of a benevolent landlord who did not evict the tenants in cases of non-payment of rent. But that by itself is not sufficient to explain the causes of failure of the experiment of the Mission in helping the converts in making a living through agriculture. As the reports of the Mission states, while some of the tenants became successful farmers, many did not take interest in farming. Gradually, these lands which were not utilised for paddy cultivation became a source of concern for the Mission. The Mission sold some of these lands to the Christian tenants at a moderate price. The remaining lands were sold to the highest bidder in auction.

The agricultural operations rapidly lost its importance in the overall economic perspectives of the Mission. The Mission did not completely abandon agriculture. Later, during the second phase of the economic activities (1852-1882), the Mission purchased paddy fields of nearly 500 acres (known as *Vengalam vayal*) at Codacal in Malabar and attempted paddy cultivation. Unlike the congregations in South Canara, Codacal congregation had a large share of converts belonging to the Cheruma caste whose traditional occupation was wet-land labour. (See Table 2.4) Yet, this experiment was apparently not successful to the expected level. Perhaps, the Mission had not understood the complexities in organisation of production in the cultivation of paddy.

In 1846, Basel missionary Metz who was posted at Mangalore, imported a frame loom from Europe for weaving carpets. Before joining the Basel Mission, Metz himself had been a carpet weaver by profession. There was not much demand for carpets in Mangalore. Later, Metz attempted to train converts in some traditional crafts like weaving and carpentry and leather craft. He established a small training establishment in Mangalore in which training in these crafts were given by the local craftsmen. It was hoped that the converts would be able to practice these crafts for a gainful living. It is obvious from the subsequent industrial activities of the Basel Mission that the task of rehabilitating converts in traditional occupations were not met with success. One reason that the missionaries given by the missionaries for the failure was that "Christians cannot live on the wages of indigenous labourers who are not wholly dependent upon their handicrafts." (Frohnmeyeer, 1893, p. 7) What the missionary Frohnmeyer perhaps meant was that most of the traditional weavers and craftsmen owned small plots of land which yielded some agricultural produce to which they could fall back in times of need. This was not the case of converts to the Mission who were wholly dependent on their crafts for survival. There may have been more substantial reasons. In the traditional societies of Malabar and South Canara, each caste had its occupation. The production and marketing activities of the respective castes were embedded into the caste structure. There were the social barriers for persons from outside a caste to take up the traditional occupation performed by members of the caste.

One line of traditional activity which the Mission was able to enter into with some success was the carpentry workshop. Carpentry as a craft was well known in Malabar and South Canara. Carpentry was practiced as a household craft by a particular caste. As Calicut was a well- known centre of timber industry, the Basel Mission established a workshop to train converts in carpentry at Calicut.

This establishment was both a training and production centre in carpentry. In 1852 the Mission sent to Calicut a trained master carpenter to take charge of the workshop. The Carpentry School trained a number of Christian converts in carpentry. Many of them made an independent living as carpenters. As missionary Frohnmeyer noted "...still you will find on every station of our Mission 1 or 2 carpenters independent from the mission, earning their livelihood by the craft learnt at Calicut" (Frohnmeyeer, 1893, p. 14). However, as a commercial venture, the Carpentry School was not a great success. By its very policy, the Mission had to take a large number of apprentices to the school adding to its overhead cost. Moreover, very soon competitors started appearing in the field. In fact some European firms as well as individual entrepreneurs started making foray into the manufacture of wooden furniture. Western type furniture like cots, tables and sofas were gradually making an entry into the homes of local people, particularly the anglicized sections of society. It would be right to say that though the carpentry shop was not a commercial success for the reasons already stated, it succeeded in training a number of skilled master carpenters who could make a living independent of the Mission. The wider purpose of establishing a carpentry workshop and training centre was therefore served. Failure of the initial attempts in industrial activities convinced the Mission that competition with native craftsmen in their own trade could not be successful. There were more significant reasons:

> Even the native industry in many branches (for instance in weaving) struggles for existence and is dying gradually. This is chiefly due to the English colonial system, at the bottom of which we see the anxiety that English productions should have a great run in the colonies. The country is overflown with cheap English weaving, all formerly done by native Industry (Frohnmeyeer, 1893, p. 7).

Here a new factor enters into the industrial perspective of the Mission. This factor is the impact of the colonial environment on the state of traditional industries of Malabar. This requires a deeper analysis and will be discussed in Chapter 7.

This sordid realisation of the disastrous impact that the colonial policies of the British Government was having on the traditional crafts had considerable impact on future of industrial activities of the Basel Mission. The Mission reflected on the approach toward traditional crafts. Carl Pheiderer, who was for many years head of the Industrial Commission summed up the reasons for the failure of the Mission in enabling the converts to make gainful living with training in traditional crafts.

> We were gradually convinced that we had to reckon with facts and that, as in other countries, so in India, the days of the small tradesmen were numbered. The single individual cannot go against the general competition and it was only the system of improved machinery and combined labour by which success could be attained. (Frohnmeyeer, 1893, p. 7).

The Mission stopped training converts in traditional artisan crafts. Their next effort was in introducing converts in modern crafts. The Mission sent two clock maker technicians, Boesinger and Muller along with tools and equipment to train converts in clock making. They had brought with them components for the manufacture of Cookoo Clocks and Black Forest Clocks which were brands of clocks popular in Europe. Efforts of the Basel Mission in introducing the new trade of manufacture and repair of clocks and watches were not successful and at one stage, some missionaries noted that in the land of indolence, clocks are not needed.[4] We have to go beyond these statements to understand the reason for failure of the Mission in entering into the business of making and clocks and watches.

Clocks were known in Europe for a long time, even during the medieval period. These were seen as curio articles. With the voyages of discovery during the 14th to 16th centuries, there was a need to determine precise time for navigational purpose.Chronometers thus became a part of ships' navigational instruments. Subsequently it was after the Industrial Revolution that watches became a necessity in every day life for synchronising the work of men and machines. Industrial Revolution had not taken place in India during the nineteenth century. But, It is not correct to think that precise knowledge of time was not at all required in India. A precise knowledge of time was required for determining identifying auspicious time for important events like marrige, entering into a newly built house and conduct of important functions. Astrologers knew the means of measuring time. There are also some other observations as well. There appears to be an emergent need for measurement of time, particularly for people working in offices, etc. So there could be a latent demand for clocks and watches. The clocks and watches assembled by Muller and Boesinger were hand crafted and must have been costlier than the machine made ones imported from America during the period under reference.[5] The Basel Mission gave up their attempt to manufacture clocks and watches and train converts in the repair of clocks and watches.

Middle Phase (1852-1881)

Following the failure of experiments in various economic activities there was much discussion on the initiation of industrial activities within the Mission and conflicting views were expressed. With a view to get a first- hand experience of the economic and other industrial activities that were being undertaken by the Mission, the Chief Inspector and Secretary to the Home Board of Basel Mission, Josef Josenhans paid a visit to the Mission establishments in India in 1851. He visited most of the mission stations in Malabar and South Canara. He came to the conclusion that the industrial activities of the Basel Mission should continue, and should be managed professionally to ensure success. He suggested certain changes in the organisation and management of the enterprises. Following his recommendations, the Industrial Commission which had existed in the Mission since 1846 was re-constituted with a separate treasury. The newly constituted Commission also had a technical member. Commercial principles came to be introduced. For example, after 1852, the money advanced for setting up industrial units came to be treated as loans advanced by the Commission for which interest was charged and repayment period fixed. The new commission was placed under the professional management of Christian merchants. With the introduction of these changes the Industrial Commission became a professional body capable of giving clear direction to the industrial activities of the Mission. The line of activity that engaged attention of the Mission first was weaving.

Weaving was an activity that existed in Malabar and South Canara for centuries. Weaving was the traditional occupation of the *Chaliya* caste in Malabar and their equivalent *Salia* caste in South Canara. There were weaver settlements and even villages referred as 'Weavers' Village',[6] throughout the district. As the climate in these regions is neither too hot nor too cold, people wore very few garments. During the nineteenth century, men and women did not wear any garments above their waste. Thus, in these districts, the demand for clothing was not high. The system of weaving practiced by traditional weavers was both simple and primitive. Traditional weavers used pit looms. There was very little dyeing. As it is argued in Chapter 7, by the second half of the nineteenth century when the Basel Mission was developing handloom weaving, Industrial Revolution had taken place in India and due to the import of machine made textiles from England, the traditional weaving in Malabar and South Canara districts were struggling for survival.

Basel Mission's attempt was to qualitatively upgrade handloom weaving, and move it from cottage industry to factory type production. Correspondingly, this required product diversification and extension of market. Basel Mission's entry into weaving is a fascinating episode in the economic history of Malabar and South Canara.

The Industrial Commission sent to Mangalore a qualified master weaver, one Johannes Haller. Haller started transforming the weaving industry of the Mission. Haller's first intervention was in the introduction of fly shuttle.[7] In the traditional weaving practiced in Malabar and South Canara, the weft thread is passed through the warp by hand. By using fly shuttle, the weft thread is made to glide fast, through the warp in a loom. Thus, the fly shuttle increases the productivity of weaver. The extent of increase in productivity varies from 50 per cent to 200 per cent depending on the width of the cloth.

After introducing the use of fly shuttle, Haller's efforts were in transforming the looms used for hand weaving. Traditional weavers used pit looms. European frame looms are bigger and the weight of the loom is borne by the large wooden frame. Frame looms come in different sizes depending upon the breadth of the cloth. The Basel Mission weaving establishments introduced many more technical innovations in weaving. Next in the line of technical up-gradation of hand loom was the attachments on looms. Jacquard weaving is done by an attachment in frame loom through which intricate designs can be woven.[8] Some changes in the frame loom facilitate weaving of carpets, Turkish Towels etc. With different types of attachments different types of products could be made. Still another innovation was introduction of mercerised yarn.[9]

In Malabar and South Canara traditionally very little dyeing was done and whatever dyeing that was done was by using vegetable dyes. Germans were world leaders in the manufacture of chemical dyes. Johannes Haller introduced new dyeing techniques that used chemical dyes. Such dyeing used steam power. As the weaving industry progressed, a Dye House dedicated for dyeing of yarn was established at Quilandy about 20 Kms from Calicut. This unit catered to all weaving establishments of Basel Mission. A notable invention of Haller was the discovery of 'Khaki' dye from the rind of the cashew nut tree *(Anacardium occidentalle)* and of the extract of the heart wood of the catechu tree *(Acacia catechu).* Khaki has the colour of dust or mud. The Superintendent of Police at Mangalore was impressed by khakhi colour that he ordered use of cloth of khakhi colour for uniform for the Police Department. Lord Roberts, the then Commander- in - Chief of the British Army in India while on a visit to the Basel Mission Weaving factory at Mangalore was so impressed by the color, that he ordered the use of khakhi colour cloth for the uniform of Indian Army.

Haller is also credited with introduction of mechanised knitting. Basel Mission factory at Mangalore specialised in production of hosiery products like vests, underwear for men and women and also various types of products using stockinet material. These were products used by Englishmen and women but these products gradually developed a local market.

Table 4.1: Growth of weaving industry in Malabar and South Canara in chronological order

Weaving Factories	***Location***	***District***	***Year of Establishment***
	Mangalore	South Canara	1851
	Kannur	Malabar	1852
	Moolky (Branch of Mangalore)	South Canara	1853

(Cont'd...)

	Calicut	Malabar	1859
	Chombala (Branch of Kannur)	Malabar	1860
	Codacal (Branch of Calicut)	Malabar	1860
Dye House	Quilandy	Malabar	1880

Source: Compiled from various RBMs.

Organisation of production

The weaving introduced by Basel Mission was technologically very different from the traditional weaving. Moreover, the Mission was frequently experimenting with new processes and new technologies. This required close supervision. Therefore, the Mission conducted its manufacturing activities in its factories only. In the establishment of factories, the Mission had a 'core-periphery approach'. The Mission had established three large factories - the first one at Mangalore in 1851 and the second one at Cannanore (now known as Kannur) in 1852 and the third one at Calicut in 1859. Out of these the largest one was at Calicut and had employed 631 workers, Kannur factory employed 462 workers and Mangalore 160 workers as in the year 1913. Each of these factories had branches. Moolky unit was a branch of Mangalore. Chombala unit was units were under Kannur and Codacal unit was under Calicut. These branches served two purposes. Trainees got introduced to basic weaving at the branches and later came to the main factories for doing specialised weaving. More complicated designs and processes were handled at the large factories as manufacture of such products required close supervision. Mangalore factory additionally pioneered product development. Demand for products like ginghams[10] which the large factories could not immediately cater, were passed on to branches. The branches had periods of full production and periods of relatively low production.

Initially, all yarn was imported. By the third quarter of the nineteenth century, spinning mills were being established in Bombay and Ahmadabad and also in Tamil Nadu. Thus yarn was available in India. But specialised yarn like mercerised yarn continued to be imported mainly from Europe.

A certain degree of specialisation was achieved in weaving. The Mangalore factory specialised in mechanised knitting and was a centre of production of vests, stockinet articles, ladies and gents underwear. This factory which was relatively small was also a centre of product development. The Kannur factory was partly mechanised when a power loom section was added in 1911. Power loom section mainly produced a type of cloth called ginghams which were regular designs with lines and stripes that could be produced in large quantities. The Calicut factory, which was the biggest of the weaving factories of the Mission, produced a wide variety of products like towels, mercerised cloth table covers, and products requiring intricate designs. Steam engines were introduced in all the three factories. Steam power was used for dyeing as well as spool winding. Excepting the power loom unit at Kannur, in all the other factories actual weaving was done by hand.

Products of weaving factories

A brochure produced for sales for the year 1896 of "Basel Mission Weaving Establishment of Kannur" (Raghaviah, 1990) lists the following products:

- Damask linen
- Counterpanes
- Towels
- Touserings
- Coatings
- Ginghams
- Jersy material
- Stockinet material

There were many more products. Uniforms for police force, a cloth called 'Webster's Shikari'[11], Abyssinian twill cotton cloth[12], hosiery products are some. At the turn of the twentieth century, Basel Mission factory at Kannur started manufacturing a simple two metre length cloth with coloured border, which was the dress that was usually worn by people of Kerala for daily wear. This cloth was called *mundu* in Malayalam. Gradually the *Mission Mundu* manufactured by the Basel Mission factory at Cannanore became a popular upper end product worn for weddings and public functions. It is said that even the Lancashire Mill industry started manufacturing cotton mull product of similar design later in power loom for export to India. The local handloom weaving industry at Kannur took up production of *Mission Mundu* in a big way after the Swadeshi Movement[13] started. Still later, when the First World War broke out in 1914 the trade channels for import of mull cloth from England was disrupted due to war, market for Mission Mundu expanded and when the new local weaving factories that were established in Kannur started producing the same product and it was called *Swadeshi Mundu.* (Aaron, 1974)

Extension of market

Excepting the case of 'mission mundu' which became locally popular for some time, the Basel Mission weaving industries did not produce any other products specifically aimed at local market. All products like coatings, suiting, draperies, table cloth, vests and inner ware products used by Englishmen in India or British colonies or a small group of Indians who, having come into contact with the English had adopted their dress and manners. The market for the products of Basel Mission weaving establishments was not very big, but these were high value products. Basel Mission showed a great deal of marketing elan in identifying the tastes and requirements of this class of people. Market for these products extended from Iraq, the

Indian Empire, Malaya and Australia. The Mission used British shipping and marketing channels.

In weaving, the overall marketing strategy of Basel Mission industries was to concentrate on a niche market where there was no competition from local products as well as British textiles. What the Mission industries produced were value added products, totally different from the products of the local handloom. But as we see local entrepreneurs emerged gradually especially in the Kannur area after 1914 and started producing some of the products that Basel Mission factories were producing. (Aaron, 1974)

The Mission entered into tile manufacturing during the Middle Phase itself. The first two modern tile factories were established during this period, first one at Jeppo in Mangalore (1850) and the second at Puthiyara in Calicut (1875). Later in this chapter while discussing the Final Phase, the evolution of tile industry is discussed in detail. The other economic activities that the Mission started during this period were printing and book binding, mechanical repairing and fabricating workshop and trading activities.

Printing and publishing

Basel Mission established a printing and book binding establishment at Mangalore in the year 1858. The Mission had established a lithographical press at Mangalore at that time. This was converted to a typographical press due to the efforts of Basel missionary George Plebst[14]. Printing and book binding were not originally conceived as an industry because the main purpose of establishing such a unit was to print books and pamphlets for the evangelical and educational related activities of the Mission. Gradually it started taking up printing orders from the private sector as well as contracts for the Government of Madras Presidency. Basel Mission Press was entrusted with the printing of question papers for the examinations of the University of Madras which it did with great merit. The printing work of Basel Mission won great acclaim and recognition in Madras Presidency. While commenting on the activities of the Basel Mission Press the official history of Basel Mission Industries published by the Mission Trading Company in 1959 quotes from a journal *Athenium* published in London noted that "the Englishmen had been defeated in their own area by foreigners (Basler Handels-Gesellschaft 1859-1959, p. 259)."

The Basel Mission Press though not conceived as a commercial venture, produced a large number of books and tracts in English, Malayalam, Tulu and Kannada. This press printed the textbooks for schools, song books and pamphlets required for missionary work. Some of these publications were books and tracts intended for evangelisation work. But there were also other substantial other works like the printing of the Bible for the Madras and Bangalore Auxiliaries of the British and Foreign Bible Society, text books for schools and even question papers for the examinations of Madras University. Basel Mission Press also did printing work for other well known publishers like Macmillan and Company.

Book binding establishment which was connected to the press had employed 30 people. The ownership of this establishment was later passed on to its foreman, one Lucas Joshua who was a Christian convert. This establishment worked as an independent unit for many years, serving the Mission as well as general public.

Trading activities

A mention was already made about a joint stock company, the Mission Trading Company *(Missions Handlungs-Gesellschaft)* which was established in Basel in 1859 as an independent entity. This company had done extensive trade with Africa, mainly Gold Coast and

Camaroon. Some of the directors of Mission Trading Company were also Directors of Basel Mission. Moreover the company supported the work of Basel Mission. The Company, after paying a dividend of 5 per cent to its shareholders gave the Basel Mission the balance of profits (Danker, 1971). Thus, a close cooperation existed between the Mission Trading Company and Basel Mission. During the Middle Phase of activities of Basel Mission in India, the Mission Trading Company had established its own trading branches in some of the centres of Basel Mission activity like Mangalore, Bangalore, Calicut, Ootacamand (now Udhagamandalam) and Mercara in Coorg. In its trade with Africa, the Company had refused to trade in armaments or gunpowder. In India, the Company was supplying some of the essential articles for the Europeans living in India at the same time not trading in alcoholic beverages that had a ready market with Europeans. Mission Trading Company imported the necessary articles for the Basel Mission factories like yarn, dyes and machinery as well as the requirements for missionary activities like paper, pencil and scientific laboratory equipments for the laboratories of schools established. The Company also marketed the products of weaving and tile industries. At one stage when there was a scam on the sale of stamp papers in Malabar, the Government of the Madras Presidency placed the responsibility of selling stamp papers through this company.[15]

The retail shops established by the Mission Trading Company were known as 'Mission Shops'. Another objective of establishing these shops were to "teach the natives the Christian way of doing business." (Frohnmeyer, 1893) Missionaries often stated that in a land where cheating while doing business was common, even a small child can buy things from the Mission Shop without being cheated.

During this Second Phase of industrial activities of Basel Mission, the Mission Trading Company took up its own direct trading. The Company attempted to market in Europe arrowroot powder produced by poor congregations in Malabar. Arrowroot powder was used as food during convalescence from sickness. There is no clear picture as to why trading in arrowroot was not successful. The Industrial commission assigned the reason to insufficient demand from Europe. The Company tried to make inroads into coffee trade about which a reference has already been made. Profits in coffee trade could not be sustained for long. The Company found itself compelled to limit its trading activities. From this point onwards, until 1882, trading activities of Mission Trading Company were confirmed to arranging for the purchase of raw materials for the various industries established by Basel Mission and marketing of their products in India and abroad.

Mechanical Establishment

By 1873, the Basel Mission had established six weaving factories and two tile factories. Therefore a need was felt to start a supportive institution to attend to the task of repair of machinery and also provide some of the support services. Tile factories require a good deal of mechanical maintenance and in the absence of any supportive facilities, the Mission established in 1874, a Mechanical Establishment at Mangalore. Like Printing Press and book binding, this was a supporting activity, but it had considerable impact on the economy of the region. It was engineer Karl Huttinger who established the mechanical workshop. Initially, the workshop attended to the repairs of machinery of tile and weaving factories. In due course it started producing engineering products on its own. Products like tools and dyes, iron safes, mechanical hand pump, iron carts, metal racks, and even metal bridges - all of which stood as a testimony of the engineering design and execution capacity that the Mechanical Establishment developed. This institution conducted night classes for its employees on engineering drawing and workshop practices and in the process produced a large number of mechanics and fitters whose services were in great demand in Mumbai (formerly Bombay) where in areas like Parel and Byculla, even now there is large number of emigrant South Canara population. In these areas, there are many Basel Mission congregations. This institution had a significant impact on the industrial development of South Canara. A number of members of the Basel Mission congregations who were trained by the Mechanical Establishment became entrepreneurs and established foundries and mechanical workshops in and around Mangalore. Availability of trained mechanics is supposed to be a factor that facilitated rapid development of road transport in South Canara. When bus transport was becoming popular in Kannur, the first road transport in Kannur was operated by entrepreneurs from South Canara. (Aaron, 1974)

The Final Phase (1882-1914)

In 1882, the Industrial Commission was merged with the Mission Trading Company. Thereafter, the entire industrial undertakings of Basel Mission in India, which was earlier under Industrial Commission was amalgamated with Mission Trading Company *(Missions Hanglungs-Gesellschaft)* retaining the name of Mission Trading Company. This was a joint stock company. Under this agreement, the Mission Trading Company paid a dividend of 5 per cent to its share holders and the rest was passed over to the Basel Mission. The equity capital of Mission Trading Company consisted of 300 shares of 100 Pound Sterling, of which 120 shares were held by the Basel Mission Society. The executive of the Company consisted of six directors, two of whom were selected by the Basel Mission while the officials placed in Basel consisted of two managers and a Technical Assistant.

The amalgamation of the Industrial Commission and Mission Trading Company into a single joint stock company enabled the Mission to overcome its main difficulty in expansion of industries which was availability of finance. The Mission was no more dependent upon the surplus generated by their units in India for reinvestment and growth. A joint stock company can have access to the European capital market in which Basel itself was an important centre. The presence of bankers and industrialists in the Board of the Mission facilitated such an access.

At this period, there were seven weaving factories and two tile factories that were already in existence. The weaving units were performing well, but there were several threats in the environment. Large scale expansion in weaving could make the Mission industries compete with British investments in the similar lines. The Mission took the path of least resistance in deciding to invest in tile industry. Unlike weaving, tile industry requires much greater initial capital. Moreover the performance of the first two tile factories was far beyond expectations. Mission's entry into tile manufacturing is another path breaking saga.

In Malabar and South Canara, manufacturing of tiles were practiced as a branch of pottery by the potter caste. In the Malabar district this caste was known as *kushava* and in South Canara, they were called *kumbara.* It was a centuries old profession. One of the early observes of the society Malabar, Duarte Barboza who spent a decade in Malabar as a writer (clerk/accountant) in the Portuguese mercantile establishments commented about the potter caste thus: "Their business is to work at baked clay and tiles with which the temples and royal buildings are roofed and by law no other person may roof their houses except with palm branches (Barboza, 1970, p. 134)." Potters used a cylindrical shaped die that was placed at the centre of the potter's wheel and around the die a cast with clay was, made. This cast was circular in shape but without a bottom. This was taken out and cut into four to get similar shaped curved tiles. These tiles were dried and baked. As these tiles were small and thin, three or four layers of tiles were placed, one on top of the other. Thus the roofing was heavy and needed heavy superstructure to bear the load. In general people used palm or coconut leaves for roofing. Lower castes were not permitted to use tile roofing and they could not afford to use it either.

Not much changed till the end of the eighteenth century. By nineteenth century, the British administration of Malabar was gradually getting stabilised and there was a demand for tiles for public works. Administrative buildings, railway and telegraphs and military infrastructure was being built. Traditional potters, with their age old technology, were unable to meet this emerging demand. Thus stage was set for the rapid expansion of Basel Mission's machine made roofing tiles.

Much of the credit for starting the new activity in tiles goes to Basel Missionary, George Plebst about whom a mention has already been made. After setting up the Basel Mission Press, at Mangalore, Plebst went back to Germany and spent some time learning the art of tile making which included treatment of clay, technique of glazing, construction of kiln and burning process. On his return from to Mangalore in 1864, with the help of a local master potter, he built his own kiln and started experiments in it. The results were impressive and beyond all expectations.

Raw material for the manufacture of tiles is clay or feldspar (Aluminium silicate.)[16] This was found in abundance in the river banks of Netravati near Mangalore. The first tile factory was established by Plebst in 1865 at Jeppo, located at the banks of the river Netravati. This factory employed two workers and produced 360 tiles per day. The growth of this unit was phenomenal. In 1871, the factory which was by then modernised, employed 60 workers and produced 2,09,000 tiles a year. By 1873, the tile factory had paid back its entire investment. By 1880 this unit had started employing 131 workers and was producing one million tiles a year.

In 1881, the bullock power was replaced by steam power. Steam power was used to operate the pug mill for mixing of clay and de airing machines for removing the air bubbles from clay. The further technical change that was introduced in this factory was conversion of existing kiln into gas firing kiln (using wood gas) for obtaining uniform temperatures for the production of salt glazed tiles and other terracotta ware. During the Middle Phase itself the Mission had started a second tile factory - at Puthiyara in Calicut. But the Jeppo tile factory continued to be a centre for product development under the direction of engineer missionaries.

After 1882, the Mission opened only tile factories. The following table gives a chronological list of the tile factories established by the Mission in Malabar and South Canara.

Table 4.2: Establishment of tile factories: chronological order

Place	*District*	*Year of Establishment*
Jeppo (Mangalore)	South Canara	1865
Calicut	Malabar	1873
Kudroli	South Canara	1882
Malpe	South Canara	1886
Codacal	Malabar	1887
Palakkad	Malabar	1887
Feroke (Calicut)	Malabar	1905

Source: Various RBMs

Originally these factories produced flat tiles, different from the curved and grooved types which are presently being used for roofing. Flat tiles are heavier and for the curved tiles which are thinner the curved design gives more strength. Basel Mission's tile factories produced a wide array of ceramic products like: Roofing Tiles, Ridge Tiles, Ornamental Ridge Tiles, Skylights, Ventilators, Ridge Terminals, Hip Terminals, Finials of various kinds, Grooved sire tiles, Hanging Wall Tiles, Ceiling Tiles, Hourdis (Ceiling Slabs), Clay Flooring Tiles, Refractory Bricks, Salt Glazed Stones[17], Drainage Pipes, Terracotta Vases, Flower Pots and Architectural Terracotta Ware.

The market for tiles covered the entire British Empire and the Mission made use of trade channels that existed within the British Empire. They were also exported in large quantities to Strait Settlements (present Malaysia), Sumatra, Borneo and to Australia. These tiles were also exported to Camaroon and Ghana where the Basel Mission had already made its presence.[18] Basel Mission tiles were used in railway stations from Mombasa to Lake Victoria in Africa. The following table gives a picture of the industrial and trading infrastructure of the Mission at the outbreak of the First World War.

Table 4.3: Employment in industrial and trading activities of the Basel Mission in Malabar and South Canara.

Establishment	*Centre*	*District*	*EMPLOYMENT*		
			Members of Basel Mission	*Others*	*Total*
Mercantile Mission	Mangalore	South Canara	14	-	14
	Mercara	Coorg	5	1	6
Mechanical	Mangalore)	South Canara	92	7	99
Establishment					
Weaving Factories					
	Calicut	Malabar	616	15	631
	Codacal	Malabar	42	-	42
	Kannur	Malabar	454	8	462
	Chombala	Malabar	88	-	88
	Mangalore	South Canara	160	-	160
	Moolky	South Canara	12	-	12

(*Cont'd...*)

Sub - total for weaving establishments			1443	23	1466
Tile Factories					
	Jeppo	South Canara	259	122	381
	Kudroli	South Canara	231	211	442
	Malpe	South Canara	82	9	91
	Calicut	Malabar	131	126	257
	Feroke	Malabar	65	252	317
	Codacal	Malabar	234	48	282
	Palakkat	Malabar	123	155	278
Sub total (Tile factories)			1125	923	2048
Grand Total			2679	954	3633

Source: RBM, 1913.

The above table gives interesting insights. Total employment in the above establishments was 3633. Out of the above 2679 persons amounting to 73 per cent are members of Basel Mission Church. In weaving factories, 98 per cent of workers are members of church while in tile factories the percentage of members of church was 31 per cent. Even within the tile factories, in Palakkad and Feroke factories which were the last ones to be established ones, the non Christian employees outnumbered members of the Basel Mission Church. In Kudroli factory, which was the largest one in terms of employment, the proportion of members of church to others was roughly equal. The apparent reason would have been that tile factories would have had to be located in areas which have availability of raw materials and transportation facilities. In such areas labour recruitment would have followed availability than the preference for converts. There is a difference in the labour content between weaving and tile factories. Weaving is a skilled task that requires some training. Most workers in weaving factories are skilled workers. In tile factories the supervisor or *maestri* is the person who is skilled. Labour is mostly the type of casual labour.

As it is seen here a total of 2679 workers were from the Church. If a rough estimation of 1:4 dependency ratio is taken (four dependents for one working person), the total number of members of the Church who are dependent upon the Mission for sustenance will be 10716. Total membership in all the Basel Mission Churches put together was 19762 during the period (Table 2.3) us, taken on the whole, 54 per cent of the members of congregations were directly dependent upon the Mission factories for their daily existence.

Financial indicators

The following two tables give a comparative picture of financial structure of weaving and tile industry. These comparisons are made on the basis of the financial statements o for the years 1877-79. Data relating to the two years are averaged.

Table 4.4: Comparison of cost structure-weaving and tile industries

Sl. No.	*Item of Cost*	*Percentage share of the Value of Production*	
		Weaving Factories	*Tile Factories*
1.	Raw materials	44.0	44.9
2.	Payment on account of labour and staff	25.3	18.8
3.	Business expenses	6.9	5.8
4.	Interest paid on capital	3.9	7.5
5.	Maintenance allowance of supervisor	5.5	5.5
6.	Depreciation	2.6	9.9
7.	Profits	11.8	3.5
	Total	**100.0**	**100.0**

Source: Derived from the Profit and Loss Statements of the units relating to the years 1877-79, provided by Union Trading Corporation International, Basel, successor company of Mission Trading Company.

The above table is to be interpreted with caution. By the year 1879, the weaving industry of Basel Mission had achieved a certain maturity while tile industry was at its infant stage. Yet, the comparisons are significant. The most glaring comparison is on the share of interest on loans. For tile industry, this is higher in comparison with weaving industry. Tile industry is obviously more capital intensive compared to weaving industry and that could be the reason for higher interest cost. Depreciation on machinery is also higher for tile industry. Share of profits to the total value of production is higher for handloom industry. This corroborates with our observations in Table 3.6. Gross profit to sales ratio is higher for weaving compared to tile industry. At this point value added by manufacture of weaving industry was higher than that of tile industry. But the actual profits from tile industry must have been higher because of the high turnover in tile industry and this could be the reason as to why Basel Mission continued to invest only on tile industry after 1882.

Table 4.5: Weaving and tile industries: some comparative performance indicators

(Amount in Rupees)

Sl. No.	*Performance parameter*	*Weaving*	*Tile*
1.	Net value added per worker	Rs. 116	Rs. 101
2.	Net value added as a percentage to total value of Production	41.02	29.93
3.	Gross profit to sales (percentage)	11.76	8.8

Source: Derived from the Profit and Loss Statements of the units relating to the years 1877-79, provided by Union Trading Corporation International, Basel. Data for the two years have been averaged. Value Added by Manufacture is the value of output less the cost of inputs excluding labour. It refers to the value that labour is adding to the raw material. In the above table, Value Added by Manufacture, averaged for two years is divided by the number of labourers to arrive at value added per worker.

Employment and wages

We have discussed so far only one aspect of employment in Mission factories; that is employment of members of the Church as against others. One observation is that 98 per cent of workers in weaving factories were members of Church as against 55 per cent in tile factories. This data related to the year 1914. As we have discussed here, there is a difference between the policies of Basel Mission in employment and wages before 1882 and after 1882.

From the data available for the year 1877-79, we get a picture of employment classified into regular and daily wage for weaving and tile factories.

Table 4.6: Employment classified into regular and daily wagers

Type of employment	***Weaving Units***	***Tile Units***
Regular Employment	379	1
Daily Wagers	1	131
Total	**380**	**132**

Source: Derived from the data relating to the years 1877-79, provided by Union Trading Corporation International, Basel, which is the successor company of Basel Mission Industries.

The tile factories seem to have operated mainly with casual labour while weaving factories worked with permanent employment, it is clear that converts found employment mainly in weaving factories while the share of employment of converts in tile factories were low. This position seems to have undergone some change by the year 1914. For the tile factories established in Palghat and Feroke, the share of converts as employees reached roughly half.

The wage differential between weaving and tile industry will further offer insights into the nature of employment.

Table 4.7: Employment and wages- comparison between tile and weaving industries

(Amount in Rupees)

Line of Manufacture	***No of workers***	***Total Yearly Wages***	***Average yearly Wages***	***Average Monthly Wags***
Tile factories	132	7415	56.17	4.68
Weaving factories	380	27999	73.68	6.14

Source: Compiled from the Profit and Loss Statement as well as the Census of Employment of the Basel Mission Industries. Data supplied by Union Trading Corporation International Ltd, Basel, successor of Basel Mission Industries. Data relating to the two years 1877-79 has been averaged.

As on the years under reference, the average wages in weaving factories were higher than tile factories. The gentle push of the piece rates appears to have made the weavers hard at work. What is given above is a macro picture on the wage differential between the two lines of manufacture. Due to paucity of data, it has not been possible to compare wages at Mission industries with the corresponding wages that were prevailing outside. Annual Reports of the Basel Mission makes occasional references about wage rates. For example, the Report for the year 1871 notes that average monthly earnings of a weaver is Rs. 9. Report for the year 1909 notes that the average daily wages in tile factories ranges from 4 to 6 annas. (16 annas make a rupee), while the income of an ordinary weaver is about Rs.12 to Rs. 15 per month. Fischer (1978) who has studied this aspect rigorously had some interesting observations. Fischer observed that up to 1882, weaving and tile factories of Basel Mission paid higher wage scale than that were prevalent locally or in other branches of industry. After 1882, real wages in the mission factories suffered general erosion, mainly after the integration of Mission industry with Mission Trading Company. The newly acquired commercial outlook of the Basel Mission industries after their amalgamation with the Mission Trading Company seems to have had some influence in determining the wage scale. After 1882, it was considered that payment of wages higher than the market levels was not compatible with healthy business principles. Christian and non Christian workers received the same wages for the same work. But Christian workers received additional benefits in terms of subsidized housing and rice donations and relief in emergencies. The condition of work was also the same for all workers - 9 to 10 hours of work a day and six days a week.

Types of employment

Paucity of data does not enable us to explore the types

of employment in the weaving and tile factories in detail. The data that is available relates to July 1877 and refers only to weaving factories. This is a period when weaving had not started using steam engine, for we do not find designations like Engine Driver (steam engine operator), mechanic, etc. At this time spool winding in weaving industry was done manually. It is in this role that women were employed in large numbers. As we see in the following table No. 4.8, out of 392 employees, 216 employees were women.

When steam engines were introduced in factories, it was spool winding, the task predominantly performed by women that got mechanised. However there were other sections that got opened later like embroidery, tailoring. These activities were performed mainly by women and this would have reduced the fall in the share of women in labour force of Basel Mission industries.

Disciplining of the labour force

During the period up to 1880, when the industrial units were small and mostly weaving units, there appears to have been very little problem in the disciplining of labour force. The general attitude of the missionary managers towards labourers was one of patronising nature intended to facilitate the converts to adjust into their new way of life. At this point of time, the weavers were a respectable, dutiful and well- behaved section of the congregations. The relatively higher wages the workers in Mission factories received as well as some of the fringe benefits like rice donations and availability of financial support at the time of emergencies must have been adequate to keep weavers at work.

With the establishment of tile factories, the picture became very different. Each of the tile factories employed more than 300 workers. Factories like the one at Kurdoli

Table 4.8: Census of employment in the Basel Mission weaving factories as on July 1877

Location of Weaving Unit	***Supervisor and Moster***	***Writer, shop Supdt. etc***	***Weaver***	***Label Maker***	***Apprentices***	***Thread Makers and Spool Winders***	***Dyer***	***Carpenters***	***Servants and Daily Wagers***	***Total***
Mongolore	1	-	26	2	8	46	3	-	1	87
Cannonore	3	5	43	3	12	71	-	2	-	139
Tellicherry	1	-	11	1 4		13	-	-	-	30
Chombala	-	-	8	1	2	5	-	-	-	30
Colicut	1	1	24	-	3	76	2	-	-	107
Codacol	8	5	- -	-	13					
Total	**6**	**6**	**120**	**7**	**29**	**216**	**5**	**2**	**1**	**392**

Source: Provided by Union Trading Corporation International, successor company of Mission Trading Company.

in Mangalore and Feroke in Malabar had more than 400 workers. The number of non-Christian workers outnumbered that of Christian workers. It became no more possible to control the laborers making use of the Christian maistry who was also often an 'elder' in the congregation and hence presented as model worker/ Christian. Here, the missionary managers and the Indian maestries struggled to control hoards of daily wagers, enforcing standards of performance above the levels of agricultural duties. Frohnmeyer observed about the environment prevailing in large factories:

> In a place where so many people live together, naturally also something like and *espirit de corps* will spring up, and the spirit is not always of the best kind, reminding one of the proletarian spirit rising under similar conditions at home. (Frohnmeyer, 1893, pp. 8, 9)

The first tile factories were immensely successful. But at Mangalore, competitors started appearing some of whom copied the designs and innovated further.[19] In order to retain the cutting edge in competition, the Headquarters in Basel decided to expand the existing capacities and start much bigger units. The intention of the Headquarters must have been to make use of economies of scale. At the same time, the general economic recession of the period provided some push effects for the mobilisation of the labour force. During the first years of the twentieth century, both Calicut and Kannur factories had more than 450 workers. The atmosphere in the larger factories was certainly very different. One desperate factory manger wrote:

> We have a spirit of insubordination, insolence, untruthfulness, disrespect and meanness, and sometimes this is beyond me....the education of these people looks like an impossible thing to me. (Fischer, Mission and modernisation: *The Basel Mission factories as agencies of social change, 1850-1913.* Shiri (Ed)1985, p. 209)

Some managers resorted to drastic punitive measures to restore a measure of control. These were objected by the local missionaries for the reason that such measures did not form part of Mission's overall objectives. After all, it was the missionaries who had to face the turmoil of congregations arising out of disciplining measures of factory managers. In some other cases the missionaries supported punitive actions of the factory managers as they felt that some workers will have to be disciplined. But in such cases also the position of missionaries became difficult. They were forced to participate in the disciplining of the labour force throughout the week and speak to them of God's love on Sundays.

The only strike in the history of Basel Mission Industry took place was at a weaving factory where majority of workers were members of the Basel Mission congregation and not in a tile factory where a larger sections of the labourers were non- converts. In 1901, at the weaving factory at Kannur, the entire labour force walked out in response to manager's refusal to grant higher piece rates for some new designs, which were more difficult to weave. This strike was a response to what the workers felt as the unbearable rule of the missionaries and missionary managers over them. The traditional control mechanism of labour using the model Christian maistry as we explained earlier seem to have failed here. In this strike, some of the maestries or supervisors whom the Mission always wished to present as 'model workers' and therefore model Christians[20] turned to be hostile to the Mission and even became leaders of agitation.[21] Therefore, it may be relevant to explore the background of the strike and the dominant ideologies that sustained it.

The ideologue at the centre of the labour action mentioned here was interestingly, a dissident Basel missionary, Volbrecht Nagel. Nagel came from working class background and was a weaver by profession. After starting his work as a Basel missionary at Kannur, Nagel started having serious differences with Basel Mission on the theological and liturgical perspective of the Mission. Most important of these aspects related to the priest's declaration of God's forgiveness of sins during the church worship. Nagel believed that only God can forgive sins. The Mission, perturbed at Nagal's stand, asked Nagel to report back at Basel, which he refused. Nagel left the Mission, married a local woman and settled down at Chovva, 20 kms south of Kannur. Meanwhile, Nagel had acquired considerable felicity in Malayalam language, and had started even composing hymns and gospel songs in Malayalam. He founded a 'counter church' at Kannur into which, members of Basel Mission congregation were attracted. Some of those who joined Nagel were even supervisors or maestries. Basel Mission closely monitored the activities of Nagel, and even had a dossier prepared on him, but could do precious little to prevent Nagel from his activities.

This new congregation, which the Basel Mission described 'Anabaptist'[22] used Biblical examples as their dominant ideology. Their present situation of Basel Mission converts being under the control of the Church as well as factory administration was seen as a form of slavery of the type that the Jews suffered under Pharos in Egypt.[23] Nagel was presented as a redeemer like Moses in the Old Testament who led the Jews from the oppressive life in Egypt.

Though the strike ended and the Mission weaving factory resumed its work, many workers and even supervisors who had followed Nagel refused to join for duty at the Basel Mission factory at Kannur because they considered the Mission weaving factory and Mission Church as one. Some of the maestries who left the church, started turning entrepreneurial. An office secretary of the Mission factory, one Thomas Christian, the leader of agitation was one of them. He started Malabar Handloom Factory at Kannur, at a location very close to Basel Mission Weaving Establishment. This unit continued to operate successfully till it was closed in 1930. Another employee turned entrepreneur was Augustine Peter who was a supervisor in the handloom factory of Basel Mission at Kannur.[24] The labour action at the handloom factory of the Basel Mission played an important role in the proliferation of small handloom units producing some of the products produced by the Basel Mission handloom industry. Entrepreneurs outside the Basel Mission fold, who wanted to establish start up ventures in handloom, body-shopped the maestries of the Basel Mission's Kannur handloom establishment. There were factors favouring these new entrepreneurs. The Swadeshi Movement which had started in Bengal from 1903 after the British Indian Government divided Bengal Province, exhorted Indians to boycott foreign goods. With the outbreak of the First World War in 1914, large British textile factories in India directed their production for war purposes. These factors increased the local demand for textiles. The extension of railway line from Madras (now Chennai) up to Kannur in 1908 was instrumental in developing the marketing net work for the Kannur handloom industry from the beginning of twentieth century. These aspects are dealt in the last chapter.

Changing attitudes of the British Government towards Basel Mission

From all available records it appears that the relationship the Basel Mission had with the British Imperial Government was one of mutually supportive nature at least in the earlier stages. At the apex level, the Mission had contact with English missionary societies. In fact, the first missionaries trained by the Basle Mission College at Basel went to work with English missionary societies like the London Missionary Society (LMS) and the Church

Missionary Society (CMS). During the initial stages of their work, the Basel missionaries had received considerable support from the local British administrators. For example, it was the British Collector who facilitated the purchase of Balmatta Hill in Mangalore where Mission started work. Similarly 'Illikunnu' the place near Tellicherry, which was the first Basel Mission station in Malabar was a gift to mission by the British judge, Thomas Strange. Conversion to Christianity sometimes brought about resistance from local communities, and occasionally to social unrest. Without the active support from the British Government, the missionaries could not have continued to work.

On their part, Basel Mission tried to distance itself from the political issues. Missionaries were working closely with the population and they were intensely aware of the emerging economic and political situation in India. The missionaries were aware of the anxiety of British colonialism to ensure British products to have a great run in the colonies. Basel missionaries generally remained circumspect in their comments. The Basel missionaries were also aware of the Swadeshi Movement. The Mission was also aware that there could be a potential conflict with the British colonial administration at some point. Though, Basel Mission did not expand the textile industry after 1882, the Mission products did have an assured niche market and was acquiring the capability to challenge interests of the British capital in India.

From the last quarter of the nineteenth century, the European colonial powers were increasingly moving into antagonistic positions. Germany was not a big colonial power like Britain or France, but, Germany did colonise a few places like Camaroon in West Africa. After the German Reunification under Bismarck, Germany was, in the process of positing itself as a colonial power. From the beginning of the twentieth century, Britain and Germany were certainly moving into opposite camps.

Matters came to a head after the outbreak of the First World War in 1914.Though registered in Switzerland, which is a neutral country; the British considered the Basel Mission as a German mission. Most of the missionaries who were working for the Mission were from Germany and the Mission was supposed to have a German character. After all, for some time, the name of Basel Mission was 'Basel German Evangelical Missionary Society.'[25]

The industrial expansion of the Mission Trading Company came to an abrupt end in 1914 with the outbreak of the First World War. At that time the Company was supposed to be having considerable plans for expansion into fields like glass manufacture.

First World War and after

At the time of outbreak of the First World War, the Mission Trading Company had 13 industrial undertaking functioning in Malabar and South Canara. When the War broke out, the German nationals working in these factories were interned. The industries were permitted to function, with young managers brought from Switzerland. In December 1915, the industrial assets of the Mission Trading Company was placed under the control of an officer of government. By signing an agreement with the British government in May 1916, when the Great War was still going on, the control of the Indian business of the Basel Mission was placed in the hands of J.P. Werner & Co, which was a company domiciled in England. Profits generated were to be entrusted with the Mission Trust of Madras in 1916. In the same year, an ordinance, 'Enemy Trading Act of 1916' was issued by the Governor General in Council to prohibit and control trading by hostile foreigners. The entire industrial assets of the Mission Trading Company were placed under the control of Custodian of Enemy Properties. At this time the Madras

Chamber Of Commerce, representing predominantly British commercial interests in South India, approached the Government of the of Madras Province for winding up the operations of the Company. It is evident that the fast growth of the activities of the Mission Trading Company in the Madras Province had challenged the British commercial interest in India.

The intervention of the Swizz Government was not successful in changing the attitude of the British Government. The Swizz intervention however succeeded in delaying the process of sale of Factories till the end of the War. Though the German managers were interned by the British, throughout the length of war, the factories of the Basel Mission functioned under the management of Swizz managers sent from Basel. On May 22,1919, six months after the armistice, on the basis of an Ordinance issued by the Governor General in Council, the entire assets of the company in India were taken over by the British Indian Government placed under the control of five member trust called the Mission Trust of South India. Under the direction of the Controlling Officer, the inventory of possessions was drawn up. The total value, after deduction the liabilities to the tune of approximately Pound Sterling 1100 was estimated at about 4, 00,000 Pound Sterling.[26]

On June 30, 1920, the by an indenture of Government, the Mission Trust of South India was instructed to transfer the properties vested with them to a Public Limited Company called The Commonwealth Trust Limited, incorporated in England specifically for the purpose of taking over the business previously carried on by the Mission Trading Company.

The following is the balance sheet drawn at the time of handing over the industrial assets of the Mission Trading Company to Commonwealth Trust Limited.[27] This Balance

Table 4.9: Balance Sheet of Commonwealth Trust Limited as on May 1919

(Amount in Rupees)

LIABILITIES			***ASSETS***	
Various creditors				
Creditors	7 053		Cash in hand	24 704
Savings a/c	2 53 591			
Sick funds	21172		Cash at bank	3 93 152
Churchfunds	6 445			
		2 88 261	Outstandings(Receivables)	2 16 694
	12 69			
Basel Head Office	382		Goods and materials(stock)	754 378
Less Profits Malabar	211131			
Less Adjustments	130	10 58121	Plant tools and furniture	12 64 319
Reserve accounts			Land and building	15 37586
Exchange Reserve	2 59 863		Labour quarters	56 580
	1117			
Plant/tool reserve	699		Various debtors	6 526
Land and building Reserve	15 37586			
Profit 1918-1919	3 41137	32 56 285	Net Missionary Council	3 48 728
		46 02 667		***46 02 667***

Source: Obtained by the author from the archives of Mission 21, Basel, Switzerland in 2010.

Sheet is prepared in accordance with the accounting standard prevailing at that period.

A few observations are made here. Liquidity positions of the industries were extremely satisfactory as revealed in the current ratio, that is ratio of current assets to current liabilities. As it is seen here the ratio is 4.8 meaning that the current assets (cash in hand, in bank and salable final products) were 4.8 times the demand for cash the companies faced. Return on Investment Ratio is 9.4, much higher than the bank interest rate that prevailed then which must have been two or three per cent. The company does not appear to have used debt as a source of capital, which means it either resorted to equity capital or re- invested profits into its business. The companies appear to have maintained a huge foreign exchange reserve of Rs. 2,59,863. This could be due to the prevailing financial situation. After the fall of Gold Standard following the outbreak of the First World War, there was no fixed exchange rate between currencies. Therefore the company had to hedge against exchange risks. The accumulated profit was Rs. 3 41137.

Basel Mission Industries -the final questions

The final questions that a reader or a researcher on the Basel Mission industries would raise are plain and direct. How was it possible for a missionary society to become an industrial entrepreneur and carry on the industry with a vibrancy of any other capitalist enterprise? This question is hypothetical like the question as to how the East India Company established as a joint stock company by merchants in London in the year 1600 could emerge by 1800 as a political administrator of one fifth of the then known world ? In the case of Basel Mission, the movement from experimentation with crafts to sustain a group of converts to establishment of large industries was not planned at the time of its inception. It happened due to a set of circumstances. From 1882, the logic of capitalism appears to have dominated the activities. That logic is investment, accumulation of profit for reinvestment. The essential vitality of the industrial activities of the Basel Mission industries came from its capability to constantly experiment, innovate, learn from failures and move forward. Obviously the faith in what the Basel Mission conceived as its 'mission' led to constant industrial reformation from experimentation with traditional crafts to modern crafts and then to large scale modern enterprises.

Notes

1. At present the region is known as Kodagu District and is part of Karnataka State in India.
2. This observation is made in the unpublished official history of Union Trading Corporation which was the successor company of the Basel Mission Industries published in 1958. Sent to the author by the Union Trading Corporation.
3. Billava caste was originally a warrier caste, meaning of Billava being 'bowman'. Later they became farmers and their traditional occupation became tappers of toddy and menders of coconut trees. They were also tenant farmers. They constituted roughly one fifth of the population of South Canara at the turn of this century.
4. This observation is made in the official unpublished history of Basel Mission Industries entitled "Basel Mission Industries 1858 to 1958" produced by the Union Trading Corporation, the successor company of the Basel Mission Industries. This unpublished manuscript was sent to the author by Union Trading Corporation, Basel.
5. This reference is made in the unpublished M.A. dissertation of Stenzl, Catherin titled *"Basel Mission Industries in India, 1834-1884: Improvisation or Policy"* submitted to the School of History, Classics and Archaelology, University of London, Birbeck. 2010.
6. Thaliparamba, and Puthiyatheru in Kannur District for examples were known as 'weavers village' as weaving was the predominant occupation in these villages.
7. In weaving, warp is a set of lengthwise yarn held in tension. Weft is a thread or yarn drawn through the warp. Weft is threaded through the yarn using a shuttle. After Industrial Revolution the shuttle became 'fly shuttle', an innovation

intended to speed up the process of passing weft through the warp.

8. The Jacquard process refers to the necessary loom attachment by which unlimited varieties of pattern in weaving is made possible. The term Jacquard is not specific to any particular loom but the control mechanism that is added for automating patterning.
9. Mercerisation is a treatment by alkali of cellulose materials typically cotton threads that strengthens them and gives them a lustrous appearance.
10. Yarn dyed cotton fabric woven into series of simple patterns in two or more colours such as checks, stripes or placids.
11. 'Webster's shikhari' is a type of cloth especially designed by Johannes Haller in response to a demand from English administrators and others for game hunting. Webster's Shikari had the colour of grass but the fibre was so closely woven so that even a blade of grass would not pierce it.
12. Abysinian twill cotton fabric was especially produced for the hot Australian climate and had a ready market there.
13. A movement which started from 1903 in Bengal as a reaction against the decision of the then Viceroy, Lord Curzon to divide Bengal. The movement used the technique of 'extended boycott', which was to include apart from boycott of foreign goods, boycott of government schools and colleges, courts, titles and government services and even organisation of strikes.
14. George Plebst, the Basel missionary was a mechanical engineer by training. He was instrumental in converting the lithographic press of Basel Mission at Mangalore to a typographical one. He was the pioneer who established Basel Mission's first tile factory in Mangalore.
15. Official history of the Mission Trading Company *(Missions Handlungs Gesellschaft)*. opp.cit
16. A chemical compound composed of aluminum silicon and oxygen, found in minerals and clays in several forms. Chemical formula Al2 Si O5.
17. Salt-glaze or Salt glaze pottery is stoneware with a glaze of glossy, translucent and slightly orange-peel-like texture which was formed by throwing common salt into the kiln during the higher temperature part of the firing process.
18. This information was received from an unpublished manuscript in German sent by Union Trading Corporation International, successor company of Mission Trading

Company. Title of the manuscript is *"Missions Handlungs Gesellschaft 1859-1959"* (German). The manuscript was translated by Dr. Bernard Fenn, Reader Department of German, University of Kerala.

19. This observation is made by late J L Pavamani, a ceramic technologist who had managed one of the first tile factories established by Indians in Mangalore. This factory is A Albuquerque and Sons established in 1868. The innovation by Alex Albuquerque Pai, the founder of the factory was in increasing the number of presses and having facility to transport clay through carts placed on rail lines. This factory is still working.
20. It is noted that quite frequently, supervisors in Basel Mission factories elected as 'Church Elders' in the Church congregations. The position of elder was significant in the church hierarchy and was considered equal to the Presbyter. For the Basel Mission, the use of Church Elder as model worker and therefore model Christian was an effective tool for control of labour.
21. Thomas Christian and Augustine Peter are two such leaders. Both of them became entrepreneurs and established their own weaving factories.
22. "A Protestant sectarian of radical movement arising in the sixteenth century ad advocating baptism and church membership of adult believers only, non resistance and separation of Church and State". www.Merriam Webster.com/dictionary/Anabaptist Retrieved on Feb6, 2017.
23. A reference is made to the Book of Exodus in the Old Testament of Bible.
24. This information is given by Dr Paul Jenkins, former Archivist at Basel Mission Archives in Basel, Switzerland.
25. In the report of the Mission published in the year 1846 the Mission is titled as German Evangelical Society and in the report published in 1869 the name is given as Basel German Evangelical Society.
26. Official unpublished history of the Missions Handlungs Gesellschaft 1859-1959. Opp.cit.
27. Obtained from the archives of the Basel Mission,(Mission 21 now) Basel, Switzerland.

Handloom weaving factory at Calicut

Interior view of the weaving factory

Weaving factory in Kannur

200 hp steam engine at the weaving factory in Kannur

Puthiyara Tile Works, Calicut under construction

Flooring tile manufactured at Mangalore

Chapter - 5

Social Impact of the Basel Mission Industries

In the last chapter, an attempt was made to trace the evolution of the industrial activities of the Basel Mission. It was also argued that the social and economic conditions in Malabar and South Canara prompted the missionaries to start some economic activities to enable the converts to make a gainful living independently. These endeavours must certainly have had reciprocal social impact. In this section, it is intended to discuss the social impact that the Basel Mission industries had on the societies of Malabar and South Canara.

Industrial, trading or related economic activities were only a part of the overall activities of the Basel Mission. These, certainly formed an important part. Basel Mission had also undertaken multifarious other activities. For example, the Mission established a network of schools starting from Primary Schools all the way up to High Schools and also specialised schools. During the nineteenth century, these schools were the only conduit through which people from the lower classes could get some education. The Mission had also established the Malabar Christian College which was an important centre of higher learning in Malabar. The Mission started a printing and publishing house at Mangalore and published books and pamphlets in various south India languages. The Mission had also established hospitals, orphanages and homes for the destitute people in Malabar, South Canara and also in other places like Gadag in the present North Canara district of the Karnataka state. In fact the first dedicated hospital as well as sanatorium for leprosy patients was established by Basel Mission at Calicut at the beginning of the twentieth century. The Mission saw the income generating activities as well as other activities as serving wider Christian objectives. The industrial and social activities of the Mission were also closely interlinked and played its role in the transformation of the societies of Malabar and South Canara. In order to assess the social impact of industrial activities, the following three areas may be looked at in particular.

(1) The impact that the activities of the Basel Mission institutions had on the caste system in Malabar and South Canara.
(2) Social mobility acquired by different segments of society as a result of opportunities provided by the industrial activities.
(3) Demonstration effect of the life -world of converts of Basel Mission.

As it would be seen in the subsequent sections, the above three aspects are not exclusive, but are closely interlinked, and therefore cannot be viewed in isolation. In Chapter 6, the issue of re-engineering of the self will be discussed in detail.

Caste and conversion

Many observers of the activities of missionary groups in India during the nineteenth century had observed that the Basel Mission converts did not retain their former caste identities (Forrester, 1980). It is equally important to understand that such synthesis was achieved in a relatively short time span of eighty years when the Mission was actively carrying on its work in India. The Mission had itself noted with satisfaction as early as 1893 that "Caste feeling among Christians is a thing perfectly unknown among us" (Frohnmeyer, 1893, p. 12).

In order to perceive the significance of the above achievement and relate the impact of such an achievement to the societies of Malabar and South Canara, it is necessary to place this in a wider perspective. The wider background as we see here is the activities and attitudes of other missionary groups in relation to the caste problem. In this, it may be relevant to compare the achievements of the Basel Mission with the activities of other missionary groups that operated in Kerala.

The Roman Catholic missionary groups that had worked in India during the 17th and 18th centuries had accepted the prevailing caste system in India as a part of the existing social order and therefore did not perceive it as hindrance or as something inconsistent with Christianity. Moreover, since the activities of these missionary groups resulted in mass conversion, it did not result in the loss of occupations for the converts. The most obvious example of mass conversion was the mass conversion of *Paravar* fishermen in Kanyakumari area as mentioned earlier (Forrester, 1980).

The different attitudes of the later Protestant missionary groups towards caste could be attributed to the relatively smaller scale of mass conversion. It could also be attributed to the influence of the Pietist Movement[1] in Europe which held the view of evangelism as a "historical process which necessarily involved Christian reshaping of society" (Forrester, 1980, p. 1).

However, within the Protestant Christian missionary groups, attitudes towards caste differed. The first Protestant Missionary group that started its work in India was a Danish mission called The Tranquebar Mission. This mission came to work in Tranquebar (now Tharagambadi) in Tamil Nadu in 1709.[2] This mission appears to have accepted caste as part of social order. In the church established by them at Tranquebar, there were separate rows of seats for lower and higher castes. From the beginning of the nineteenth century, there was a vibrant discussion among and within the Protestant missionary groups on the perception of caste. The basic issue that was discussed was whether a converted Christian should retain his former caste identity. Are such caste identities compatible with Christianity? After all, it was St. Paul, one of the founding fathers of the Christian church who stated in his letter to Galatians (3.28) that "There is neither Jew nor Greek, there is neither slave nor free, there is neither male or female, for you are all one in Christ Jesus". Forrester notes that by 1850s most of the Protestant missionary groups had arrived at a general view of caste as "a great evil which must be ruthlessly uprooted from the church" (Forrester, 1980, p. 40). The missionary objections to caste were of various kinds, theological, ethical and strategic. There were situations where caste was not seen as a significant obstacle to the spread of gospel; and situations where caste was even tolerated.

In Kerala, during the nineteenth century, two major missionary groups functioned, the Church Missionary Society (CMS) and the London Missionary Society (LMS).[3] The experiences of the above groups were different from that of Basel Mission. The LMS predominantly operated in South Travancore and adjoining regions and converted mainly people from the Nadar community, equivalent of the Thiyya community in Malabar. There was also a portion of converts from the castes of agrestic slaves like Cheruma and Pulaya. The LMS undertook a number of economic activities, but these activities did not achieve the level of professionalisation of the Basel Mission. Conversion to Christianity did not raise the social status of the converts of the LMS, though it gave them access to missionary sponsored educational institutions, freedom from caste oppression and to some extent ability to choose their future. The converts had to fight for a higher status in society. During the nineteenth century, the women in the Nadar community were not permitted to wear upper garments. The community went through turmoil, now referred as 'breast cloth controversy' to establish their right to cover the upper part of their bodies.[4] Often, the relationship of Nadars with other communities was still permeated by the caste insignia, terminology, etc. There was widespread use of 'Nadar' suffix to the names of Nadar converts to Christianity.

The CMS which operated mainly in Central Travancore region, initially tried to take the non-Catholic Syrian Church in its fold. This led to certain conflicts and after a break with the Syrian Church; the CMS turned its attention to converting lower castes, predominantly Ezhava and Pulaya communities. The consequence of such conversion was: "By 1880s there were some 16,000 CMS Christians of who more than half were of Pulaya stock and roughly quarter were Syrians. The reminder were mainly from Ezhavas and other low castes" (Dalton, 1963). The different caste groups within the fold of CMS did not get integrated into one entity. The result of the above pattern was expressed by a contemporary observer as thus: "The slave converts form a separate body with whom the rest of the Christians have no social intercourse" (Forrester, 1980, p. 109). At present the congregations established by the CMS are part of the Central Travancore Diocese of the Church of South India (CSI). The CSI do not appear to have been successful in effecting any changes to the situation described above (Mohan, 2015). The Basel Mission succeeded in eradicating caste feeling among its converts. Though the Mission converted people from lower castes, the caste hierarchy also permeated to the lower castes. It was stated earlier that converts to the Mission came mainly from two castes; the Thiyyas and the Pulayas. Between these two castes there was untouchability as well as polluting distances that were imposed rigorously. There was also converts from upper castes (seeTable 2.4 Chapter 2). Basel Mission's success in eradicating caste barriers can partly be ascribed to the relatively smaller portion of upper caste converts, and partly to the impersonal industrial environment created by them, under which converts from different caste background worked side by side, performed similar type of work and received the same wages. The second factor was that the Basel Mission was determined to eradicate caste consciousness within their congregations. The strong stand that the Mission took against caste and the marriages the missionaries are supposed to have had arranged between spouses with different caste background further facilitated such a synthesis.[5] Employment offered by the industrial undertakings established by the Mission must have shattered the concept of caste related occupation.

What is significant from the point of social impact is the powerful demonstration effect of creating a group of converts without a caste identity. These aspects will be discussed in the next chapter entitled 'Re - engineering of the Self. In the background of the caste differentiated environment of Malabar and South Canara, such a powerful demonstration would have naturally resulted in the eventual challenging of caste restrictions by the lower classes.

Social mobility

The Thiyya/Billava castes constituted a majority of converts of the Basel Mission. The latter half of the nineteenth century was a period of social upheaval among these castes. In the cases of the Thiyya caste, the social transition was made easy by the peculiar position of this caste in the caste hierarchy and their traditional attitudes, which were rather cosmopolitan. During this period, social reformers like Sree Narayana Guru had also emerged within the caste in the neighbouring state of

Thiruvithamkur (Travancore) (Issac, 1986). Sree Naryayana Guru had proclaimed that there is only one caste, one religion, one God for humanity. He advocated temperance to Thiyya/Billava castes whose traditional occupation was toddy tapping. He encouraged the members of the above castes to enter into new professions like industry. The Basel Mission's experiment in the creation of a group who did not carry their former caste identities further accentuated the process of social mobility by offering a chance for the Thiyya and Billava converts to seek an existence outside their caste based occupation.

Cheruma/Pulaya caste in Malabar and their equivalent the Holeya caste in South Canara formed a significant portion of converts. They were slaves attached to the agricultural lands of landlords. In Malabar district, when the land was sold, the slaves attached to the land was also deemed to have been sold to the new owner. The slaves were not allowed to acquire education. Being a polluting caste, they had to keep certain distances from the upper castes. This difficulty was also overcome by conversion. This group had a great deal to gain through conversion, like opportunities for education, chance to enter into different professions and even to be treated with respect. The social mobility that converts from these castes had acquired was visible.

The improvement in the social status is also closely linked with the creation of a technically oriented labour force. A technically oriented labour force could command a higher reserve price in the sense that employment of such labour would also be sought after by people other than the missionaries. This further enhanced the social status of converts. This was possible for a society which had created sufficient demand for such skills. The second half of the nineteenth century was a period in which such demand had spread in both Malabar and South Canara. In the process of their work, the Basel Mission created a group of labourers who possessed basic literacy and having worked in factories had acquired industrial skills. Basel Mission industries had offered employment not only to converts but also non-converts. These labourers had new avenues of employment.

Several examples can be seen. The workers who had acquired technical skills as fitters, mechanics, foundry men and machine operators at the Mechanical Establishment of the Mission at Mangalore found easy employment in Bombay (now Mumbai) which was growing as an industrial centre from the turn of the twentieth century. It is said that at the turn of the twentieth century, labour contractors had arrived at Codacal from Bombay for recruiting labourers to Natal in South Africa.[6]

Female participation in the activities of Basel Mission

Women participated in the missionary, social and industrial activities in a number of ways. In the arena of evangelisation they worked as door-to-door campaigners referred in the missionary parlance as 'Bible Women.' Duties of Bible Women were to preach the gospel mainly to women in households. For the women who were earlier confined to their homes, even working as Bible Women were entry into the public sphere.[7] In the social and educational spheres women worked as teachers, boarding school supervisors, helpers in creches or schools. Many women even rose to the position of Headmistresses of primary and secondary schools. In hospitals of Basel Mission, women were employed as nursing assistants, particularly maternity assistants, writers, sweepers and cooks. Women were employed in large numbers in weaving establishments in the early stages. The record of employment of the weaving industries for the year 1877 (See Table 4.10) shows that out of the total of 392 workers, 216 were women. These women were employed mainly as 'thread makers and spool winders'. Interestingly, it was these activities that got mechanised with the introduction of steam engines. Women continued to be the mainstay in the embroidery and tailoring departments which were attached to the weaving factories.

The question which requires to be examined relates to the extent of female empowerment which was effected by the activities of the Basel Mission. In the traditional societies of Malabar and South Canara, among certain matrilineal castes like the Nayars in Malabar and Bunts in South Canara, women had played an active role in the management of properties. Women in those communities had certain recognised rights out of properties. Such women might not have gained after conversion in terms of status. But the position of middle and lower caste converts were different. They had limited avenues for acquiring basic education or jobs requiring some basic education. Basel Mission provided both. Women had an opportunity to enter the public sphere. The schools, hospitals and industrial undertakings in which women got entry were essentially entry into the public sphere. There are other dimensions to the entry of women in the public sphere. In the traditional Hindu society, a single woman, be it a widow, a divorcee or a never married person, is not accepted and her presence is considered inauspicious in social and religious functions. The impersonal atmosphere of industrial units in which a large number of women from different caste or marital backgrounds worked, removed much of the stigma attached to the single women and often brightened the chance of her remarriage. In centres like Calicut and Kannur where a number of single women worked in factories, the Mission had also established women's hostels. Such arrangements further enhanced the chance for entry of women into the public sphere.

The spread of literacy

The basic objective the Basel Mission had in spreading

of literacy was that every convert should be able to read the Bible. For this purpose, the Mission established various types of schools in the Malabar and South Canara districts. These schools were the only means through which people belonging to the lower castes could get education. The purpose of establishment of schools attached to churches and industries were explained by a missionary as thus:

> We have no primary education, an education not aiming at a literary career but containing the elements of knowledge for everybody. What is called primary education with us are 4 or 5 standards of a curriculum laid down for a course of instruction ending with a BA Degree. (Frohnmeyer, 1893, p. 11).

In actual practice, the Basel Mission went far beyond the scope that the missionary Johannes Frohnmeyer stated here. In the Malabar and South Canara districts, the Mission had established a number of schools. These were not only primary schools. These were high schools secondary schools, middle schools, girls schools and schools attached to orphanages. There were vernacular schools and Anglo - vernacular schools, the difference being that in Anglo-vernacular schools English was also taught as a language. In a few instances, the Mission started night schools for imparting basic literacy to a group of converts. The Mission established a technical school at its Mechanical Establishment in Mangalore. The objective of such a school was to impart theoretical knowledge on engineering subjects to the employees who were already performing engineering duties. This technical school can be compared to modern polytechnics or industrial training institutes. Similarly, the Mission established an agricultural school attached to its orphanage at Parapperi in Malabar. Here, the students were given practical training in husbanding garden crops. It was much later, (in 1909) that Basel Mission established the

Basel German Mission College (now the Malabar Christian College) at Calicut, a premier institution of higher learning in the Malabar region. These schools as well as the Malabar Christian College opened their doors to students from all castes and creeds. These institutions did not allow untouchability of any type to be practiced within its portals. Students of all social groups sat together, studied together and played together. It has been noted that members of the thiyya caste which benefited most out of the educational institutions of the Basel Mission. Given under is the enrollment in various schools of Basel Mission in Malabar as on 1913.

Table 5.1: Enrollment in schools run by the Basel Mission in the districts of Malabar and South Canara

District	***Christian***		***Non-Christian***		***Total***
	Boys	***Girls***	***Boys***	***Girls***	
South Canara	901 (47.3)	659 (46.2)	4714 (43.1)	1022 (46.2)	7296 (44.3)
Malabar	1002 (52.7)	770 (53.8)	6212 (56.9)	1191 (53.8)	9175 (55.7)
Total	**1903 (100.0)**	**1429 (100.)**	**10926 (100.0)**	**2213 (100.0)**	**16471 (100.0)**

Source: RBM 2013.

The above table shows that out of the total enrollment in the educational institutions, a higher share came from Malabar district. This is understandable because the population of Malabar during the period was roughly double of that of South Canara. This proportion is well distributed over all categories of enrollment. The table below gives a picture of the proportion of Christian and non-Christian categories of students across the two districts.

Table 5.2: Enrollment in schools: enrollment by Christian and non- Christian students in the Malabar and South Canara districts

District	Christian Students		Total	Non - Christian Students		Total
	Boys	Girls		Boys	Girls	
South Canara	901 (57.7)	599 (42.3)	1560 (100.0)	4714 (82.2)	1022 (17.8)	5736 (100.0)
Malabar	1002 (56.5)	770 (43.5)	1772 (100.0)	6212 (83.9)	1191 (16.1)	7403 (100.0)

Source: RBM 1913.

The above table gives some interesting insights on the enrollment in schools run by the Basel Mission. The table shows the progress achieved by the Basel Mission in female literacy. In South Canara, among the students enrolled in Mission schools, 42.3 per cent were girls and in the Malabar district, the percentage was slightly higher at 43.5. Among the non- Christian students girls formed only 17.8 per cent in the South Canara district and 16.1 in the Malabar district. In both the districts, the proportion of Christian girls enrolled in schools are higher than that of non Christians.

The Christian missionary enterprise started after the voyages of discovery. Christian missions followed the flag and wherever the missionaries went, they had to learn the languages of the places of their work in order to effectively communicate with the people. Thus, the learning of local languages was part of the missionary enterprise, globally. Use of dictionaries and knowledge of rules of grammar are required, when a new language was to be learnt by people who are from outside. In India, the missionary enterprise resulted in substantial contributions to local languages. William Carey,[8] who was one of the earliest Protestant missionaries, was a linguist. (Firth.C.B., 1983 (1961). pp. 149-150) The first dictionaries and grammar books in many Indian languages were the result of labour by missionaries.

The German interest in Indian languages, goes far beyond that of the interests that British colonial administrators showed to these languages. Philosophers of the Romantic Movement in Germany were impressed by Indian thought and literature. For example, Max Muller had translated Sanskrit play *Shakunthalam* from Sanskrit to German. A German missionary B. Ziegenbalg (1862-1917) who had come to Tharagambadi as a missionary of the Danish Mission wrote a book on Tamil grammar. Another missionary J. Ph. Fabricius (1711-91) compiled a Tamil dictionary. The first chair in Indology was established at Bonn University as early as 1818.[9]

When the Basel Mission started to send missionaries to different parts of the world, the missionaries were asked to learn the languages of the place of their work and understand the culture of the region. The newly arrived missionaries usually spent their first six months learning the local language and customs.

The two districts, Malabar and South Canara, though contiguous, are different in many ways. The language spoken in the whole of the Malabar district is Malayalam which is a Drividian language evolved from the sixteenth century. By the time of arrival of Basel missionaries, the Malayalam language was already rich in literature. But the language did not have a lexicon. Many Portuguese missionaries like Rev. Fr. Arnose and later Protestant missionaries like Rev. Benjamin Baily had endeavored to prepare a lexicon for the language.[10]

The case of South Canara was different. This region evolved differently and a number of languages were spoken here. The most important language used here was Kannada, a language which got evolved from the ninth century and thus was older than Malayalam. The Kannada language has its own script. In South Canara, a sizeable part of the population, particularly those from the Billava as well as Bunt community use the Tulu language. Thus, the

Tulu language formed a 'speech island' within Kannada. This language does not have a script of its own. So, for writing, the Kannada script is often used. At present efforts are going on to develop a script for the Tulu language. A third language that is used in South Canara is Konkani. People belonging to the Gowda Saraswat Brahmin (GSB) community as well as the Roman Catholic population in South Canara who originally came from the GSB stock, speak Konkani language. Konkani is usually written in Devanagari[11] script. There are other languages which are in use by the different sections of the South Canara society. Urdu is spoken by a section of the Muslim population who emigrated from central India centuries back. The language Byari spoken by a section of the coastal community in South Canara is a corrupted version of Malayalam. The contribution of Basel missionaries to each of the three languages, Malayalam, Kannada, Tulu were significant.

The Basel Mission started working in Malabar from 1840. Soon after, the missionaries started publishing books in Malayalam. Following this, many other missionaries started being deeply involved with Malayalam language. The contributions of these missionaries can be divided into religious and secular fields. A number of hymns were either translated from German or composed by missionaries themselves in Malayalam for the use during worship. Prominent among the translator/ composers of hymns were Dr Hermann Gundert, E Diaz, J M Fritz, L Frohnmeyer, Christopher Irion, C Renz, F Muller and J Knobloch. These hynmns are still used for worship in congregations established by the Basel Mission.

Dr Hermann Gundert and his work

The missionary who contributed most to Malayalam language is Dr.Hermann Gundert. The contribution of

Dr Gundert is so substantial that he is often referred as As the *Valarthachan* (foster father) of Malayalam language. Born in Stuttgart in 1814, Dr Gundart completed his doctoral studies in philosophy from Tuebingin University in Germany. He came to India first as a missionary with the London Missionary Society and worked at Tirunelveli in Tamil Nadu. The stay in Tamil Nadu and later in Chittoor, which is in the state of Andhra Pradesh, enabled him to acquire proficiency in Tamil, Telugu and Kannada languages. Dr Gundert had already known many European languages well. Of all the languages that he knew well, Malayalam language appears to have been his passion. The biggest contribution that Dr Hermann Gundert made was also to this language. However it must be noted that Dr Gundert came to Malabar as a missionary. So, to begin with, a mention must be made about some of his literary work as a missionary. Dr Gundert wrote many pamphlets in Malayalam for the purpose of spreading the gospel.

An important contribution of Gundert was a journal called *Rajyasamacharam.* Literally translated, the word means 'news about the kingdom'. In this context, it was meant God's kingdom. This journal contained stories from the Bible as well as news on how the gospel was being propagated to people in different lands. Two other journals that were published by Gundert had short lived existence. These are *Keralopakari* and *Kerala Yuvavu* (Kerala Youth). Of the two, Keralopakari stood somewhere between a journal and a news magazine and covered a wide range of topics. The publication Kerala Yuvavu was exclusively addressed to the youth. It is the contribution that Dr.Gundert made to the secular field that gave him the name of foster-father of Malayalam language. Only a few works are mentioned here. Gundert compiled the proverbs in Malayalam in a publication called *Pazhamchol Mala.* He further standardized the learning of Malayalam through a series of textbooks called *Patamala*. He further made foray into Kerala history and wrote historical works like 'Kerala Pazhama or History of Malabar'. What he did here was to convert oral tradition to writing. This work covered history of Kerala up to the advent of the Portuguese. The first newspaper in Malayalam was edited and published by Gundert from a lithographic press at Tellicherry in 1847. This paper was called *Paschimodayam* meaning 'Rising from the West'. In the very first issue itself Gundert made the objective in publishing this paper:

> Apart from the sciences and arts known here, there are many sciences and arts known in the West. There are great differences between these two. In order to make these things (sciences and arts of the west) understandable to the Malayalis, we are bringing out portions from selected areas as under. (Chummar Chundel (Ed), 1977) (Translated by me)

The areas covered by this paper were astronomy, scientific discoveries and inventions, accounts of distant lands and people, geography, Kerala history and folklore. This paper was edited by Dr. Hermann Gundert and his assistant F.Muller. The lead given by the Basel Mission was carried forward later by the CMS which brought out the newspaper *Gnananiskshepam* under the editorship of CMS missionary, Rev. Benjamin Baily. This paper was closer to the modern concept of a newspaper.[12]

The most important contribution of Hermann Gundert to Malayalam language was his work "A Malayalam and English Dictionary" published in 1872 after Gundert had returned to Germany and had become the editor of a publishing company in Calw. The Malayalam and Tamil languages had several similarities and the biggest difficulty that Gundert faced was "to draw a line of demarcation between Malayalam and Tamil words as those languages of the old differed rather as dialects of the same member of the Dravidian family than as separate languages."[13] Gundert took great care to note the idioms and significations peculiar to the north and south Kerala. Gundert took note to include foreign words which had become common parlance in Malayalam. These were Persian, Hindustani, Arabic, Portuguese and English words. While translating a Malayalam word to English, Gundert went on to explain the context of usage of these words. Gundert's work thus, is unique in its contents.

It will be of interest to know that the theme of conversion to Christianity appears as the main theme in a novel written by one Joseph Muliyil a convert of the Basel Mission and an educator.[14] This novel was published interestingly by the Basel Mission itself. The title of this novel is *Sukumari* and it can be seen as one of the first novels written in Malayalam.[15] The locale of the work is the Mission Compound of the Basel Mission in Chirakkal in Kannur. The novel deals with the reaction of the traditional Hindu society against the conversion related activities of the missionaries. This novel is both, a work of fiction as well as a document on social transition.

To give a sample of the contents of books and pamphlets published by the Basel Mission Press Mangalore in Malayalam language, translation of the title, and names of authors are given hereunder.

Table 5.3: List of some of the books and pamphlets published by the Basel Mission

Name of the book/pamphlet	***Author***
The story of a Christian Saint Women	Author not noted
Repentance	Not known
What is Truth?	C.Stolz
Two Friends (Can be sung like poetry)	LJ.Frohnmeyer
The Good Sheppard	LJ.Frohnmeyer
Mohammed or Jesus: Who is Greater?	LJ.Frohnmeyer
On Bribe	Not known

(Cont'd...)

Customs of Ancestors	Not known
Sermon on the Mount	Not known
Is There Untouchability?	Not known
The Good Sheppard (in Hindu metre)	LJ.Frohnmeyer

Source: Archives Mission 21.

Contribution of the Basel Mission to Kannada literature

The Basel Mission started its work in Mangalore from 1834 onwards. And the first activities of the missionaries related to education. Therefore the Basel Mission became deeply involved with Kannada language from the very beginning. Several missionaries contributed to Basel Mission's efforts in developing Kannada language. They were Hermann Mogling, Godfrey Weigle, W G Wuerth, Ferdinand Kittel, Frederick Ziegler and converts like Kristhanuja Watsa and Chennappa Uttangi.

There is a parallel between the work done by the Mission in Malabar and Kannada in terms of contributions to the Kannada language and literature. The efforts of the Basel missionaries working in South Canara were first focused on the preparation of textbooks for the Basel Mission. Thereafter the missionaries started producing books for evangelisation. One of the first booklets, published by them *Hridyaya Darpana* (Viewing of the Heart) was produced in the form of a series of playing cards. The cards were illustrated with pictures. The booklet was intended to give the reader a reflecting moment on himself, or his behavior, comparing this to the behavior of different animals. This book was the result of partnership between Hebich and Moegling. Hebich had produced a similar one in Malayalam. Moegling's Jathi Vicharana is a treatise critically evaluating the concept of caste. Moegling's *Deva Vicharana* critically evaluates the concept of God as it is revealed in other religions.

The Basel Missionaries published two newspapers in Kannada. These are *Mangalora Samachara* (Mangalore

News) (1843-44) and *Kannada Samacharavu* (Kannada News). (Chummar Chundel (Ed), 1977). These were secular publications and were intended to give reader a broad picture of what was happening around the world as well as within the country at that time. The Mission had to be very circumspect. While reporting an item of news, the interpretation the news magazine gave about the news could be taken against the Mission by the ruling administration. A case in point is the report on what now the Indian historians refers as the First War of Independence of 1857.[16] The sympathies of editor Moegling were with the Indians and Moegling saw the uprising as an anti colonial struggle, but he was careful enough to express his opinion only between the lines.[17] Topics covered by these papers are interesting and wide ranging. There were reports on the state of the British economy, the Kabul War, affairs of the Khalsa and events in the State of Gwalior- to give a few examples.

Just as Hermann Gundert made an anthology of proverbs in Malayalam, Herrrmann Moegling made an anthology of proverbs in Kannada, thereby creating a parallel. Moegling, who had spent many years in Coorg, reminisced about his life in Coorg in his book "Coorg Memoirs". This book gives an insight into the society of Coorg during the nineteenth century.

Basel missionary, W G Wuerth (1845-1869) spent most of his time in North Karnataka region which was part of the earlier undivided Canara district. The credit goes to Wuerth for bringing out a volume of verse in Kannada language. This memorable work, *Prakavya Malika* is a collection of poems n which he compares Christianity with the Veerashaiva religion.[18]

Ferdinand Kittel's contributions to the Kannada language

It was the Basel missionary Ferdinand Kittel who made the greatest contribution to Kannada literature.

Kittel was a great scholar and the most important contribution of Kittel to Kannada literature was the Kannada-English Lexicon. This dictionary has been described as most accurate, orderly and scientific. Kittel was a versatile scholar. He worked on the grammar of Kannada language and wrote "A Grammar of Canarese Language" in 1903. He further went on to write a long poem in Kannada entitled *Kathamale* which narrates the life of Jesus Christ.

Frederick Ziegler, another missionary, was a scholar in Kannada. He wrote "A Practical Key to Kannada Language". Ziegler was held in high esteem and was chosen as the President of *Karnataka Vidhyavardhaka Sangha* a leading cultural organisation in Dharwar.

Here, it is important to remember the contribution of two converts to Christianity. First was Christanuja Watsa. After being converted to Christianity, Chritanuja Watsa studied theology and became a faculty in the theological college of the Mission in Mangalore. He wrote books and articles and was the editor of *Kraista Sabha Patra* (Christian Church News). The second person, Rev. Chennappa Uttangi was also a good scholar. He came from the Lingayat community. Uttangi was attempting to develop a theological perspective that combined the Christian thought with the philosophy of Veerashaiva Dharma which was the basis of the religion of Lingayat sect.

Basel Mission's contribution to Tulu literature

Tulu language was spoken by a large segment of population of South Canara and hence referred as a 'speech island' within the South Canara district. This language had not developed classical literature as the language did not have its own script. In South Canara, Kannada was the language of the administration. It was also the language of creative expression. Thus, by not having its own script, the Tulu language did not get an opportunity to grow. The renaissance of Tulu literature began with the advent of the arrival of Basel missionaries to South Canara. Since Kannada was the language used by most of the population of South Canara, the missionaries felt that it would be appropriate for Tulu to be written using the Kannada script. This was a turning point. People who could read the Kannada script could now read Tulu literature written in the Kannada script.

The contribution of Basel missionaries to Tulu language can be divided into four categories.

1. Translation of books from the Old and the New Testament, hymn book, hymns for children and stories from the Bible.
2. Linguistic work. Rev. A Maenner prepared a Tulu-English Dictionary and English -Tulu dictionary. Rev. J. Brigal wrote a Tulu grammar book through the medium of English. This book contained chapters on phonology, etymology and syntax.
3. Research on Tulu folklore: Rev A Maenner produced a transcription of Tulu folk epics and ballads. Missionary A C Burnell wrote a book on the spirit worship (Bhuta worship) among the Tuluva community. This was titled "The Devil Worship of the Tuluvas", clearly indicating the negative perceptions that the missionaries had of the religion practiced by the Tuluvas.
4. Primers for learning Tulu.

A religious conference was held in Mangalore in the year 1865 with Tulu as the medium indicating the importance that the Basel Missionaries gave for the development of that language.

Medical work of the Basel Mission

Historically, many Christian missionary groups have taken up medical work which was described in the mission parlance as 'healing ministry'. Christ revealed his love for humanity through several miraculous acts of healing. In the parable of the Good Samaritan the Bible in the Gospal of St. Mathew, the good Samaritan nurses the man who was attacked and wounded by robbers. The medical work is viewed by missions as a means of revealing the love of Christ to mankind. But, as far as the Basel Mission was concerned, medical mission was not considered as an important part of its activity at the time of its founding. It was in 1892, fifty-six years after its work in the Malabar and South Canara districts that the Mission started medical work.

There were reasons for this lack of interest in medical mission. The societies of Malabar and South Canara were caste ridden. Pollution of different types like polluting distances, pollution by touch, and by sight existed. Therefore, there were no hospitals to care for all sections of the society. The system of Ayurveda was prevalent. People from different castes had their own medicinal practices which combined Ayurvedic medicinal practice along with chanting of *manthras* or similar practices. Such practices varied from one caste group to another. Among the higher castes, there were objections to male doctor touching a female patient either for physical examination or attending delivery. For these reasons, concept of a hospital attending to the medical needs of all sections of population did not exist. During the nineteenth century, district hospitals were established by the government at the headquarters of each district. These hospitals were very small compared to the size of the respective population of this district and catered only to the needs of privileged sections of the society.

At the same time, there was an objective need for modern medical facilities. During the nineteenth century, In Malabar as well as the South Canara districts, death rate was very high. The high death rate was due to diseases like cholera and tuberculosis, typhoid, and small-pox, and dengue. For some of these diseases no effective remedy was found even in western medicine. These districts also had a high rate of maternal and infant mortality.

For the Basel Mission, the seeds of starting a medical mission came from the gruesome experience of a Basel missionary, Eugene Liebendorfer. While on a tour on evangelisation, the boat carrying Liebendorfer rammed into a bridge and sank injuring and killing many co-passengers. Liebendorfer suddenly became aware of the need for medical help. Following this ghastly incident, Liebendorfer decided to volunteer to get medical training for which he went to Germany. He returned with a medical degree and in 1886 established the first hospital at Calicut. This hospital was primitive in many ways. Facilities were minimal. The hospital had 14 beds, one consulting room and one operation theatre.

But yet, this hospital was making a difference. Its doors were opened for people from all castes. People who kept polluting distance outside the hospital were treated as equals within its walls. Patients came with snake bites and jackal bites, injuries caused by accidents and various other illnesses. Liebendorfer regretted the high incidence of diseases connected with consumption of alcohol. By 1902, Calicut hospital had moved into its own dedicated premises. A few nurses arrived from Germany to assist the doctor and this new hospital catered up to 5000 patients a year. The treatment given by the hospital was free, but the hospital accepted donations (Shiri (Ed) p. 1985). Almost every year, there were epidemics like typhoid, small pox, tuberculosis or dengue. There were also frequent famines that exacerbated the situation. (Raghavan, 2016) Doctor, along with the staff struggled to handle the flood of in-patients and out-patients.

There were two outstations attached to this hospital, one at Codacal and one at Vaniyamkulam. Both the outstations were managed by 'Dressers'. Some converts were given basic training in treating simple ailments and they assisted doctors. Vaniyamkulam outpost was closed in 1914. When Dr. Liebendorfer returned to Germany, other doctors arrived to take his place. We have names like Dr. Wittenberg, Dr.Stokes and Dr Schneiter and Indian doctors like Dr. Joseph and Dr. Ambat. There were also nurses from Germany like Sr. Kathe Fritz who won the hearts of women through her dedicated service. Gradually, the number of women patients started increasing. Payment, for the treatment, expected from the patients was minimal. Like schools established by the Basel Mission, in the hospitals also no caste discrimination was permitted. All patients were treated alike.

A leprosy hospital was established at Calicut by the British administration in the middle of the nineteenth century. This hospital was in fact a small house near the beach. At the request of the British administration, the Basel Mission took over the hospital and in 1903 transferred it to a new facility located at specious area at the outskirts of the Calicut town. For this, the Mission also received financial assistance from the Leprosy Mission in Edinburg, This hospital was a modern facility, complete with an operation theatre and rehabilitation facilities for the patients. The Basel Mission had also established a small leprosy hospital at Mangalore. But this appears to have been a short-lived affair. The more important activity by the Basel Mission in the medical field took place in North Canara district which was separated from South Canara district and became a part of the Bombay Presidency. Here, at Gadag -Betgeri, the Mission started a full -fledged hospital in 1903. This hospital continues to flourish now under the Church of South India.

The Basel Mission hospital at Calicut was closed by 1930. By this time, nursing homes were being established by the doctors from Calicut who had acquired medical training mainly from the Madras Medical College. Some of the Christian converts of the Mission had also acquired medical education and at least one of them, Dr. Robert Herman had started his own clinic and nursing home at Calicut. After the industrial assets of the Mission was taken over by the British government and placed under the Commonwealth Trust Ltd, the contribution from the industries to running the missionary activities declined. Moreover this income was to be shared with other missionary organisation. This brought about a severe financial crunch on the resources available for the Mission Hospital.

Now, we sum up the discussion on the medical work of the Basel Mission. The essential message of the medical activities initiated by the Mission was evangelical. It was shown as an expression of Christ's love for mankind, irrespective of race, caste or creed. Through the medical work, the Mission was also propagating the message that diseases are caused by germs and not by the anger of the Gods and hence the Gods need not be pleased through animal sacrifices and such other means. Establishment of large hospital with female nurses in attendance, special care given to women, particularly assistance in delivery and reaching out to all patients cutting across caste barriers, had a powerful demonstration effect. At the same time it should be stated that the missionary medical personnel were not totally free from their biases. Many of them believed that the sickness often transmitted through germs was a punishment of God for the sins committed by the person concerned.

When the social impact of the Basel Mission in Malabar and South Canara is examined, it is not possible to separate the three activities that the Mission undertook - industrial, educational, literary and medical. These remained intertwined. For example, it was due to the insistence of missionaries on basic literacy of converts that the Mission ended up with a labour force which was more literate and capable of learning technical subjects. Both the industries as well as the schools succeeded in creating a public sphere for women. Technical education imparted at the Mechanical Establishment at Mangalore certainly helped in the development of entrepreneurship among the converts as well as non-converts. The industrial, educational and medical activities of the Mission directly challenged the existing caste system. The journalistic and literary activities of the Mission ended up in showing a direction for future. This impact was most felt during the inter-war years. This period was an era of social upheaval. A large number of newspapers, journals and pamphlets were published in Malabar during this period. While some of these books, journals and pamphlets espoused the cause of freedom for the country, there were many that took a focus of social issues. It is not difficult to trace the origin of these books and journals to the newspapers and pamphlets published by the Basel Mission.

Notes

1. See Chapter 2 for further reference on Pietism.
2. For a discussion of activities of various missionary groups in Travancore, see: Agur, C. A. (1903). *Church History of Travancore.* Madras: SPG Press.
3. The LMS had also established a large number of schools to which the converts had access. Education gave opportunities for joining government service. It also opened up opportunities for employment in private sector.
4. See Robin Jeffry. Opp.cit
5. Told to author by some senior members in Basel Mission established congregations.
6. Told to author by members of the Codacal Parish.
7. Public space is a discursive space in which individuals and groups associate and discuss matters of mutual interest and when possible reach a common judgment about them. Jurgen Hebermas identified three characteristics of the public sphere. These are 1. Entry disregarding ones status. 2. Domain of common concerns. 3. Inclusivity. See:Wikipedia.org/wiki/Public_sphere.(referred on October 27, 2016)

8. William Carey came to India 1794 as missionary of the Baptist Missionary Society.
9. See Kurup, K K N (1985). Contribution of the Basel Mission in Malabar to Malayalam Language and Literature, in Godwin Godwin Shiri. Opp.cit. pp. 225-231. Mangalore: Karanata Theological Research Institute.
10. Arnose Pathiri (Fr. Arnose) alias Father John Earnest Haxlenden was a person of German origin who came to Cochin during the seventeenth century as a Jesuit Priest. He acquired scholarship in Sanskrit and Malayalam. He wrote a Sanskrit Portuguese dictionary as well as a Malayalam dictionary.
11. Devanagari script is a script used in India and Nepal. It is written from left to right and is recognizable by a horizontal line that runs along the top of full letters. This script has roots in ancient Brahmi script.
12. Benjamin Baily (1805-1871) came to Kottayam in central Kerala as a missionary of the Church Missionary Society. He translated Bible into Malayalam. He also standardized the Malayalam types.
13. From the preface in Gundert's s Malayalam English Dictionary. (1872). Mangalore. Quoted by Kurup, K K N, Ibid, p. 229.
14. Joseph Muliyil was the Principal of the Malabar Christian College, the only institution of higher education established by the Basel Mission at Calicut for some time.
15. The first novel written in Malayalam is "Indulekha" by Chandu Menon. This novel follows the narrative style of western novels.
16. The British described the great uprising of Indian soldiers against them in 1857 as 'Sepoy Mutiny' or soldiers mutiny. Indian historians refer to the uprising as the 'First War of Independence'.
17. Havannur, Srinivasa.(1985). Contribution of Basel Mission to Kannada literature. Godwin Shiri (Ed). 1985. *Wholeness in Christ.* Mangalore: Karnataka Theological Research Institute.
18. Veerashaiva religion is also called as Lingayatism. An off shoot of Hinduism, Basava who lived during the twelfth century in Karnataka was the founder. He was a social reformer, unfolded the banner against caste and suggested path of devotion to God (Bhakti). Wikipedia.org/wiki/lingayatism, retrieved on October 27, 2016.

Women workers in a Mission tile factory

Students of a girls school

Basel Mission High School at Tellicherry

Inmates of Boy's Orphanage at Parapperi posing along with a missionary couple

The Basel German Mission College,(now Malabar Christian College) Calicut, established in 1909

Teachers of the BEM High School, Calicut

Chapter - 6

Re-engineering of the Self

The sense of self of an individual in society is a discursive construct; therefore it is always in the processes of de-construction and re-construction. Various social institutions like caste, kinship, marriage, social, political and religious institutions play a dominant role in creating the sense of self. Individual's mediations with the society are influenced by his or her sense of self. One's identifications with oneself and with others are conditioned by self-identification as an individual in society. This 'individual' is not an atomized and homogenous entity, but it had multiple identities and self-identifications.

Those converted to Christianity by the Basel Mission came from various social relations, especially from different caste backgrounds; each of these castes had its own collective self in their respective social groupings. In the social hierarchy, each caste stood at different positions in caste relations. Thus inter-caste relations become decisive. Consequently, while accepting its position in the social hierarchy, each caste had 'a way' of looking at other castes depending on its sense of self. I argue in this chapter that what the Basel Mission did was to socially re-engineer a new sense of self among its converts. Such a re-engineering had two aspects. First aspect was the de-construction of not only the caste structure that existed within the minds of the converts but also the altered the psychological space. By the psychological space, it is meant the belief systems that transcend the caste boundaries to the society as a whole. For example, belief in astrology, auspicious time, understanding of time and distance, belief in multiplicity of Gods, belief in the power of *Bhutas* (demons), understanding of the influence of nature, notions of pollution and non-pollution, concept of cleanliness of body, separation of work and leisure and many others. These aspects relate to the culture of the people of this region in different ways and in degree and they transcend all castes.

Culture, as it is employed here, is the medium through which the people solve their problems of existence as these are conceived by the members of the society. Culture can be identified with everyday living to creation of the world of art and artifacts. Various cultural institutions such as kinship and marriages, political and economic organisation, social relations and religion combine to form a cultural system. Culture has multiple dimensions; it is material and non - material, symbolic and so on. Material culture is reflected in the way a person relates with order of things and appearances. Non-material aspect of culture refers to aspects such as cognition, belief systems, nuances in language and the ethical and moral practices followed.

Among their converts, the Basel missionaries appear to have taken up the de-construction of the existing culture of the people of the region. Through their activities in Malabar and South Canara, the Basel Mission was not only encountering the belief systems that existed in the districts but also the technological practices. We are arguing that the Mission used the European post-Industrial Revolution technology to encounter the existent belief systems. Like other Europeans, the Basel missionaries also considered the European civilisation or culture as something unique because it had the knowledge of Christ. They also considered European technology as unique. To quote a missionary source:

> We should not think that a converted Hindu is not by far a European, not forget that our civilisation created by Gospel and existing since one and a half millennia is a gift of special divine grace, which confers on us also manufacturing skills of an unusually great advantage. (Industrial Commission, 1856, p. 7)

The second aspect was the constructing of a new sense of self. The new self was that of an industrious man, or a man who accepted the discipline and ethics of an industrial society. In this section, it is intended to explore the praxis of re-engineering of the self. The influence of Calvinism in the creation of a sense of self of the Basel Mission has already been discussed in Chapter 2. In their various prescriptive pronouncements, the Basel missionaries tried not only to articulate what the converts were eventually expected to become and also occasionally doubted whether they would succeed in creating the anticipated selfhood.

> Loyalty in word and deed, loyalty in fulfilling duties to oneself and others, awareness of the value of time, circumspection and looking forward, understanding and acquisition of what is new and changing......may emerge as effective fruits of first conversion. (Report of the Industrial Commission, 1856, p. 4)

The Calvinist theology certainly had a role in the re-engineering of the self of converts to Christianity. The process of re-engineering that we are attempting to discern here, does not end in only imparting new industrial skills or a work ethos that transcended caste distinctions. We may look far beyond such a scenario. It is pertinent here to reflect on the interaction of technology and culture in the context of industrial and religious activities of the Basel Mission.

Technology is a product of culture as much as culture is embedded in technology.[1] The Basel Mission attempted to use the western post -Industrial Revolution technology to engage the existent culture of the converts. This process can be called as social engineering.[2] In this sense, a large factory, an orphanage, a school and even hospital are tools or site for social engineering. Having raised the issue of technology, it may be appropriate to delve a little deeper into the questions that relate technology. It may also be appropriate to discuss the concept of technology.

The instrumental definition of technology is explained by Heidegger thus: "The whole complex of these contrivances is technology. Technology itself is a contrivance, or, in Latin an *instrumentum.*" (Heidegger, 1977, p. 5) But as Heidegger himself has argued, this instrumental definition of technology is not sufficient to understand the essence of technology. As Heidegger argues, technology has the ideal of bringing forth or revealing. For example a chalice used for sacraments in a church is made of silver. The technology of manufacturing a chalice, including the craftsmanship of the craftsman who has made it, reveals what is in the silver ore. Thus a technological object can be looked into as what goes into the technology (in the case of chalice, it is silver ore or bauxite, coal, etc), what form it takes (the shape of chalice) and what ultimate purpose the chalice is to serve (the sacrament in church).

'Technology' is also used in relation to the constitution of human or individual self; which is termed as 'technology of self' by Michel Foucault (Martin, 1988). Technologies of the self permit individuals to effect certain operations on their own bodies and souls, thoughts, conduct, and way of being, so as to transform themselves. These operations are carried out by oneself or with the help of others. The concept re-engineering has tangential semblance with the concept of 'technologies of self.' When the concept 'technology' is employed, we combine technologies of self as well as technologies that go into the production of commodities. At the same time here it is intended to give relatively more emphasis on the latter one than the former. Specificities of both the technologies are inextricably linked to culture.

Perhaps technology manifests or brings to light the culture embedded in it. And culture makes technology possible and functionalises it. We examine the post Industrial Revolution European technology and culture as exhibited by the Basel Mission in its activities, juxtaposed against the retained culture and technologies that existed in Malabar and South Canara. Basel Mission was a medium through which post-Industrial Revolution technologies transmitted to India and demonstrated application of it to a small group of Christian converts, having a background in 'traditional' technologies of production. We may have to introduce a third factor too- that of science- because post Industrial Revolution increasingly used the knowledge provided by science in explaining and broadening technology.

Technology is the art of making and doing things as well. In the process, it brings forth and unravels what is in nature of things as well as nature of human beings. Man has been making artifacts as these are required for his everyday life, because man can also be a gatherer so as to survive. Civilisations are known for the technologies that they produced. Science offers a different field. Science existed as a human enquiry of knowing the cause of things. It strives to explain and predict. For these reasons, the Greeks philosophers referred to science as 'Natural Philosophy'. It was after the fifteenth century that science and technology developed as an interdependent and looping relationship. To give an example, the Italian astronomer, Galileo Galilei[3] who lived in the sixteenth century is supposed to have travelled to the Netherlands to learn the art of making optical lenses that enabled him to manufacture telescopes to observe the celestial bodies more clearly. This in turn resulted in Galileo developing a different view of the universe. Interdependence of science and technology became more pronounced with the Industrial Revolution of the eigtheenth and nineteenth centuries.

It is well known that the Industrial Revolution that started in England during the second half of the eigtheenth century completely changed the system of manufacture by the second half of nineteenth century. The Industrial Revolution started with a series of technological inventions in spinning and weaving, and progressed to iron and steel manufacture. Household and craft based manufacturing system gave way to factory system based on division of labour. The production activities which a single individual performed in a craft based manufacturing system was sub divided into several components, with each individual assigned a single function. This facilitated mass production and consequently, substantial reduction in cost and time expended for production. A second aspect relating to Industrial Revolution is about the use of power. In a craft-based industry, human force or animal power was the motive force. With the invention of steam power, and its adoption for industrial purposes, it became the motive force. The first major source of fuel was coal. Thus, division of labour, use of an external motive force, increased application of science in developing a technological apparatus are the important aspects of Post Industrial Revolution technology.

During the 18th and 19th centuries, significant scientific discoveries took place in Europe. The understanding of molecular structures, metallurgy, human anatomy, understanding the circulation of blood and are some of these. And these discoveries transformed the human being's world view. This expanding knowledge of science not only influenced the system of industrial production, but also man's belief systems and the conception of man as an individual. For example, during medieval times, diseases were believed to have been brought by the curse of God. Modern science would show that micro organisms caused diseases, and its spread can be controlled by chemicals in the form of medicines.[4] The basis of modern science is empiricism[5] or positivism, which means that experiments can be replicated, and that the same results can be obtained under given conditions. In general, modern sciences redefined human being's relation with Nature-nature that exist outside and nature of human beings.

It is possible to relate the perspective of modern science and technology with that of the local technology in the context of the industrial activities of the Basel Mission. Weaving and tile manufacturing were the two lines of manufacture pioneered by the Basel Mission. Both these lines of manufacture were practiced as cottage industries in the Malabar and South Canara districts during the nineteenth century. When the Basel Mission started tile factories in the Malabar and South Canara, potters here were producing small, curved tiles using the potter's wheel. Potters had Extensive traditional knowledge of clay. However, this knowledge was plasticity and breaking strength. However, this knowledge was rarely articulated in writing; it was transmitted from generation to generation orally and learned by doing or producing clay based objects. A modern ceramic technologist would understand clay as aluminum silicate, and relate its plasticity and strength to the proportion of aluminum and silica it contained.[6] For a ceramic technologist, plasticity and breaking strength are also quantifiable through respective parameters. Similarly, in modern ceramic industry, burning process is measured in terms of heat transfer calculated through mathematical equations. The final product is evaluated in terms of various scientific parameters. This example is given here to explain the epistemology of modern technology and posit it against pre-modern technology.

Handling of contradictory viewpoints

Before going into details regarding the praxis of the Basel Mission in dealing with the existent culture, it may be appropriate to explore some of the complex belief systems and sense of self the converts held and also the general social beliefs that the Basel Mission encountered and relate these to the praxis of the Mission in dealing with such complexities. First, the belief systems that posed a problem to the missionaries. In South Canara, a delegation from a few Billava dominated villages approached the Basel missionaries and agreed to be converted with the only condition that they would be allowed to follow some of their continued practices. (David, 1985) The missionaries did not accede to this request. The missionaries wanted the Billava members to completely renounce their former practices.

The Thiyya caste in the Malabar district, like the Billavas in South Canara were predominantly engaged in toddy tapping and mending of coconut trees. Toddy, is a fermented drink tapped from the coconut palm. In Malabar local parlance it is called as *kallu.* Basel missionaries referred to this brew as 'coconut brandy' and initially instead of prohibiting manufacture of *kallu,* tried to make sugar out of it (See Chapter 4). They did not succeed in their attempt as it was not cost effective. This led the missionaries to seek other avenues of employment for the converts.

There were other issues which the missionaries had to tackle. There were castes whose traditional occupation was as temple shamans or oracles (Velichappadu/Theyyam in Malayalam)[7] Basel missionaries treated the profession of this group as 'devil worship' or 'devil dancing', and hence not compatible with Christianity. Belief systems of the *velichapadu* were different from the belief systems of Christianity. Such instances led to compelling needs of de-construction for the Missionaries.

While the above examples are specific to castes, there were certain commonalities which all cultures in the districts of Malabar and South Canara accepted as true and adherence to it unavoidable. One such was the belief in astrology. There are a whole range of concomitant beliefs associated with astrology like the belief in auspicious time and inauspicious time. Astrology was practiced, by members of *kanian* caste as the caste profession. However, astrology was also practiced by all the upper caste people as well, in the caste hierarchy it was practiced by Nambudiris downwards. For any important activity to be embarked upon, an auspicious time is to be determined. There is an auspicious time called *muhurtham* for the conduct of many ceremonies including marriage. Belief in astrology entails that the exact time and place of birth of a person will determine his/her path of existence in this world. It is interesting to know how belief in astrology influenced the life of common folk. Compatibility in astrological terms is still a very important element in arranged marriages even to this date.

In their discourse, the Basel Missionaries went out of the way to clinically analyse astrology as a science, and explain that it as a fraudulent or as something bereft of a scientific base.

In the societies of Malabar and South Canara the concepts of time and distance were understood differently from an industrial society. Agricultural labourers went to work in the field soon after day break, when there was enough visibility and returned home once visibility becomes dim at twilight. There was no concept of fixed hours of work of a day, it differed from one agricultural operation to another. Similarly, Distance was often expressed as, for example, *oru nazhika dooram,* which meant that the 'distance that can be covered by walking one hour'; distance or spatial extent was recognised with the help of time. But, time itself was not clock time. This suggests that space-time divide was different from the post-enlightenment European concept of 'space' and 'time'. Even if time was measured, the speed of the persons who is walking differs and hence the distance covered becomes subjective; yet such recognition of distance was operational and 'enabling' as in the Heidegger's conception of technology. Such complex intersecting conceptualisations of space/time might have been foreign to the European Missionaries and they concluded that here the concepts of time and space are vague. Here, we are aware of the counter argument that the Kerala astrologers measured time in very precise terms.

Inversely, in European post Industrial Revolution societies, time was objective, measured in a precise manner with the help of clocks; we are also aware that there were people in Europe known as Luddites, who used to smash the clocks to disuse. The translation of one concept of time-space to another time-space created mismatches and faced irreducibility. In Europe, though clocks were invented earlier, they had only a curio value. Along with the voyages of discovery, it became necessary to measure time in precise terms for navigational purposes. After the Industrial Revolution, 'time-keeping' emerged as a job as the work of men and machines had to be synchronised in the operation of a factory. Instead of work time, clock time became important. Missionaries introduced the latter concept of time here as well and both the concepts prevailed here but giving more circulation to the clock time.

The Basel missionaries were surprised with the approaches of the local people towards work because their notion of work differed substantially from the notion of work prevailed here. In Calvinist ethos, work was something beautiful and deemed for man. But in India, the missionaries found work, being treated as a drudgery to be borne only as long as it is absolutely necessary. In many occasions, Basel missionaries rather ruefully noted that In India, people see their life's work as something to be done after retirement.[8] Basel missionary, L. Johannes Frohnmeyer noted in his paper presented to the Decennial Missionary Conference at Bombay, (1892-93) noted: "It is Christianity, which has sanctified labour, whilst in Hinduism exertion is looked upon as an evil, which is undergone only as far as it is absolutely necessary." (Frohnmeyer, 1892-93) Missionaries identified work from calling. In German language any work is referred as *arbeit* while calling is referred as *beruf.* In the Calvinist ethos, a person predestined for salvation, revealed himself as a man of calling or a *berufman.*

Love, courtship and marriage

Having commented earlier about the system of arranging marriage in a pre-modern society, the concept of marriage itself will have to be commented upon. In the society of Malabar and South Canara as well as the rest of India, the institution of marriage existed as an arrangement between two families or between the joint families, if the spouses came from joint families. These were often marriages of convenience for the families concerned. Inter-caste or inter religious marriages were not even visualised as the social penalties accompanying such marriages were heavy. The only exception seems to be the sambandam alliance which the members (except the senior most offspring) of the Nambudiri caste used to have with Nair ladies.[9] The institution of sambabdam was at best a conjugal right which could be terminated at will by either of the party concerned. In sambandam marriage, Women had greater freedom in terminating it. It can be said that romantic love did not play any role in the arrangement of any type of marriage in Malabar or South Canara. Moreover it appears that the concept of romantic love did not exist. Perhaps, there were some exceptions. It is generally believed that members of some lower castes like the Pulayas who were agricultural labourers did have the space for romantic marriages as long as it was with members of the same community.[10] In this community, both men and women were wetland agricultural labourers and performed the agricultural duties together. There were occasions for courtship before marriage. For the missionaries, romantic love was the natural way to marriage.

A reference has already been made of the sambandam form of marriage. Sambandam is at best a right for co-habitation. The woman stayed in the safety of her own house after Sambandam. The husband visited the wife well after dark and left the house in the early hours of the morning the following day. The children born out of this union were taken care of by their uncle. Sambandam relationship could easily be terminated. Women had relatively greater power in terminating these relationships. Once terminated, the women concerned could enter into other sambandam relationships. Polygamy also existed among some communities, particularly the higher caste Nambudiri community.

The Basel Missionaries considered this system of sambandam alliance as something very close to prostitution. They also viewed casual termination of a marriage as highly objectionable because in Christianity the institution of marriage was considered sacred. Basel Missionaries encouraged pre- marital courtship among the small group of Christian converts. In their respective countries pre- marital courtship was the norm. According the church laws that were imposed by the Mission upon the converts, a man or a woman had to attain the minimum age of 18 years for the marriage to be consecrated in the Church. Thus, in the small community of converts, child marriages became completely banned and marriages became results of adult sexual preferences. Strict church rules enforced by the mission demanded that a married man should not absent himself from his family for more than three months. This was intended to prevent emergence of casual extra-marital relationships among the married couple.

The Basel Mission used spatio-temporal rearrangements to introduce a new work culture among the converts and those went to factories. A factory is a space which is impersonal and operating in its own synchrony between man and machines. Within factory workers are graded and marked and then distributed across spaces and jobs. Individual workers were also differentiated in terms of gender. Division of labour is one among such operations/ arrangement that took place within the factory space. At times age based ordering also took place. Surveillance became a permanent feature within the factory for disciplining, ordering or serialising individuals to enhance productivity. The factory workers and Christians were separately identified by distancing them from the rest of the society in terms of religion, culture and work ethic. Work time gets identified with clock time with decimal precision. Factory and church functioned as a site of convergence of mobilised people under a roof. Workers are alienated from the commodity that they produce as place of production and place of marketing are distanced. All these arrangements began to constitute insular individuals of a different kind hitherto existed; the tendency was to constitute individuals, as we understand it in the contemporary world. Nevertheless, all this was part of social engineering that the Basel missionaries practiced.

The process of conversion

Let us discern certain process/procedures involved in the introduction of this new arrangement. At the entry level, it is the conversion to Christianity. This process was a long one, sometimes lasting up to a year. Basel Mission churches had verandas on three sides. These verandas are usually meant for the 'inquirers' or people who might be converted. They view the prayer session without necessarily participating in it. Some of them may decide to seek conversion and approach the missionaries for the same. Very often the 'inquirers' were sent to work in factories to test their sincerity for conversion. To justify this practice one missionary blatantly stated: "Hypocrites seldom like to work" (Frohnmeyer, 1893). The logic was that a good worker would naturally become a good Christian, and *vice versa* a good Christian would be a good worker. Industrial labour was mechanical usually extending up to nine to ten hours a day. From the initial days onwards work at the factory began with a prayer and ended with a prayer. This persuading act was intended to make laborers imbibe a new work ethic which conceives work as worship and worship as work. Hence, the motive was to convert workers such that they do not consider work as bane or something to be suffered. Factory labour certainly tested the capacity to do consistent and monotonous labour. Labour in factories also demanded different degrees of precision and concentration of a different nature when compared to what was needed for agricultural labour.

Thus, when a convert entered a factory, he encountered a different environment. Inside the factory there were no polluting distances. Caste consciousness gradually tended to gave way to work consciousness and over a period of time to class consciousness. The Basel Mission factories provided a public space for women as their day time at home was replaced by work time at factories. A large number of women were employed as spool winders, label makers and in the tailoring and embroidery departments of weaving factories.[11] Women were also employed in tile factories in large numbers. Some of them did the similar job as the men. There was a certain sense of freer mutual association as there was opportunity for men and women to meet freely which often resulted in romantic liaisons leading to marriage. Missionary managers did not object to these and allowed such marriages to take place if both the partners belonged to the church. Moreover such romantic liaisons took place under the watchful eyes of the maistries and the factory manager.

Within the ambit of missionary activities, women were employed in various capacities, as teachers in primary schools, nurses in hospitals and dispensaries, attendants in creches-since all large factories had creches to take care of the children when young mothers worked in the factory, offices and canteens. The factory, the office, the creche and the church to which attendance was compulsory was part of the newly generated public space. Not only that the new work culture individuated the converts and factory workers, segregated men from women, differentiated individuals in terms of job and so on, the new culture and space provided individuals to get identified with others as in marriage relations.

Binaries of work and Ieisure

According to the Old Testament in the Bible, God created the world in six days and rested on the seventh day. This has been the logic of the six-day week. Following this logic, the Jewish community observed the seventh day of the week, as Sabath, on which no work was to be done. Subsequently, the Christendom accepted Sunday as the day of rest as well as for prayer and other religious activities. The industrial societies that came up in Europe from the eighteenth century, observed Sunday as a day of rest. This was not due to any altruistic consideration. Work days were hard and working conditions very rigorous. It would therefore not be possible to maintain the productivity of labour without providing rest at regular intervals.

In agrarian societies there was no concept of a regular leisure. There are seasons of hard work, like seasons for ploughing, transplanting, de- weeding, harvesting there were also seasons of relatively very little or no work. Basel Mission 'imposed' rest on Sundays as they imposed industrial discipline at the workplace and church. There was insistence on every member to attend church service on Sunday mornings. But there was also insistence that after church, no work be done on Sundays. For example, washing of clothes was not allowed to be done on Sundays. To be good at work, a worker needed leisure at regular intervals; this seems to be the logic behind imposing the discipline of rest on Sundays. Such an approach reveals a new distribution of labourers across days of a week. This seems to have redefined the work leisure divide or both of them. This redefinition might have been the result of utilitarian notions prevalent in Europe. This disciplinary technology of or process of re-engineering in factories and churches entered even into individual behavior not only when they are either in the factory and church but also when they are at their own homes.

Rites of passage in the re-engineered society

In the Basel Mission churches that got established, the first rite of passage for a newborn child is the christening ceremony. A special thanksgiving prayer is rendered by the priest for the safe delivery of the woman. The custom is for the mother to wear her wedding *sari* (dress) at the occasion of the christening of the first born. This ceremony is usually held on the 40th day after the delivery, The child is named at the christening ceremony. In Kerala society of those times a person's caste could be known through his or her name. Nambudiri Brahmin can have a name Krishnan. The same name for a person belonging to Thiyya caste is 'Kittan'. In the congregations established by the Basel Mission, some protocols seem to have emerged in giving names to newly baptized children or adults converted to Christianity. The first name appears to be usually western, at times even German. This is perhaps done to show a break from the past. Among the Basel Mission Christians, even now there are names in circulation like Rhine, Gottleb, Ulia, Wilhelmina and Karl, which are distinctly German. The second name is usually Indian or local, and the third name the name of the tharavadu or joint family. Names like Gottleb Prabhakaran Puthanpurakkal is one example, and for a woman a name like Wilhelmina Sukumari Maliekkal can exist. To overcome the stigma of caste revealed through names, the Basel missionaries attempted to create 'Indian' names which are in no way connected to the names of Hindu Gods but indicating certain spiritual quality that is seen as Christian. For example, for men, missionaries introduced names like Nirmalan (a person of purity), Supriyan (beloved person), Spadigam (like glass, transparent) for women names like, Snehi (loving person), Sushili (well behaved person), Suguna (full of virtue) for women. In South Canara, converts had names like Jesupriya, (favourite of Jesus) Christananda (one who is in blissful joy with Christ), Christanuja (brother of Christ) Suvarthappa (the person who delivers good news or gospel), Subhodappa (one with wisdom) Shanthappa (the peaceful one), Jesuananda (one who is at bliss in Jesus), Gnanamithra (one who is a friend of wisdom). Women had names like Jesudasi (servant of Christ), Devadasi (servant of God), Shanthi (the serene person) These names had not been in use in either Malabar or South Canara earlier and were creations of the missionaries. These new names made possible identification of individuals who are Christians just by hearing about him/her name. At the same time these names completely obliterated the caste related names that existed before.

In all traditional societies attainment of puberty of girls is acknowledged and celebrated with fanfare. Each community has its own peculiar way of celebrating attainment of puberty by girls. This usually happens between the ages 10-14. A girl is supposed to be ready for marriage after attainment of puberty. The Basel missionaries considered attainment of puberty as a biological evolution not immediately related to marriage.

Basel Mission did not permit child marriages. Attainment of adulthood as the Mission conceived was when a boy or girl grows big enough to make adult choices. The route to adulthood is by becoming a full member of the church. This is called confirmation because a child who is baptized as Christian at birth confirms his or her faith in Christianity and is given full membership of the church, which includes participation in the sacred rite of Holy Communion and the right to vote in the Church Assembly. Confirmation and attainment marriage age is usually co-terminus and for girls and boys the age for confirmation is roughly the same, that is 16-18 years.

In the churches established by the Basel Mission, Confirmation is a rite of passage to adulthood. A child is made a communicant member of a congregation through this rite. Only communicants are allowed to partake in the sacrament of Holy Communion.[12] In the Basel Mission church, the boys and girls in their teens had to attend classes for two years before being allowed to be a communicant member. Confirmation was conducted when a youth is 16 or 18 years of age. Girls were not permitted to be married in church before attaining the age of 18. Hence the Confirmation ceremony in the Basel Mission church, viewed anthropologically, would mean the celebration of arrival of a new group of maidens eligible for marriage. For boys, it meant entry to manhood. The function is seen as a symbolic preparation for marriage and had certain embellishments of the marriage function. The function is elaborate. The dress/colour code is white for both girls and boys, and a lot of care went into selecting the apparel. A church elder is invited to the house of the girl or boy to be confirmed, to conduct a prayer before the candidate left for church as is done for marriage. After confirmation, a good many boys in the congregation were ready to join the factories as workers. The marriage function is similar to any Christian marriage.

Thus, among the converts, the concept of adulthood underwent a change. For girls, confirmation takes place much after puberty. Similarly a menstruating woman is not considered as polluting. She can participate in church worship and receive the Holy Communion during menstruation. Thus the concept of what is pollutant and what it is not also changed.

The last of the rite of passage are the ceremonies following death. Excessive weeping and wailing were not appreciated as such acts are considered as not reflecting the Christian hope for resurrection and life after death. This is in contrast to the existed response of the relatives of the demised although the notion of rebirth was in vogue. The body is placed in a coffin for the burial. Usually, a prayer meeting is held at the house of the deceased person. There is no specified number of mourning days. In the traditional society of Malabar and South Canara, the practice among most castes were that after death, bodies are cremated and the ashes interred in the sea or in river. Missionaries did not allow such practices and insisted that the dead bodies should be placed in a coffin and buried.

Celebrating the Harvest Festival

Among the agrarian societies around the world, harvest is a joyous occasion which is followed by festivities. In Kerala, *Onam* is the harvest festival. The first harvested bunch of paddy is usually offered to the temples as a symbolic offering. In Hebrew societies Harvest Festival is celebrated by offering the first fruits of the agriculture to the temple. This custom is adapted to the Christian culture. In the Basel Mission church, the Harvest Festival which is usually conducted during the month of November (this happens after the Onam festival) is usually celebrated on a grand scale, and usually is a full day affair. There is usually a group singing and choirs from the neighbouring churches are invited to render songs. Members of the congregation invite their friends and relatives to attend the festivities, which included fun and games after the church service.

Most centres of the Basel Mission had a factory or workshop. Where there were factories, New Year's evening thanksgiving prayer was conducted at the factory premises. Basel Mission did not separate factory work from religious work. Moreover, Basel Mission had described their factories as the crown and centre of their activity. Besides the factory labourers, their families and other members of the congregation also participated in the annual prayer.

Mission Compound and the idea of Christian Village Community

The Mission Compounds emerged as convergence centres of various activities. Convergence of so many people under a roof and working for long hours in factories was something alien to the contemporary society of those days. The idea of collectivity of different kinds was prevalent; it could as expressed in community activities like temple festivals, ritualistic performances, collectivity in the paddy fields and so on. Notion of 'compound' entirely owned by a single entity such as individual was also something new. A large area of land was owned by the Mission. Mission Compounds existed in Kozhikode, Kannur, Codacal, Chombala, Palakkad and Vaniyamkulam and many other stations of Basel Mission. These sprawling compounds had coconut trees and other garden crops planted. Church, houses of pastors and missionaries, schools, hostels for working women, buildings for Men's Fellowship and Women's Fellowships, and Widows Quarters were located within the Compound. A good number of converts lived here under the surveillance of the missionaries and pastors. Before the advent of electricity, at dusk, lamps were lit and families, usually extended families, had the daily family prayer under the gaze of missionaries. Mission Compounds had significant role in social engineering of converts. Here, missionaries knew every convert, his or her background, behavior pattern and habits. Missionaries insisted that evening prayers were conducted as soon as it was dark and lamps were lit. The missionaries also ensured that cultural practices and symbolic objects relating to the former way of life and beliefs of the converts did not enter the mission Compound. Such was the nature and visibility of the Compound; it was a given landed area, it was property, it had wall, it was also inclusive of built up spaces, open spreads, multiple cropped land, it was source of income, site of production of commodities ranging between marketed commodities and subsistence food for the family.

Role of orphanages in re-engineering of the self

There were two other institutions that played a role in re-engineering the self. These were the Girls Orphanage at Chombala, near Vadakara, and the Boy's Orphanage at Parapperi near Codacal in Malabar and Mulki in South Canara. The inmates of these orphanages were not always orphans in the full sense of the term. Most of the inmates had at least one parent. They were mostly single women with children. These women went to work in the factories or other institutions run by the Mission admitted their wards to these orphanages. The orphanages took care of bringing up a new generation of 'Christian' children. The notion of 'new generation' needs some qualification or elaboration. The convert's children at individual families were different from the Christians children brought up in orphanages. This is because, first, they were entirely converged within the orphanage. Second, they were without constant and continuous presence of the converted Christian parents who had retained at least some of the 'tradition' that they had. Thirdly, the inmates were brought under surveillance by the priests or teachers round the clock. And therefore, more real Christians (more proximate to the European self) than converted Christians became a reality. The 'new generation' Christians were disciplined at orphanages. Simultaneously, orphanages brought out laboring subjects perfectly employable in the factories of production. Both boys and girls were given minimum education up to the fifth standard. The more intelligent among them continued to study up to Standard 8 or more. Boys from varied caste background lived and studied in the boys' orphanage located at Parapperi, about 3 kms distance from Codacal which was one of the oldest stations of Basel Mission in Malabar. The orphanage had a large compound comprising several acres. At one time the Mission ran an agricultural school here. Boys attended their class in the morning, and in the afternoon they went to the field to be engaged in garden farming like rearing and mending coconut trees.

The girls' orphanage was located at Chombal in Malabar and Mulki in South Canara. Here, apart from the usual curriculum, girls were taught domestic work like cooking and needlework, senior girls were given instructions on personal hygiene particularly during menstruation, about human reproduction and handling deliveries. Photographs taken during the nineteenth century abound with pictures of girls in kitchen- related work and boys in garden work. These photographs taken mainly for the benefit of donors at home are nascent images of the creation of a new self. In other words, although boys and girls received different kinds of skills based on gender specificity, in nutshell it can be said that they were enabled to take care of themselves.

Introducing polyphonic music

Traditional Indian music, whether from the Hindustani or Carnatic tradition is monophonic. A melody is sung or played and the accompanying instruments play the same melody sometimes with a time gap. Polyphonic music is a distinct contribution of the west. It is based on the concept of harmony. The songs are sung or played by instruments in four voices or tunes. These are bass, tenor, alto and soprano. There are of course variations to this like contralto and baritone. The foremost exponent of polyphonic music was the German classical musician, Johan Sebastian Bach.[13] Germany has a great tradition in polyphonic music. Great masters of western music like Beethovan, Schubert, Mozart were all German. Many German missionaries who came to serve in India had training in the western classical tradition. For example, Christopher Irion who served in Chombala and Parapperi was a distinguished musician.

German missionaries taught students of orphanages polyphonic music and also playing of instruments like Piano, organ and violin. They also taught the students polyphonic music. Basel Mission believed in congregational singing. The whole congregation sang in loud voice, and sang polyphonic music, the whole congregation became a choir. Even now, the congregations founded by the Mission carry the tradition of polyphonic music.

Summing up

The Basel Mission had a benefit which no other missionary organisation enjoyed. They could combine secular and religious activities in such a way they could re-engineer the converted Christians with a view to create new selfhoods which resembled that of the European ideals of an individual. Although the target group of re-engineering was confined to the converted Christians, it had spread effect on those who (belonged to different religions and castes) were directly and indirectly associating with the Christians and factory workers. Factories represented new technologies, new ways of interacting with machines, new identity and new ways of being in this world. These factories and the labour therein were a means by which the Mission could steam-roll through in making a new community with different value base. It used the new technologies effectively; however the coverage was limited. During the nineteenth century, there was a wider discourse among the missionary groups in India whether caste was compatible with Christianity. In such meetings, the Basel Mission was proud to state that their churches did not suffer from caste discriminations. Certainly, converts of the Basel Mission were a small homogenous group. The Mission had succeeded in re-engineering of the self of these converts. The converts did not behave like another caste. The converts appear to have acquired work consciousness instead of caste consciousness.

The Mission introduced new ways of distributing people in spaces as in the factory, church and in orphanage; they were also redistributed in time as in the case of work days and leisure day; distributed people in new relations of power and so on. The Basel Mission introduced new differentiations in terms of gender relations, marriage and other ceremonies, religion, interpersonal relations, periods of pollution, attitude towards themselves and others etc. In general, the subjectivity (to oneself and to others) of the converts to Christian religion and to work force engendered new individualities and self-identifications. These new arrangements of re-distribution and differentiations re-engineered the self. New technologies of self along with new technologies of production are part and parcel of new modes of re-disciplining self. For subjecting one to oneself is quite important, as important as subjecting one to others. That is, technology of production of commodities is one thing that is inseparable from introduction of encoding people's behavior through cultural codes. It is also possible to think that with coming of factory system, not only laborers got redistributed in new spaces and time but also their offsprings. All these involved re-engineering self of the present day converts and their future generations.

Notes

1. For a discussion on this topic see: Murphie, Andrew & Potts, John. *Culture and Technology.* (2003). New York, Palgrave Mcmillan.
2. Definition of social engineering in Wikipaedia is "A discipline in social science that referes to the effort to influence particular attitudes or social behaviour on a large scale whether by governments, media or privilege groups in order to produce deserved statistics in a target population", http://www.wikipidia.org/wiki/Social engineering (Political Science) engineering. Retrieved on 21-12-2015. Social engineering can also be understood philosophically as a deterministic phenomenon where the goals of the architects of new social construct are realised.
3. Galileo Galilei, (b.1564) was an astronomer, mathematician and engineer. He played a major role in the scientific revolution during Renaissance. Galileo's championing of heliocentricism and Copernicanism was controversial during his lifetime.
4. For a full discussion on this subject, see: Russel, Bertrand. *Impact of science on society.* (1961).Bombay: Blackie & Son (India) Limited, Bombay
5. "Empiricism in philosophy the view that all concepts originate in experience, that all rationally acceptable beliefs or propositions are justifiable or knowable only through experience. This broad definition accords with the derivation of the term empiricism from the ancient Greek work *emperia,* or experience. http://www.britannica.com. Retrieved on 22-12-2015.
6. The raw material for producing tile is clay or Feldspar. Feldspar is the name given to a group of minerals distinguished by the presence of Alumina and Silica in their chemistry. This group includes aluminum, silicates of soda, potassium, or lime. It is the single most abundant mineral group on earth.
7. Velichappadu in Malayalam translates as Revealer of Light, is the oracle or mediator between a deity and devotees at a Hindu Temple in Kerala. Prominent in Valluvanad, the Velichappadu is also known as Komaram in some parts, is an integral part of the rituals in a Bhagavathi temple. There are both male and female Velichappadu and often belong to a particular family. People, in Kerala and beyond, have enormous respect for these mediating oracles when they're in their trances and heed to their words. Wikipedia (Retrieved on April 19, 2022)

Theyyam is a popular ritual form of dance worship in Kerala and Karnataka. Theyyam consists of thousand-year-old traditions, rituals and customs. The people of these districts consider Theyyam itself as a channel to a god and they thus seek blessings from Theyyam. There are about 456 types of Theyyam. Wikipedia (Retrieved on April 19, 2022)

It is quite possible that the Basel Missionaries used the generic terms "devil dancing" to refer to both the above ritualistic performances.

8. Such observations recur in many writings of the missionaries.
9. Nair women had greater freedom in terminating sambandam relationship and there was not stigma against remarriage of such women.
10. This observation on the Pulaya community is made after making extensive personal enquiries. Pulaya community are traditionally wetland agricultural labourers. In this community, men and women participate in agricultural activates together, giving opportunity for men and women to get to know each other.
11. Detailed picture of women's employment in Basel Mission factories is given in Chapter 3.
12. Holy Communion is a Christian rite that is considered a sacrament in most churches and an ordinance in others.
13. "Music is said to be polyphonic if it is composed of two or more voice parts, each having individual melodic significance". Willie Apel, Ralph T Daniel.(1961). *The Harvard Brief Dictionary of Music.* New York: Washington Square Press.

Girls from Chombala orphanage pose with kitchen implements

A missionary wife training women in lace making

A musical rendition at Harvest Festival.
A contemporary photograph

A confirmation service in progress.
A contemporary photograph

Chapter - 7

Economic Impact of the Basel Mission Industries

The industrial activities of the Basel Mission were pioneering initiatives in modern manufacturing, both in Malabar and South Canara. Even before the British colonial capital turned its interest towards establishing modern manufacturing units in the Malabar and South Canara districts, a Christian missionary group which originated in South Germany or Switzerland had started investing on these lines. We have already seen how and when such activities were started in Malabar and South Canara. It would be appropriate to examine the influence the industrial activities of the Basel Mission had on the course of the economic life in the region.

The Basel Mission experimented with various lines of traditional and modern manufactures, but eventually settled for handloom and tile manufacture. These two lines of manufactures were already in vogue in Malabar and South Canara as cottage industries. What the Mission attempted was to technically upgrade these manufacturing processes and eventually raise them to the level of modern manufacture. Such a powerful demonstration would no doubt have multiple levels of impact on the traditional system of manufacture. There are some pertinent questions that arise while attempting to assess the economic impact that the Basel Mission industries had in the districts of Malabar and South Canara. Here, we focus our enquiries on some of the following issues.

1. While on the one hand the production capacity in handloom and tile sectors grew after the Basel Mission industries started producing the above two products, did the traditional cottage manufacture of these products suffer due to the inroads made by the Basel Mission products in handloom and tile manufacture?
2. Did the entry of the Mission in the manufacture of tile and handloom products result in the dichotomy between the objectives of industrial production and the felt need of the society?
3. Did the Basel Mission industries result in the creation of a new labour force, working for a wage and having no control over the means of production and disciplined according to the new concepts of time and duty?
4. To what extent, did the technologies demonstrated by the Mission come to be adopted?
5. What was the type of impact the demonstration of an external market with alternate marketing channels had on the future course of development of the weaving and tile industry in the Malabar and South Canara districts?
6. The impact of accounting and managerial practices introduced by the Basel Mission in the evolution of industrial activity in the region.

State of traditional handloom industry in Malabar and South Canara

The above questions are addressed here, though not in sequence. The first issue that we discuss relates to the handloom industry. The handloom weaving as a craft has a history of thousands of years. Humans needed clothes to protect themselves from the vagaries of weather. Requirement for clothing varied, depending on the weather of the particular region. Malabar and South Canara districts have a temperate climate. Thus, in the districts of Malabar and South Canara, where there are no extremes in climate, requirement for clothing was very limited. Consequently, very little weaving was done in these districts. Men and women wore a white piece of cloth around the lower part of the body, and this cloth was called the *thuvarthu* in Malayalam. Women used a similar piece of garment to cover the upper part of their bodies. The full length lower garment reaching up to the ankle level was worn generally by the upper caste people. This was called *the mundu.* The normal clothing of the working class population was the thuvarthu. Very little dyeing was done in Malabar and South Canara. Neither of the districts of Malabar or South Canara are cotton growing. However, cotton was grown in the Coimbatore district of the Madras Presidency which was contiguous to Malabar, and the North Canara district, contiguous to the South Canara District.

Therefore, conceptually traditional weaving could have existed only at three levels.

1. Rural households having looms and producing garments during off season, either for their own consumption or for sale in the rural markets.
2. Weaving undertaken throughout the district, in small centres, and supplying cloth to the neighbouring areas.
3. Agglomeration of weavers who weave superior garments, usually located at urban centres.

The first model that is described here, that is, agriculturists practicing weaving as an off-season activity is in practice even now in some states in India like the north eastern states of Assam, Manipur, Meghalaya,

Mizoram and Arunachal Pradesh. The strict caste hierarchy and related division of labour practiced in the Malabar and South Canara districts could have been the reason for the non existence of part- time weavers in Malabar and South Canara. Wetland labourers did only wet -land work and garden labourers did only garden related work. The weaver caste in Malabar is known as *chaliya* and their equivalent in South Canara was known as *Sales (Salia), Jadas* and *Billimagas*. No other castes did the weaving in these districts either as a full-time or part-time activity.

These chaliya weavers used their primitive pit looms to weave the thuvarthu which was the common garment worn by the people. Weaving of the broader mundu was undertaken in Malabar and South Canara only by some weaver groups located near urban centres. Such hand woven cloth was also brought from neighbouring cotton producing district of Coimbatore by traders from the Chetty community and marketed in the Malabar district. The Chetty traders also sold yarn to the chaliya weavers, often on credit. The position of South Canara district was a little different we have some quantitative information. A part of the requirement of cloth seems to have been met through imports from Bombay.

In Malabar, the administrative units that existed earlier were called as *amsam* and its sub-unit *desom*. Each desom or hamlet had its own weaver families. The feudal landlords of the desom took interest to bring Chaliya weavers from outside and settle them in their desoms. In Malabar, there are also some references about larger weavers' villages where a large concentration of weavers lived. The Taliparamba village in Kannur district was one such weavers' village. We do not have a picture of organisation of production of the weavers settled in urban centres and weaving superior garments. In Thiruvithamkoor State, (Travancore) south of Malabar, king Balarama Varma of Thiruvithamkur kingdom, had invited weavers from Andhra and settled them at a village called Balaramapuram, a short distance from Thirvananthapuram, which was the capital of the kings. These weavers specialised in producing superior cloth required for the royal families. Balaramapuram remains as a centre for weaving superior hand woven cloth to date.

Nither the Malabr district nor the South Canara districts has similar urban agglomeration of weavers producing superior garments or mundus. It is quite possible that some chaliya weavers might also have woven mundus in their looms. By the end of the nineteenth century, the women had started wearing a broader cloth referred in Kannur as *podava*. They were obviously, not in large numbers. Therefore, it is fair to come to the conclusion that, to some extent, the superior garments or mundu/ podava were imported from neighbouring districts or came from weaving centres along the Coromandel coast. In the South Canara district, part of requirements of handloom cloth must have come from north Canara district which was a cotton producing area in the Deccan plateau and was known for its traditional weaving. The cost of such imported garments must have been high, and made the garments affordable to very few people. We thus, come to the conclusion that only two types of weaving took place in the Malabar and South Canara region. That was the weaving of a coarse garment called thuvarthu and the broader cloth called mundu. Our enquiries must certainly be directed to understanding the organisation of production and marketing patterns of the chaliya weavers in the Malabar and South Canara districts.

Chaliya weavers - organisation of production and marketing of products

The chaliya weaver castes in the Malabar and South Canara districts lived in small agglomerations scattered throughout the district. These weavers usually lived in houses built along the two sides of a street leading to their temple. For these weavers, living together as a community was a professional necessity. Warp for weaving was set in the open street in front of the homes. The entire family members of weavers including women and children participated in different operations relating to weaving. It appears that multiple models of organisation of production existed in Malabar and South Canara. First was the model of the chaliya weavers weaving thuvarthu/mundu and vending the products from household to household. This type of marketing usually covered an area of about 5 km - 10 km radius - a distance that could be covered by foot in a day.

Still another model which is not mentioned above is explained by an important social observer Kanipayyur Nambuthiri (Shankaran Nambuthiri, 2009). He observes that many the weavers in weaver settlements received as payment for their products not in cash, but in terms of a prescribed quantity of paddy after each harvest from the tharawadus that sponsored these weavers. When such families urgently needed cloth for special occasions - festivals like *Onam, Vishu* or marriages, such families would advance money to the weavers for buying yarn. Weavers could also get yarn from the Chetty traders on credit, but that would depend upon a number of other factors like the command the Chetty traders had on the finished product. It appears that often the Chetty traders also practiced a putting out system. They advanced yarn to weavers against the promise to supply finished products which they marketed. Thus multiple models of organisation of production existed in the Malabar district. We do not have sufficient information on organization of production of handloom in the South Canara district.

The major towns in Malabar were Calicut, Tellicherry, Kannur and Palghat and in South Canara, Mangalore and Udippi. Of these, during the nineteenth century, Calicut was a district headquarters with a population of around 50,000. Kannur and Tellicherry had a population of about

30,000. Kannur was an important cantonment town. Telicherry was an important trading centre in pepper. Mangalore again was the district headquarters of South Canara district administration. We do not have references of agglomeration of weavers producing superior garments in any of these places. There are references about weaver's village in Taliparamba near Kannur There is alsoa scant reference about some weavers in Telicherry, producing towels and napkins for the English residents settled there (Logan, 1887). This was the state of weaving in Malabar when the Basel missionaries arrived there.

Changes started taking place from the middle of the nineteenth century. These changes can be understood only in the context of the debate on impact of colonial policies on traditional industries. Generally this debate is referred as debate on de-industrialisation. The debate on de-industrialisation has a long history. The measure of de-industrialisation is the proportion of population that is involved with the secondary sector. In the case of the nineteenth century India, since large industries were very few, the measure will automatically refer to the share of population in the handicraft manufacturing sector. As early as 1924, Dr D R Gadgil, in his classic work entitled "Industrial Evolution of India in Recent Times" had noted: "All industries for which India has been noted from ancient times had declined under the jelous commercial policy of the East India Company" (Gadgil, 1924 (1942), p. 376). He specified products like silk, wool manufactures, brass and copperware, wood carving, and sugar and noted that "the Government had cruelly repressed the infant mill industry of India under the mandate of Lancashire" (Gadgil, 1924 (1942), p. 386). Jawaharlal Nehru, the first Prime Minister of India, in his book "Discovery of India" had noted similar sentiments. Noted Nehru: "Foreign political domination led to rapid destruction of the economy she had built up, without anything positive or constructive taking place" (Nehru, 1956, p. 36).

This debate continued in 1968 with the publication of a journal article by Prof. Morris D Morris titled "Towards Re-interpretation of Nineteenth Century Economic History" (Morris M. D., 1968). Morris took a view that up to the nineteenth century, India was a static and self contained economy, not capable of withstanding the shattering influence of commercial and industrial competition from the West. India could not warm up to the positive impact of the Industrial Revolution in Europe due to its 'other worldliness'. He further argued that till the arrival of the British, India did not have a tradition of continuous administration; India was also not a pre-industrial manufacturing nation. Morris was specific about his view of the impact of the British yarn and machine made cloth on the traditional handloom manufactures in India. He argued that Britain had also exported machine made yarn to India which was cheaper compared to the Indian hand - made yarn and this would have made Indian handloom industry more competitive. His final conclusions were:

> My tentative conclusion is that, at worst, the vast expansion of British cloth exports to India skimmed off the expanding demand. The handloom weavers were at least not fewer in number and no worse off economically at the end of the period than at the beginning. The net effect for the economy was a positive one in terms of per capita real income. (Morris, 1968)

This comment brought three qualified responses from the anti - imperialistic historians in India like Bipan Chandra, T.Raychoudhury, Irfan Habib, Amiya Kumar Bagchi and Japanese historian Toru Matsui and several others.

The gist of arguments brought forward by the above historians against the views expressed by Morris were as under: First of all, Morris does not make any reference about the 'drain theory' about which substantial arguments were brought about by nationalist historians like R.C Dutt and others as early as the turn of the twentieth century (Dutt, 1882 (1960)). This theory deals with the drain of wealth which the British imperialism caused on India through various means. The British imperialists appropriated the agrarian surplus in India through tax settlements. But the money so raised was repatriated from India as 'home charges' like the cost of placing British armed forces in India, high salaries paid to the British nationals working in India and even for financing British wars at places outside India, like the wars conducted in Ethiopia and Afghnistan. As a result, finance was not available for investment in infrastructure as well as social sector.[1]

Backing his argument with hard data, Bipan Chandra showed that during the period 1849-1889 British export of cloth to India had increased by 25.5 million pound sterling (12.1 times) while the export of yarn had increased only by 1.8 million pound sterling (4times) contradicting the view that import of machine made yarn could have made Indian handloom products more competitive (Chandra, 1968). Bipan further argued that even British administrators like C Jack had noted that the once vibrant handloom industry in Faridabad was killed by British imports (Chandra, 1968). Toru Matsui argued that import of machine made yarn could have thrown Indian spinners out of job. Most of the spinners were women doing part-time job (Matsui, 1968).

It is generally difficult to prove the decline of handicrafts through empirical analysis. This was attempted by Amiya Kumar Bagchi. (Bagchi, 1976) Bagchi took two different sets of data, both relating to Bihar. First was from the report of Francis Hamilton Buchanan for the year 1803 on the survey that he conducted for the EIC. The second set was the census report of Bihar for 1881.Though the two sets of data are not exactly Comparable, a decline of population involved with the manufacture of handicrafts was observed.

Observations of Morris D Morris that India could not warm up to the positive effects of Industrial Revolution in Britain due to the 'other worldliness' also came under sharp criticism. T Raychaudhuri in his paper argued that during the seventeenth and eigtheenth centuries, India and China were the only two Asian countries where very rich merchant class were trading in their own ships. He further argued that the Coromandel merchants had showed the capacity and intuitiveness to organize limited liability companies.

The debate on de-industrialisation continues to date. Some general observations on the debate will have to be brought into conclusion. While discussing de-industrialisation, generally, western scholars avoid discussion on the drain theory. The Industrial Revolution had taken place in England and from the beginning of the nineteenth century, England was emerging as a large scale exporter of cotton cloth. The white broad cloth known as 'mull cloth' and sometimes as 'Lancashire mull' cloth was machine made, and hence cheaper. This cloth was being imported from England to the Malabar and South Canara district as well as the rest of India. Machine made mull cloth was cheaper than the mundu produced by local weavers. Gradually the mull cloth was replacing the traditional mundu. The aristocratic classes as well as the new formed groups like junior functionaries in the government who were earlier wearing mundu woven by traditional Chaliya weavers, had started using the mull mundu. Following this trend, a portion of people who earlier wore only thuvarthu/ mundu started shifting to the imported mull mundu. Thus, we assume that the demand for thuvarthu must have gradually declined during the latter part of the nineteenth century.

There have not been empirical studies to assess the impact of imported mull cloth on the local weaving industry in Kerala. In the absence of such studies, it may be necessary to depend on the observations made about the problems faced by the traditional weaving industry in Malabar and South Canara. An important document on the state of industry in the Madras Presidency, *The Industry Investigation Census of Madras Presidency for the year 1911,* took a view that the number of weavers in the Presidency in recent years had not declined. Nevertheless, the further statements made on the matter is highly revealing. While commenting upon the state of the handloom industry in Malabar, the Report stated that:

> Owing to the stress of competition, (from machine made imported cloth) they (the weavers) turn out a larger amount of finished goods than was formerly the case; that is to state that the majority of them will have to work harder to make a bare living. (p. 208)

Another Government publication, The District Gazeteer of Malabar and Anjengo (1908) also reports a similar picture:

> Chaliyans or weavers especially have been hit by the introduction of machine- made goods from Europe, but they still struggle without thought of improving their time honoured methods or deserting their hereditary trade for more remunerative employment. (Innes, 1908, p. 252)

The Gazeteer goes on to explain the state of degradation of traditional weaving:

> The Chaliyans are thus reduced to supply only the lower castes with clothes and to weaving coarse towels. They are miserably poor and with antiquated loom the whole family, including women and children have to work the whole day to make a living. (Innes, 1908, p. 252)

The import of British machine made textiles, it appears, did not just skim off the increasing demand for textiles that was emerging during the second half of the nineteenth century. It seems to have affected the demand for the thuvarthu which the Chaliya weavers were weaving. Many Chaliya weavers had to move out of traditional weaving. Subsequent history of the evolution of modern handloom industry in Kannur shows that many chaliya weavers who were thrown out of their profession due to the changing economic environment, were employed as weavers in the Basel Mission weaving factory at Kannur. (Raghaviah, 2011). As it would be seen in the next chapter, from the beginning of the twentieth century, some of the members of the chaliya community who had gained experience in modern hand-loom industry turned entrepreneurial and started units of their own. This could be deemed as forced entrepreneurship. Many of the modern handloom factories that were started in the Kannur region at the turn of twentieth century were started by members from this community.

The state of weavers in South Canara district appears to be different. In Chapter 3, we have quoted an observation from the District Manual of 1895 (Stuart, 1895, p. 145) which states that the traditional weavers have not been effected by the import of British textiles. Such an observation will have to be carefully examined. It is beyond the purview of the present enquiry.

The impact of Basel Mission textiles on the local handloom production - an assessment

Thus, there is a difficult scenario which we have to understand. The most important issue relates to how the Basel Mission could have entered into handloom weaving at a time when the traditional hand weaving was in the decline. To begin with, the Basel Mission had taken up traditional weaving in Mangalore before they embarked on modern handloom weaving. The result of this experiment was not satisfactory. The Mission made fabrics could not compete with the products of traditional weavers. The Basel Mission felt that the traditional weavers had something more, like a piece of land to depend upon for sustenance were not fully dependent upon the weaving for sustenance. At the same time, the Basel Missionaries were keenly aware of the impact on the British colonial policies on the manufacture of handicrafts in India.

As it is argued here, from the second half of the nineteenth century, the traditional handloom industry was facing a decline in demand due to the import of British textiles. Yet, when the Basel Mission decided to take up industrial activity to give employment to its converts, the Mission first took up handloom weaving as the activity and started establishing weaving units. It is in the above context that the qualitative up - gradation of handloom weaving as attempted by the Basel Mission that assumes importance. This has already been discussed in Chapter 4. The series of technical changes that the Mission introduced in their factories included introduction of fly shuttle, modern dyeing techniques, use of jacquard looms, and introduction of power in certain operations like winding of thread and dyeing, introduction of new materials like hosiery, and stockinet are to be viewed in the above perspective.

There is something particular about the new products and processes introduced by the Basel Mission. Excepting in the case of hosiery products (manufacture of hosiery is essentially a machine process), all weaving was done by hand. Steam engines were used as motive force only for operations relating to spool winding and dyeing. The Basel Mission's weaving industry did not compete with the British textiles which were being imported to India on a large scale. A large part of the output of the Mission textile products were exported mostly to British colonies, using British trade channels. In India, these products (for example bed sheets, towels, suiting and jinghams) were used either by the Europeans living in India or by the new class of Indians who had started imitating the Europeans in dress and manners. The textile products of Basel

Mission were addressing to a 'niche market' in which the quantity of output was not very high, but the product was value added and therefore commanded a higher price. Even retaining such a niche market demanded ability to bring out new products for which the Mission industries showed great skill. Products like Webster's Shikari, and Abyssinian Twill Cotton, about which a mention has already been made in Chapter 4, are examples of such product innovations. The Basel Mission factories did have the capacity to make such innovations. The impact of the Basel Mission's entry into handloom weaving was in demonstrating new weaving technologies, factory type manufacturing systems, global marketing and mobilisation of labour force. A good many of these factors were adopted by the local industry that came up - though to a lesser level. Needless to say that there was a dichotomy. The producers did not know the final customers who were in far off places.

The case of the tile industry

The tile industry presents a different scenario. Making of tiles was a traditional activity of the potter caste called *kushavans* in Malabar and *kumbhars* in South Canara. The kushava community basically produced earthenware vessels, mainly pots used for cooking and other domestic purposes. Production of tiles by this community was at best an activity undertaken in response to some specific demand. That demand was small as ordinary people were not permitted to use tile for roofing. Moreover, a roof with traditional tiles was very expensive as it needed heavy wooden superstructure. This was a factor that negatively impacted the demand for traditional tiles. By the second half of the nineteenth century, there was an emerging demand for roofing tiles from the government, mainly from the Public Works Department and from railways. The traditional potters were not equipped to handle such a massive demand. Moreover, the potter profession was caste based and it would have prevented new entrants into the business of pottery. The number of members of this caste was also small. There has not been any specific study of the impact of machine-made tiles on the business of the traditional potters. It may be right to speculate that the impact was only marginal. The kushava potters could not have met the demand for roofing tiles which started emerging from the beginning of last quarter of the nineteenth century. This demand was, later met by the new modern tile factories that came up first in South Canara and later in Malabar (Raghaviah, Industrial Development of Malabar 1914-1947: Processes and Trajectories, 2011).

Creation of a new labour force

In the traditional weaving and pottery, performed as cottage industry, family was the unit of labour. The entire family members including women and children participated in the production process. As against such a system, the Basel Mission industries employed wage labour. The employees of the Mission, whether they were converts or not, were wage labourers. The wage labourers came from different backgrounds, but carried with them a class consciousness. As seen in Chapter 4, about eighty per cent of workers in the weaving establishments were converts. Missionaries had a strong grip over the converts as members of the church. Yet, the first known full-fledged strike took place at the weaving factory at Kannur in the year 1901. Subsequent history of the labour movement in Malabar and South Canara shows that labour movement was nourished in the weaving and tile industries first, and later in other sectors like the *beedi* (country cigarettes) industry (Raghaviah, Industrial Development of Malabar 1914-1947: Processes and Trajectories, 2011). The modern handloom weaving factories that sprung up during the inter war years (1914-1939) were centres of trade union activity.

Market, marketing channels and demand pattern

A traditional economy like that of Malabar and South Canara can be said to be in a static equilibrium. Traditional industry operates on a technologically weak foundation because of the limitations of the market. Demand for traditional industries was confined to the respective regions. An industry catering to the local market faces seasonality of demand, but since the economy itself exists in static equilibrium, the demand is generally constant or increases only marginally, depending upon the increase in population and purchasing power. The marginal increase in population does not warrant changes in the organisation of production.

Modern industry, on the other hand caters to a wider market. An industry operating in a wider market is subjected to the vagaries of global demand and to address to such vagaries, the industry has to constantly up-skill itself, bringing out new products and introducing new processes. The industry must operate on technologically superior foundations and achieve a higher level of specialisation of labour. The tile and weaving industrial units established by the Basel Mission were of this type. They catered to an international demand.

One of the most important impacts of the Basel Mission industries was that it established marketing channel within the country and outside. Basel Mission industries used the services of travelling salesmen who journeyed throughout the British Indian Empire which comprised also Burma (present Myanmar) and Ceylon (now Sri Lanka). Later, particularly during the inter- war years (1914-1939), the smaller handloom factories that came up in Kannur also started employing travelling salesmen. The Kannur handloom industry was also supplying a large part of their output to other parts of India including Assam and Bengal.

Transfer of technical knowledge

In this chapter as well as the previous chapters, the concepts 'traditional technology' and modern technology has been used, often juxtaposing one against the other. There is a difference between the two types of technology. That difference is in the application of science. For centuries, science and technology grew in different lines. While technology was the art of making and doing things, science was an enquiry into understanding the cause of things. For this, science used the relatively sophisticated skills of numeracy and literacy. In this sense, the approaches to technology can vary. As we have stated earlier, a traditional potter can understand the clay by getting a 'feel' of it. For a ceramic technologist, clay is a combination of aluminum and silica and hence it is aluminum silicate. The plasticity and breaking strength of clay is empirically tested and re-tested by the technologist and the relevant parameters recorded. Thus, what we call as modern technology uses science in the creation of machinery and artifacts.

It was during the Industrial Revolution of 18th and 19th centuries that culminated in the marriage of science and technology. A few inventions in spinning and weaving initiated the process.[2] The Industrial Revolution completely transformed the production process from cottage industry to large scale industry. Increased specialisation of labour, use of external motive power and application of scientific knowledge in the production process are the important aspects of modern technology.

Weaving and tile industries were traditional activities in Kerala. It is these same manufactures that were transformed by the Basel Mission into large scale manufacturing technologies. Technology which is demonstrated in one place can be copied and adopted - this process is called transfer of technology. In the following table an attempt is made to list out all technologies that were introduced and demonstrated by the Basel Mission industries and observe the technologies that got adopted by weaving and tile industries that came up in the Malabar and South Canara districts.

Table 7.1: Technologies demonstrated and adopted - weaving

Technologies introduced by the Basel Mission	***Adopted in latest years or not***
Frame loom	Adopted
Fly shuttle	Adopted
Jacquard weaving	Adopted
Dyeing using chemical dyes	Adopted
Introduction of Khakhi dye	Adopted
Use of mercerised yarn	Adopted
Introduction of hosiery products	Adopted
Use of steam power as motive force	Adopted with a time lag

As far as weaving was concerned, most of the technologies demonstrated by the Basel Mission industries were adopted. Even the use of steam power was adopted with a time-lag of about 30 years. For example, Aaron Spinning and Weaving Mills Ltd, as well as Premier Hosieries, the two important weaving factories that were established in Malabar during the inter-war years, used steam power. The Basel Mission industries were managed by technical managers who had training in textile technology and had knowledge of the basic sciences relating to weaving. They could innovate and introduce new products. The modern handloom industry that came up in and around Kannur area copied the manufacturing process of these products, but could not bring out new products. This was a serious limitation. It should also be noted that in India, textile technology came to be taught as a branch of study only from 1887[3] The tile industry that followed the same route also shows a similar picture, as it will be seen here.

Table 7.2: Technologies demonstrated and adopted - tile industry

Traditional technology used	***Technology demonstrated by the Basel Mission***	***Adopted or not***
Testing of clay by experience and 'feel'.	Scientific testing of clay	Adopted, not fully
Mixing by man/ bullock power	Mixing of clay using a pug mill	Adopted
Done manually	Pressing into shape using machine process	Adopted
Traditional kiln. Unequal distribution of heat.	Use of Hoffmann type continuous firing kiln	Adopted

Here again, a parallel can be seen. The tile industry that came up both in Mangalore and the Malabar region duplicated the products and process of the Basel Mission, albeit, with a time lag. For example, at the time when the Basel Mission factories were using steam power, some of the new units that came up were using bullock power. Use of steam power appear to have been adopted a little later. Secondly, the factories established by the Mission were constantly innovating and bringing out new products. The tile factories that came up were only attempting to duplicate the production process of the Basel Mission factories and remained at a technologically inferior level for some time. There were a few exceptions also.[4] In the case of tile industry also, there was a technological gap. The conduits of transfer of technology were the supervisors or maistries as they were called. These supervisors possessed the knowledge gained from experience. They did not have a theoretical knowledge of the science of ceramics or for that matter weaving. This was a serious limitation. For the reasons stated here, the new tile factories that were established by the local entrepreneurs could not bring out new products.

The Basel Mission industries demonstrated new technologies in two other fields as well. The Mission had set up a Mechanical Establishment in 1875 at Mangalore, about which a mention has been made in Chapter 4. This institution imparted skills from the field of mechanical engineering. The Mechanical Establishment appears to have had a tremendous impact in terms of transfer of technology. As we have mentioned earlier, many of the individuals who worked there or received training seem to have started enterprises of their own. The establishment of large number of foundries and industrial workshops in Mangalore by workers who gained experience in this establishment is often given as an example.[5] Direct rail connectivity between Mangalore and Mumbai, was established only in 1990, with the building of the Konkan Railway. By the turn of the twentieth century, Mumbai had established itself as an industrial centre in modern spinning and weaving industry light engineering and ship building. These industries required skilled man-power in the form of fitters, mechanics and tool cutters. It appears that many of the trained mechanics and fitters who had experience in the Basel Mission Mechanical Establishment sought employment in the industrial units in Mumbai. There was a migration of skilled workers of Mangalore in Mumbai. When road transport started developing in South Canara, the services of mechanics and similar tradesmen trained at the Basel Mission Mechanical Establishment was certainly supportive of the development of the road transport.[6]

The second was a book bindery. This establishment was transferred to the hands of a foreman of the unit, one Mr. Lucas Joshua. This unit became a private enterprise, and a large number of similar units came up in Mangalore itself. While discussing the transfer of technical knowledge from Basel Mission Industries, the impact made by these two institutions will also have to be noted.

Table 7.3: Technologies demonstrated and adopted- Others

Activity	*Traditional technology used*	*Technologies demonstrated by the Basel Mission*	*Adopted or not*
Mechanical Establishment	Non-existent	Trades like fitting, turning welding foundry technology, and machine tool operatin. Skill in machine drawing	Adopted
Book-binding		Typographical printing	Adopted
		Open binding, Calico binding	Adopted

In the case of book-binding, the technology was completely transferred. The book-binding establishment of the Basel Mission was entirely transferred to one Lucas Joshua, a Basel Mission convert who was for many years, the foreman in the factory. Since then, book binderies have flourished in South Canara.

Operating of even a simple machine requires some basic understanding of the working of the machine. In this sense, all the work force in the Basel Mission factories had some understanding of machinery. While the Basel Mission industries imparted basic technical knowledge and operating skills of machinery, wider management perspective, or a higher technical knowledge was not imparted. This adversely affected the vertical mobility of the converts within the industrial hierarchy, with the result that the workers could only expect to rise to the level of supervisors. All the factory managers were Europeans who had the technical qualifications as well as the experience of working in large similar establishments in Germany or Switzerland. The skill component was with the maistries, while the factory managers possessed the technical know-how. This trend appears to be part of a deliberate policy.[7]

Accounting and managerial practices

In addition to the technological knowledge which got transferred across cultures, these were also human resources management and accounting practices which got introduced to the people of Malabar and South Canara as a result of the activities of the Basel Mission. The modern factory organisation itself is the result of the Industrial Revolution. Specifics of such practices were introduced to the region by the Basel Mission industries. Practices including recruitment, training and disciplining of labour force and a higher degree of specialisation of labour, were fundamentally different from the practices of traditional manufacturing.[8] A high degree of professionalisation of jobs as well as greater sensitivity of managers to varied factors, particularly to subtle changes to demand patterns in the market were all hallmarks of this new type of industrial organisation. An alternate form of production relation, aimed at higher productivity and labour which was not caste based emerged as a result of the Mission's activities. The Basel Mission industries, thus, demonstrated a model. We will discuss as to what extent this model could be adopted by the industries that came up in the region.

Max Weber pointed out the use of an appropriate accounting system as an indicator of the capitalist industry. The Basel Mission industries used double entry system of accounting. This system has been in practice in Europe ever since it was introduced by the Medici Bankers of Florence, Italy (Ferguson, 2009). In the industrial activities of the Basel Mission, it is possible to see new approaches to financing. Initially, that is before the setting up of the Industrial Commission, the investment for economic activity was considered as a type of a grant. The activity could succeed or fail. After the setting up of the Industrial Commission with its own treasury, the capital for establishment of industries came to be treated as loans on which interest was charged. Gradually, after the establishment of the joint stock company (Mission Trading Company), considerations like rate of return on alternate investments (referred to as capital budgeting techniques) must have been used. This must have been a factor that prompted the Mission to move from weaving to tiles.

The Basel Mission industries demonstrated an alternate model of raising capital for business. This was a joint stock company, but with a difference. The idea of a joint stock Company with limited liability is as old as the beginning of the seventeenth century. The Dutch East India Company which was established in the year 1600 is supposed to be the first joint stock company in the true sense of the term (Ferguson, 2009). In the case of a joint stock company, the holder of stock is a joint owner, but his liability is limited to the value of the stock that he has purchased. The risk of investment was spread on the one hand, and on the other, the joint stock model enabled raising of large volume of capital from a large number of investors. The joint stock company, as a legal person could also borrow from banks as well.

Summing up

While summing up the discussion on the economic impact of the Basel Mission industries it may be appropriate to examine the impact in terms of the questions raised at the beginning of this chapter.The first issue that is to be discussed relates to the question of the Basel Mission industries addressing itself to the felt need of the society. Did that happen? The answer will naturally have to be on the negative. The objective that the Mission had while setting up industries was not to address to the felt needs of the people but to give gainful employment to converts who had lost their jobs on account of conversion. That was not the felt need of the society, but the felt need of the Mission. The Basel Mission certainly succeeded in addressing that objective. But, in the process, the Mission succeeded in demonstrating new technologies, opened wider market for their goods and created a new type of labour force. The impact has been so strong that if the industrial map of Malabar and South Canara is examined as at the eve of India gaining independence, the dominant lines of manufacture would be tile and weaving, the ones first demonstrated by the Mission. The industrial establishments started in the lines demonstrated by the Mission, also addressed themselves to a wider market. At the time of starting these, it was not the immediate market that these industries intended to cater to.

It would be equally relevant to examine as to the impact the Basel Mission industries had on the traditional weaving and tile making. It has already been argued that at the time of entry of the Basel Mission in the field of hand - loom, the traditional weaving industry was in the decline, struggling for survival. This was due to the large scale import of British mill-made cloth. Our answer would be that the Basel Mission weaving did not compete with the traditional weaving. Most of the market of the Basel Mission produced cloth was outside the state as well as India itself. Yet the type of weaving introduced by the Mission showed a path of expansion that the traditional weaving could take up. The weaving industry that came up in the Kannur region during the inter-war years did exactly that. This industry did not fully replicate the products of the Basel Mission factories, but they could replicate to some extent and even produce some of the products for the local market. The Swadeshi Mundu that the Kannur industry produced is one example. These aspects are discussed in the next chapter. The case of the tile industry was different. Traditional tiles were produced by potters whose major manufacture was the manufacture of cooking vessels. Potters themselves are few in number. They were not capable of responding to the emerging needs for roofing tiles. Like weaving, the tile industry that came up in the South Canara district supplied not only to the district but using the sea born connectivity to Bombay it supplied tiles to outside the country as well.

Thus, we find that the Basel Mission industries showed a path of expansion for the traditional industries. These had three types of demonstration effects. 1. Post-Industrial Revolution technologies that used division of labour as well as power. 2. A new type of market. 3. Method of rising of capital as well as the accounting practises accounting practices followed by them. 4. System of recruiting and disciplining the labour force.

As it would be seen in the next chapter, the modern weaving factories that started coming at Kannur from 1914 were remarkably small, some having as little as 3 or 4 looms. But, handloom weaving is an industry that has the capacity of growing horizontally. A unit can be started even with one or two looms and gradually expand by reinvesting the surplus income into business. Up to a point such growth was possible. Beyond that level, there were issues of working capital to be addressed to. This required some type of institutional finance. As we see in the next chapter, it was first the Marwari money lenders who emigrated to Kannur and later the local and sometimes caste-based banks that addressed to this need. The handloom units had to follow modern accounting practices for availing credit. As far as tile factories are concerned these factories will not be viable if built in very small scale.[9] Therefore the need of initial capital as well as working capital is high. We find that from the beginning of the twentieth century local banks started being established in South Canara. Some of these local banks grew to size and became large national banks. We have examples like the Canara Bank, Syndicate Bank, Canara Banking Corporation (now known as Corporation Bank) and Vijaya Bank. Institutional finance must have been available from these banks to the industrialists establishing tile factories.

Now, we come to the issue of recruitment and disciplining of labour force. The tile factories and modern hand loom industries that came up required a large labour force. Factory labour, particularly in the tile industry is very drudgerous. For the Basel Mission industries recruitment and disciplining of labour force was mainly achieved through the medium of the church. The gentle push of piece rate and some other facilities like subsidized housing, rice donations and availability of money in times of exigencies were sufficient to the Christian labourers at work. But the Mission industries had funds for health insurance for all employees, for which the Mission industries also made contributions. The modern tile and weaving industries appear to have succeeded in attracting labour was more due to push effects. Many who sought employment in these factories mainly during period of depression were desperate people who needed some work for their day to day living. At the same time, congruence of a large number of people in the work place had its own impact. It was in the tile and weaving industries in the Malabar and South Canara districts, that the labour movement first evolved.

Notes

1. Apart from R.C Dutt, earlier nationalist historians like Dadabai Naoroji, Lala Lajpat Rai, Radhakamal Mukherjee contributed to this debate.
2. For a detailed discussion on science and technology, see: Raghaviah, Jayaprakash (2012). "Technology in History", Working Paper Series 27. Centre for Socio Economic and Environmental Studies. Kochi.
3. Victoria Institute of Technology was established in Mumbai in the year 1887. At the time of establishment, the institution had two departments, Sir J J School of Mechanical Engineering and Ripon Textile School. The institution has since grown into a major engineering college in India.
4. A Albuquerque and Sons, a tile factory established as early as 1868 at Mangalore an innovative system of multiple pressing of tiles. This is discussed in Chapter 4.
5. I am indebted to the discussion with Dr.Ratnakar Sadananda, formerly Director of Karnatak Theological Research Institute, Mangalore for this information.
6. Samuel Aaron, a noted industrialist and freedom fighter from Malabar noted in his autobiography that when road transport came to be introduced to Cannanore area, the first entrepreneurs were from South Canara. See :Aaron, Samuel, (1974) *Jeevithasmaranakal* (Malayalam),

7. A reference is made to the unpublished manuscript 'History of Mission Trading Company 1859-1959'. Made available to author by the Union Trading Corporation, the successor company of the Mission Trading Company.
8. For a detailed account of the practices of recruiting and disciplining of labour by the Basel Mission Industries see:Fischer, Rudolph. (1978). *Die Basler Mission Industrie in Indien 1850-1913, Recruitering Und Disziplienung der Arbeiterschoft* (German). Zurich: Verlag Reihe. W.
9. Modern tile factories use Hoffmann type continuously firing kiln in which heat travels through the many chambers, enabling continuous operation.

Early entrepreneurs - Choorakkadan Aaron and his son Samuel Aaron

One of the modern weaving units established in the 1930s in Kannur

Jacquard loom in a Kannur weaving factory

Examples of the Kannur handloom prodcuts

Chapter - 8

Postscript

In this postscript, I will selectively recall some of the themes that are contained in the previous chapters; but at the same time I will also situate the industrialisation process that has taken place in Malabar and South Canara within the macro conditions that have implications for the micro conditions discussed so far.

This book, started with a few enquiries about the appearance of Basel Mission in Malabar and south Canara. This Mission did something that no missionary society had ventured till then. The industrial enterprises that they have modified and new ones introduced have semblance with modern capitalist industries mingled with a variety of Christian worship. Therefore our attempt was to understand the theological base of the society that enabled it to equate industrial work as missionary work. The next issue that was examined related to the entire process of economic activities of the Mission that resulted in establishment of large industries in the Malabar and South Canara districts. Here, the structural differences between the two predominant lines of activities in terms of content of labour, capital and technology were found to be significant for understanding the performance of these industries. The material processes initiated by the Basel Mission were viewed in the background of the industrial evolution of

India during the same period. We have taken a close look at the land and societies of the Malabar and South Canara districts with a view to understand what the enabling and disabling factors were. Institutions like the caste system, joint family system, concentration of wealth in the hands of a few families and lastly the very debilitating nature of the colonial dominance were certainly disabling factors. At the same time, these are the factors that enabled recruitment of the labour force irrespective of the specific castes that they belonged. Thus, it appears that a technology comparable to the post Industrial Revolution technology of Europe and a system of industrial organisation comparable to the capitalist enterprise was demonstrated in the districts of Malabar and South Canara which did not possess adequate preconditions for industrial development. This book addressed the question, what sort of impact introduction of such technology and enterprise could portend for the regions? In the earlier chapters, we have addressed each of the above issues excepting this last one. The proposition that we put forward is that the impact of the industrial and other activities of the Basel Mission became visible after some of the pre conditions changed.

It might be appropriate to look back within a specified time span. Till India gained independence in 1947, the colonial policies continued, albeit, with some changes necessitated by the outbreak of the First World War. The industrial development that took place in Malabar can only be viewed in the background of emerging Independence movement, social legislations that came up, the world depression of 1930 and the outbreak of the Second World War. The period from the outbreak of the First World War to the attainment of Independence for India was significant. To sum up, during this period (39 years to be precise), India continued under British domination, but with some changes in policies that slightly favoured industrial development in India. The impact that the industrial activities of the Mission had on the two districts was revealed in the trajectories of industrial development of Malabar and South Canara districts during the first half of the twentieth century.

With the outbreak of the war, there were substantial changes in the economic and fiscal policies of the government of India. Regarding the Indian economy before the outbreak of the First World War, Amiya Kumar Bagchi makes the following observation:

> The Indian economy before the First World War was an open one with very low import duties on a restricted range of commodities, geared primarily to the U.K. as far as its imports were concerned, but exporting raw materials and food-grains to many parts of the world, and contributing precious dollars to the pool of the sterling area centered on Britain. (Bagchi, 1980, p. 73)

In economic terms, the outbreak of the First World War had far reaching consequences. Till then, the International Gold Standard maintained exchange stability between currencies which were the need of trade.[1] India was earlier part of the silver standard system. In the year 1900, the silver standard that existed in India was substituted by the gold standard. The Currency Commission that recommended such a change, made its recommendation based on the argument that about 80 per cent of India's trade was with the gold standard countries. What eventually emerged was the gold-exchange standard.[2] The change had significance, because a gold exchange standard of any kind is less automatic and fool-proof than the straight gold standard. Rupee being the integral part of internal circulation was given an exchange value of 16d.in sterling and was maintained at that till 1914. In the post-war period, exchange value of the rupee reflected the exchange instability of all world currencies.[3]

Following the outbreak of the war, there was far reaching consequences for the economic and fiscal policies.

The ideal of national self-sufficiency got slowly crystallised as the national economic ideal. The pre-war period was a free trade period with a limited number of import revenue tariffs which was one of the lowest in the world. The post war period witnessed an inversion in this matter. It was one of soaring revenue tariffs with the tariff free list considerably reduced. After 1924, there was a crop of protective duties following the changeover from free trade to 'discriminating protection' (Bagchi, 1980). As in the rest of the world, these tariffs in the world of falling prices were revised periodically.

As the war was in progress and the shipping supply lines were being disrupted, the government of Lord Hardinge, the then Viceroy of India suggested to the British government that a definite and self conscious policy of improving the industrial capabilities of India will have to be pursued after the war. Consequently, three major changes came into being. While the war was still going on, in 1917 the Indian Industrial Commission was set up to examine the possibilities of further industrial development of India. The difficulty of obtaining stores for war and the urgent necessity to produce in India whatever that could be produced for war purpose led to the formation of the Indian Munitions Board also at the same time. The issue of giving the Government some measure of fiscal autonomy was taken up by the British Indian government and resulted in the setting of the Indian Fiscal Commission. The Commission was set up in 1922 and in its first report articulated the issue of 'discriminating protection' to help the growth of industries in India. From all these developments it is clear that the Government of India, in the post-war period, was freer in the matter of regulating its revenue and protection tariffs. The change in this position is very clearly reflected in the fact that while the pre-war period, 1900-14, was one of almost no tariff change, the post-war period was one of repeated and annual changes. Indian protective duties were planned to equalize the prices of indigenous and imported goods rather than to shut out imports.

Industrial promotion in the Madras Presidency

Out of the three presidencies that were directly governed by the British, the Madras Presidency was the least industrialised one at the end of the nineteenth century (Ray, 1979). The Bengal Presidency had the lead in industrial development and there the industrial activities had started in the late eigtheenth century with the activities initiated by the Managing Agencies as well as successful partnerships between Indian and British entrepreneurs.[4]

In 1906, well before the outbreak of the war, a Department of Industrial and Technical Enquiries was established in the Madras Presidency. As Tayabji notes; "What makes the Madras Presidency unique in the pre-World War I days is the early development of an industrial policy centred on a government department specifically for industries" (Tayabji, 1993, p. 13). But the credit for the industrial promotion goes to Alfred Chatterton, the first 'Director of Industrial and Technical Enquiries.' Sir Alfred Chatterton had earlier, established on behalf of the government, a factory at Coimbatore for the manufacture of aluminium utensils. Later, this factory was sold to a European entrepreneur (Bagchi, 1980). The Department of Industrial and Technical Enquiries under the guidance of Alfred Chatterton took up the following activities.

1. Introduced improved method of chrome tanning.
2. Improved method of weaving handloom cloth.
3. Introduction of lift irrigation for using ground water.
4. Digging, with modern boring tools, deeper wells.

There was considerable opposition from the European-dominated Madras Chamber of Commerce to many of the proposals submitted by Chatterton. A remarkable change came when Alfred Chatterton was appointed in the newly formed Department of Industries as its Director.

During the next two decades, this department had the benefit of being headed by, apart from Alfred Chatterton, another deeply committed administrator- Frederick Nicolson. The activities undertaken by the Department falls into several categories as detailed hereunder:

Table 8.1: Activities undertaken for industrial promotion in the Madras Presidency

Sl. No	*Classification of activity*	*Specific activities undertaken*
1.	Industrial research	Appointment of a scientist at the Indian Institute of Science to conduct applied research. Technical officers in the Department of industries encouraged to develop appropriate machinery for various purposes.
		Establishment of Industrial Research Laboratory at Coonoor mainly for research on various types of inks for industrial and commercial purpose.
2.	Creation of skills	Establishment of various training institutions. Sending students for training at home and abroad in new skills. Supporting voluntary institutions churches and missions who are working in the area of skill development. Peripatetic weaving training system.
3.	Starting of model industries	Examples: Kerala Soap Institute, Calicut, Government Pencil Factory at Madras, Glue Factory, Madras, Fish Oil Factory at Calicut, Food Canning and Preservation Factory at Coonoor.
4.	Industrial exhibitions	Industrial exhibitions conducted at different parts of the Presidency. Participated in Imperial Industrial Exhibition at London.
5.	Loans and advances	Loans and advances for starting new industries or for existing industries.
6.	Policy prescription	Preferential store purchase by the government.
7.	Geological surveys	Geological surveys conducted at different parts of the Presidency to identify new minerals.
8.	Technology	Examples are sugar cane crusher machine and introduction of machine for decotorisation of seeds and oil pressing.

Source: Various Reports of the Department of Industries (1923-1939). Government Press, Madras.

A mention must be made about the activities of the Kerala Soap Institute at Calicut as this was a celebrated institution that had considerable impact in the region. A mention has already been made about this institution in Chapter 7. This institution combined in it the role of a training institution on soap manufacturing technology, a research institution endeavoring to make use of various types of oils available in the Malabar district for the manufacture of different types of soaps as well for hydrogenation[5] of various types of oils. The technology of soap manufacture got easily disseminated and soap manufacturing units came up in the Malabar region at cottage industry level.

Another line of manufacture that was promoted by the Department of Industries in Malabar was manufacture of fish oil and fish guano.[6] The Department of Industries established a fish oil factory at Feroke, a few miles from Calicut. The Malabar district, with its long coastline was ideally suited for the extraction of fish oil. The technology was relatively simple. It is not surprising that a large number of fish oil units got established along the coast.

The Department of Industries established a number of institutions during the period for industrial promotion as given under.

Table 8.2: List of institutions established by the Department of Industries during the period 1915-1947

Name of the institution	***Activity***
Government Industrial Institute, Madras	Manufacture of various types of inks and ink powder
Food Preservation Institute	Processing and preservation of horticultural products. Demonstration and dissemination of technologies related to canning and preservation.
Glue Factory, Madras	Manufacture of different types of glues for industrial and commercial purpose.

(*Cont'd...*)

Sugarcane Crushing Factory, Pallapalayam	Demonstration of mechanised sugar crushing. Services made available to a wide variety of customers.
Textile Institute, Madras	Training in new weaving techniques. This institution was involved with development and dissemination of new technologies in hand loom weaving.
Coonoor Silk Farm, Coonoor	Training and research relating to silk filatures.
Government Pencil Factory, Madras	Manufacture of pencils. Supplied pencils to government departments as well as to public.

Source: Various Reports of the Department of Industries, Government Press, Madras.

Without going into great detail about the industrial promotion, an attempt is made to give the overall picture of the activities undertaken by the department of Industries. Basically attempt of the Department was to technically up-grade the industrial activities that was already been done in the Madras Presidency either at cottage level or at small scale industries level. Improvement in chrome tanning leather, improvement in the productivity and quality of handloom production, using of machines including oil engines in crushing of sugar cane are examples. This did not involve heavy capital outlay. The only exception is establishment of the Kerala Soap Institute. Soap manufacture was altogether a new activity that was introduced.

The entire expenditure born by the government of the Madras Presidency for industrial promotion was quite low. It was Rs 9, 03, 057 in the year 1924-25. It increased to Rs.15, 14,643 in 1938-39. (Department of Indistrues,, 1939) Such a limited outlay was not sufficient to create infrastructure for large industries, like investment in the power and transportation sectors as it was done in the native state of Travancore during the 1930s under the leadership of the then Diwan Sri. Ramaswami lyyer.[7]

The activities relating to industrial promotion, particularly the setting of model industries invited opposition from the Madras Chamber of Commerce which was dominated by the European owned firms. Yet, what the Department of Industries could do was mainly due to the dedication and commitment of people like Chatterton and Nicolson who headed the department at different times.

National Movement and its impact

The industrial promotion activities initiated in the Madras Presidency took place along with gaining of momentum of the national movement. The objective of industrial promotion was to create some industrial infrastructure in India so that in the event of outbreak of another war the British colony could hold on its own. The objective of the national movement was to make India a sovereign nation. These very contradictory goals augured well for the development of industries in India from the beginning of the twentieth century. During the inter-war period, changes had started taking place at the political, economic and social level.

The first event at the national level was the Swadeshi Movement. This movement started in Bengal in 1903 and gradually started having a longstanding influence in the praxis of the national movement elsewhere as well. The Swadeshi Movement started as a response against the decision of the British government to partition the Presidency of Bengal to East Bengal and West Bengal. The decision for partition was made publicly known in 1903 and the actual partition took place in the year 1905. The reason that was given by the government was that the Presidency had become too big and unwieldy to govern. The province of Bengal with its capital at Calcutta (now Kolkata) had become a centre of nationalist activities. The division of Bengal was done on communalistic lines. The majority of population in East Bengal was Muslim. This decision for dividing Bengal along communal lines were seen by the nationalists as an attempt by the government to break the emerging national movement. In course of time, the Swadeshi Movement acquired many hues and colours. As Bipan Chandra notes: “From conservative moderation to political extremism, from terrorism to incipient socialism, from petitioning to public speaking to passive resistance and boycott, all had their origin in the movement” (Chandra, 1989, p. 124).

The Swadeshi Movement started with the boycott of foreign products and a preference for products made in India. The burning of foreign cloth, introduction of spinning and weaving of the Khadi cloth as a replacement were part of the Freedom Movement that was appropriated from the Swadeshi Movement. In this process, there was some amount of import substitution. The fact that, products, like Swadeshi Soap, Swadeshi Pen, Swadeshi Paper, had appeared in the market, are examples. In Bengal large and medium industries were established under the inspiration of the Swadeshi Movement.[8]

The market of the Basel Mission industries does not appear to have suffered on account of the Swadeshi Movement. These industries were treated as ‘local’ having been ‘owned’ by a section of Indians. As mentioned earlier in this book, for some time before the outbreak of the War, the Basel Mission weaving industry in Kannur had produced a local garment cloth; a two metre long cloth with a coloured border. This was initially called ‘Mission Mundu’. Later when the Swadeshi Movement started gaining momentum, the modern handloom industries that came up in Kannur started producing a similar product which they called ‘Swadeshi Mundu’.

The next factor was the Freedom Movement. The Indian National Congress that spearheaded the Freedom Movement was founded in 1887. The Swadeshi Movement was started in the year 1903. The most critical event in national movement occurred with the return of Mahatma

Gandhi from South Africa and he assuming leadership of the Indian National Congress. It was Mahatma Gandhi who successfully incorporated the Swadeshi Movement as part of the Freedom Movement.

The Malabar district was vibrant in Freedom Movement. As early as 1916, All India Home Rule League was formed in Malabar. In 1930, Salt Satyagraha was held in Payyanur in Malabar. In 1935, a National Conference of the Indian National Congress was held in Payyanur. It was in this conference which was held under the chairmanship of Jawaharlal Nehru the 'Purna Swaraj' (complete independence) for India was accepted as the goal. Due to the political pressure, the Malabar Tenancy Regulation Act was passed in 1929. This act gave kanom tenants a measure of security of tenure. Malabar Marumakkatayam Act was passed in 1932, allowing dissolution of joint families. This had wide consequences. Earlier, a member of a joint family had right out of the property, for example, claim for subsistence only and not rights to the property. As joint families got partitioned, the adult members could demand their share of property and through this share some capital for their own for productive investments. All these changes occurred in the face of the great depression of the 1930s and the poverty that followed. The poverty that followed provided push effects for the movement of labour to handloom factories that were being established.

Spread and localisation of weaving and tile Industries

As it is was discussed earlier in this chapter, after the outbreak of the First World War, the economic and political environment started undergoing changes. These changes were favorable for the spread of industrial activities. As far as the handloom industry was concerned, with the outbreak of the war, the import of British cloth declined drastically as the shipping and supply lines were disrupted. The local production of mill - cloth like that was produced by firms such as the Buckingham and Karnatic Mills (Binny's), had to be diverted to meet the requirements of war. This coupled with the impact of the boycott of foreign cloth and a preference for locally made cloth created a demand for the local hand-loom cloth. Another factor that helped in the extension of market was the completion of railway lines up to Mangalore. The interest of the government in developing rail connectivity with the Malabar district was mainly strategic. From the year 1836 onwards there were frequent insurrections in the districts (referred in Chapter 3) and this necessitated movement of troops and material. It was the Malappuram region that was affected most. Calicut became connected to Madras (now Chennai) in 1882. The railway line was extended to Mangalore by 1908. Thus, the entire district of Malabar and Mangalore, which was the headquarters of the South Canara district, were connected by rail to the rest of India.

Here, it may be appropriate to examine the trajectories of growth of tile and weaving industries in Malabar and South Canara districts. In both these districts the Basel Mission had established both weaving and tile factories. In Malabar district, the Mission had established four tile factories (Puthiyara, Feroke, Codacal and Olavakkot) and two weaving factories (Calicut and Kannur). Beside, the Mission had set up a dye house at Quilandi near Calicut. In the South Canara district the Mission had three tile factories (Jeppo, Kudroli and Malpe) and one weaving factory at Mangalore, with a branch at Mulki. The weaving factory at Mangalore was small in terms of employment. It was in the Malabar district that the weaving activity got localised and much of this activity was centred on the Kannur region. On the other hand South Canara district got known for the localisation of modern tile industry to the extent that even now the roofing tiles are referred as Mangalore tiles. It may be appropriate to speculate the reasons for such localisation. Our analysis ought to go beyond the obvious reasons. Our enquiries go in three directions.

1. What factors led to the localisation of hand-weaving industry in and around Kannur region and tile industry in the Mangalore regions?
2. Who were the entrepreneurs? From which community did they come predominantly?
3. What were the sources of capital?

The structural differences between the two lines of manufacture weaving and tile are pertinent to be observed. The initial capital requirements of hand-loom weaving units are relatively low. An entrepreneur can start a hand-loom weaving unit with just one or two looms in a thatched shed. Yarn and dyes can be purchased in credit. There are multiple levels of marketing. A new entrant in handloom manufacturing could get sub-contracts from large weaving units. Alternately a new weaving unit can manufacture products exclusively for a niche market. By re-investing the surplus made in business, the unit can expand its activities. In reality many hand-loom industries started as very small units and over a period of time grow into large units. As against this, the tile industry requires large initial capital. These units cannot be conceived as small units as very small sizes are un- economical. The Hoffmann type continuously firing kiln requires a set-up in which at regular intervals some chambers are emptied and some filled in. In this type of kilns, fire travels around different chambers. Before burning the pressed tiles will have to be dried for a number of days to remove moisture. These companies also require higher levels of working capital. Essential raw materials like clay and firewood has to be accumulated in advance to ensure continuous production. There is relatively high proportion of stocks as raw material, semi- finished goods and finished goods. Thus, for a tile factory, fixed capital requirement in terms of building and machinery is high and equally high are the working capital requirements. Without a much higher quantum of initial capital, a new tile unit cannot be established.

Though tile and weaving industries were set up in both the districts of Malabar and South Canara, it was the weaving industry that got localised in the Malabar district, mainly in and around Kannur, and it was the tile industry that got localised in the South Canara district. In order to understand the process of localisation, the events and trajectories that led to the localisation can be examined. We begin with the handloom industry.

The Basel Mission had established two large weaving factories in Malabar district. The first one was at Kannur, (established in 1852) and the second one at Calicut (established in 1859). Each of the factories had employed more than 450 workers. It was at Kannur, that the hand-loom weaving as introduced by the Basel Mission got localised. The circumstances that led to localisation of weaving industry in Kannur is worth noting. The first instance relates to the strike that took place in the factory at Kannur in the year 1900. A reference has already been made about this strike in Chapter 4. The strike took place as a reaction of workers against what they considered as the oppressive working conditions and also the rule of missionaries over congregations. A reference of this labour action has already been made in Chapter 4. Some of the maistries who led the strike also did not join for work, in fact they joined a nascent 'counter church' that was functioning there. Thus, there were a few maistries as well as a number of workers who preferred to opt out of the Basel Mission church as well as the factory as they felt that church and factory were in effect a single entity. This group formed a technically oriented labour force outside the church and became carriers of technology. The first modern weaving units outside the Basel Mission church were established by this group. We have already made references to a few of the new entrepreneurs. One was Thomas Christian, who was originally from Mangalore but came to Kannur for working in the Basel Mission Weaving factory and became a supervisor in the dyeing section. He established the Malabar Handloom Factory, at Kannur in the year 1900. This factory existed till 1930 when it was closed. Another supervisor, Augustine Peter also started his own weaving factory which continued to function though not as successful as Mr. Christian's factory. The most important entrepreneur, who was so successful was Choorakkadan Aaron. We will discuss about this entrepreneur later.

The railway line which had earlier reached up to Calicut in 1882 got extended to Mangalore by 1908. By 1905, it was already extended up to Kannur. The Swadeshi Movement had its reverberations in the Kannur region also. An industrial exhibition was organised at Kannur in 1907 under the inspiration of the Swadeshi Movement. Industrialist and freedom fighter from Kannur, Samuel Aaron who witnessed this exhibition as a boy volunteer reminisced about this exhibition:

> Products from different parts of India exhibited in this exhibition aroused my curiosity. Agricultural and tuber crops that I had never seen before, different types of machines and also cloth, all these were totally new to my eyes. I felt proud to think that these products were made in my country. I wondered why these could not be manufactured here (in Kannur). (Translated by me) (Aaron, 1974)

This industrial exhibition seems to have brought the businessmen from north India in contact with the handloom entrepreneurs from Kannur region. There was a fledgling local handloom industry already in Kannur, wanting to widen their market. After the outbreak of the war in 1914, the Indian mill-cloth production was diverted for war purpose. There was unmet demand for cloth and thus new handloom industries started establishing to meet the demand. The new industry did not necessarily cater to the local market only. It started catering to the all-India market as the local businessmen had already established contacts with the north Indian businessmen. The local handloom industry produced some of the products like curtains, bed-spread, shirting and coatings that the Basel Mission industries produced. Samuel Aaron remembers that by the year 1915, there were as much as 150 weaving units in Kannur region only (Aaron, 1974). Some of these units grew in size. For example Rajarajeshwari Textiles had about 200 looms and the largest one M/S Aaron Spinning and Weaving Mills grew into a composite mill that did spinning and weaving. It also had a power loom section. At one stage this factory employed up to 1400 workers and was the cradle of the trade union movement in the north Malabar region. The broad dimensions employment in the new handloom industries that came up are shown in the following Table. This list is only a sample.

Table 8.3: Names of some handloom industries in and around Kannur region

Name of unit	Location	Employment
Imperial Weaving Establishment	Kannur	50
Vijayaram Weaving Establishment	-do-	105
Gokuldas Jamuna Das Weaving Est.	-do-	56
Victoria Weaving Est.	Kannur	108
Malabar Weaving Est.	Kannur	80
T.B. Brothers and Co Weaving Est.	-do-	85
P.C. Karuvan and Co Weaving Est.	Baliapatam (Kannur Dist)	77
Kallayi Weaving Est.	Calicut	22
Tellicherry Weaving Est.	Tellicherry	22
West Coast Weaving Est.	Kannur	45
Lakshmi Sahayam Weaving Co	-do-	32
Mushim Weaving Co	Baliapatam (Kannur Dist)	45
India Weaving Co	Baliapatam (Kannur Dist)	45

(Cont'd...)

Kulapuram Weaving Co	Kannur	20
Rajarajeshwari Weaving Co	Kannur	22
Azhikode Weaving Co	Kannur	22
Sherodayam Weaving Co	-do-	32
Edakkad Weaving Est.	Kannur	25
National Weaving Est.	Kannur	25
United International Weaving Est.	Kannur	20
Oriental Weaving Est.	-do-	45
K.1. Ahmed Kutty Weaving Est.	-do-	28
Oriental Weaving Est.	-do-	45
Punnakombra Kunhikannan Weaving Est.	Kanathur (Kannur Dist)	20
Parasuram and Son Weaving Est.	Taliparamba (Kannur Dist)	30
Oriental Weaving Establishment	Payyangadi (Kannur Dist)	23
Paul Supriyan's Weaving Est.	Azhiyur (Kannur Dist)	40
K.K. Ramaswami Iyer's Weaving Est.	Vadakara	40

Source: Various Reports of the Department of Industries, Government of the Madras Presidency.

It is interesting to note that in the above list, five units offered employment to more than 75 labourers. We do not intend to argue that the modern handloom industry was established only in and around Kannur. There were units established in Tellicherry which produced only *lungis* which are two metre long cloth with checked designs worn as garment for lower part of the body. Lungi is not much different from the jinghams that the Basel Mission weaving industry produced. Lungi is the national dress in Burma (Myanmar). The handloom units established in Telicherry, for producing lungis, catered exclusively to the Burma market. There were many small modern handloom industries established in various parts of the Malabar and South Canara district. But a visible concentration is seen only in the Kannur region.

Here, we address the next questions. Who were the entrepreneurs who started the handloom units? What was their social background? From where did the capital come from? At this stage, only broad generalisations can be made based on enquiries made. Majority of entrepreneurs seem to have come from two caste backgrounds; Thiyya and Chaliya. As it was stated in Chapter 7, the traditional occupation of the Thiyya community was climbing coconut trees, mending coconut trees and also extraction of toddy from it. They were tenants -at- will and held plots of one or two acres. By the turn of the twentieth century, this community was distressed and seeking upward mobility. Social reformer Sri Narayana Guru advised the community to give up their traditional activity of making toddy which is an alcoholic drink. His message was 'do not make toddy, do not drink toddy.' During the nineteenth century, the Thiyya community made use of opportunities for education offered by the Basel Mission schools. Many reached higher echelons of government. Their route for social mobility was through education. The other route could have been entrepreneurship.

There are a few more aspects relating to the Thiyya community that are pertinent for observation. In north Malabar, the Thiyya community seems to have been a little more independent and prosperous. Many had one or two acres of coconut garden. Though they could be technically evicted from land at any time, by custom they were usually not evicted and they had created some space for themselves in the caste ridden society. Some of them used their surplus funds for money lending. Regarding the availability of capital for the Thiyya community to start new handloom units, one hypothesis is that during the 1920s when soap industry gradually started developing in Bombay (now Mumbai) the price of coconut oil increased resulting in an increase of real income of small coconut farmers. From the year 1918 to the year 1930 the price of coconuts marked a steady increase in Malabar. This is due to the policy of discriminating protection (Dilip Menon, 1994). It was perhaps the surplus income that first got converted into money- lending capital and then to industrial capital. During the 1930s a bank called Kannur Bank was established in Kannur. This was a bank essentially run by the members of the Thiyya community and gave loans to entrepreneurs of that community. Meanwhile during the 1920s there was a migration of Marwari money lenders to Kannur. The emerging small entrepreneurs might have initially borrowed from these money lenders. Some of these Marwari money lenders like Jamnadas Purshothamdas who came to Kannur purely as money lenders, first lent money to the fledgling handloom units. Later they started their own handloom units in Kannur.

The other social group that emerged as entrepreneurs was the Chalia community, whose traditional occupation itself was weaving of a crude type. As we have argued in Chapter 7, in the Malabar and South Canara districts, the traditional handloom weaving industry was in the decline and many of the members of the Chaliya community must have been thrown out of their traditional weaving. Some of them became weavers in the Basel Mission factories and acquired knowledge of modern weaving. Many of them took the prefix 'Nayar' to their name. They were already in the handloom weaving trade and knew the technology and marketing network. The route, some of these members of community took to entrepreneurship was different. Some of them installed one frame loom in their house compound and side by side they had the pit loom.[9] Initially they sub contracted work from the Basel Mission industry as well as other units that were established. Later, these entrepreneurs increased their number of looms by reinvesting their surplus. Some of the early entrepreneurs like A.R. Nayar who started Rajarajeshwari Weaving Mill with 10 or 15 looms grew into size having 250-300 looms apart from outsourcing a good amount of work.[10] It appears that a few of the entrepreneurs came from the Chetty/ Vaniya community who were traditionally sellers of cloth and yarn. A.R. Nayar came from the Vaniya community of traders. It is the knowledge of market that enabled members from this community to become entrepreneurs. It was also a case of trading capital that was converted into industrial capital.

Tile industry in Malabar

Tile industry, also did come up in the Malabar district in a big way. The localisation of this industry was mainly in Feroke. Basel Mission had also established a large factory here in 1908. Most of the factories that were localised in Feroke were located at the banks of the Feroke River and connectivity was the most important factor. The factories at Feroke were large. They used external sources of power. If examined closely, it can be seen that, most of these factories that were established with capital from outside. (Raghaviah, 2011) For example, it was a German national Henkey who established Henke's Tile Works, which was established at the beginning of the twentieth century. This factory was the largest tile factory in south India.[11] The Calicut Tile Factory was established by Mudaliar brothers, Venugopala Mudaliar and Nataraja Mudaliar from Tamil Nadu. They were timber contractors for Kolar Gold Mines. This was a case of contracting capital converted to industrial capital. Yet, establishment of a few large tile factories in the Malabar district were result of powerful demonstration effect of the technologies introduced by the Basel Mission. Each of these entrepreneurs had sourced technology from outside.

Localisation of the tile industry at Mangalore

Well after a century and half since the first tile factory was set up by the Basel Mission at Jeppo near the mouth of the river Nethravathi at Mangalore, the grooved roofing tiles are still referred as Mangalore tiles. This has happened due to the fact that the tile industry got localised at Mangalore. Just as Feroke is located at the mouth of the Feroke River, Mangalore is located at the mouth of the Nethravathi River. The first tile factory was set up by the Basel Mission in 1865. But within three years, by 1868 a Roman Catholic Christian called Alex Albuquerque Pai had set up a tile factory comparable to the Basel Mission factory. That factory continues to function even now.

Kappayya Bhandari established a tile factory soon after. We have names like Raigo Tile Works and Pinto Tile works. By the turn of the twentieth century, according to the Gazateer of South Canara (Sturrock 1906) there were as much as 65 tile factories at Mangalore itself. Raw material for making tiles, clay or feldspar was available aplenty at the banks of the Netravathi river as well as other rivers. As explained in the previous chapter, there were smaller tile manufacturing units in the interior parts of the South Canara district. Therefore, It would be to appropriate to enquire into the social background of entrepreneurs who established these tile factories, also their source of capital. There have not been many studies on these aspects. Therefore only careful speculations can be made. Only rigorous studies undertaken in future can address this question. What is attempted here is to give some tentative explanations from the enquiries made. Our enquiries reveal that most of these entrepreneurs had came from two communities. One was the Gowda Saraswat Brahman community and the second was Roman Catholic Christian community.[12] The Roman Catholic Christians are mostly converts from the Gouda Sarswat Brahmin community whose traditional occupation is trading. A part of the community got converted to Roman Catholic Christianity but retained their caste identity.

The trajectory through which the members of this trading class became land owners is interesting. The tenure mulawarg in the South Canara district is similar to janmom in Malabar but not exactly so. The ownership janmom could not be sold. What was sold and purchased was the kanom tenurship. Janmom was absolute ownership while the case with the South Canara district was different as we have discussed in Chapter 3. In the South Canara district, the ultimate landlord was the State. Agricultural taxation was high in both, the Malabar and South Canara districts. In the Malabar district, the Janmi occasionally sold his kanom right to pay the taxes. He still remained the janmi of the land sold by him. In South Canara, often, the Government confiscated the land of the mulawargdar to realize the tax dues. These lands were sold in auction. Very often, those who purchased these lands were from the Gowda Saraswat Brahmin or Catholic Christian converts from the same class. Some Muslims also purchased these lands. Thus, trading capital came to be invested in land and there came into existence Muslim and Christian mulawargdars in the South Canara district. These land owners could raise capital by mortgaging their land. They could also invest part of the trading capital in industries. To give an example, Alex Albuquerque Pai who started a tile factory in Mangalore was from the Catholic Christian community and was a liquor contractor earlier. It was the trading capital that got converted to industrial capital.

Another group of entrepreneurs appears to have been from the Bunt community. In terms of land ownership, the Bunts were mulaganidars. The tenancy mulagani is roughly equal to the kanom tenure in Malabar. But there is a difference. Due to the interpretation of the kanom tenure by the British as one of mortgage or lease, but not perpetual lease, the kanakkars lost security of tenure even if they had paid their dues to the Janmis. The kanom tenure itself became something that could be terminated at the end of twelve years. The position of mulawargdar in the South Canara district was different. The mulaganidar tenure holder had security of tenure as long as he paid his dues to mulawargdars. (Kurup, 2000) Under such circumstances, the Bunt who is a mulagani tenure holder stood in a position better than that of their equivalent kanakkar in the Malabar district. This also affected the productivity of the Bunt farmer. A Bunt farmer is described as a hard working person who toiled along with the labourers. (Sturrok, 1896) In Malabar, the severe polluting distances prevented the kanakkar in Malabar to work closely with the wetland labourers. Naturally, agriculture in South Canara was more productive in comparison with the Malabar district. It is not surprising that the South Canara district became a rice exporting region as against Malabar which was a rice importing region. It could have been either the agrarian surplus in the hands of the members of this community or land itself that got converted into industrial capital in the case of the entrepreneurs from the Bunt community. To give an example, Shivaram Shetty (Matheus Jesupriya after conversion to Christianity) was a Basel Mission convert from the Bunt community. He worked in the Kudroli Tile Factory under the Basel Mission as a supervisor and later started the Prabhakara Tile Works in Coondapoor in South Canara.

Though the Malabar as well as the South Canara districts were severely taxed by the British, internal conditions in South Canara appear to be more conducive for accumulation of commercial capital. While the Malabar district was referred as the most rack rented district, (see Chapter 3) but the South Canara district is not referred this way. It is not surprising that the South Canara district could develop capital required for investment in tile factories. The fact that five commercial banks that acquired a national stature emerged from the South Canara district[13] from the beginning of the twentieth century supports our argument.

At this point, while concluding this discussion on the localisation of handloom industry in Kannur region in the Malabar district and tile industry in Mangalore in South Canara, it may be appropriate to ask the critical factors that led to the growth of these lines of manufacture. NasirTayabji in his book, "Colonialism, Chemical technology and Industry in South India" (Tayabji, 1993) argued that the industrial growth in south India during the first half of the twentieth century was chemical industries led. He specified the industrial growth that happened in south India as the result of increase in the production of oil seeds in south India. Oil seeds production leads to expansion of production in so many by- products, ranging from glycerin to cattle feed.

This generalisation is not applicable as far as tile or weaving industry is concerned. Increase in the price of coconuts in Malabar from the years 1918 to 1928 achieved due to the policy of discriminating protection certainly had its impact in Malabar through the increase in the disposable incomes of coconut farmers who were mainly from the Thiyya community. This must have helped some of the members of the community to become entrepreneurial. But, more important factor appears to have led to the localisation of the weaving and tile industry in the Malabar and South Canara district was the expansion of market. Market for the handloom and tile industries were certainly beyond the confines of the districts and covered the whole country in the case of handloom and the whole of south and south east Asia in the case of tile industry. However, it may be appropriate to link the growth and localisation of the handloom and tile industries with some other aspects as well. Handloom industry in Kannur and tile industry in Mangalore got localised for quite different reasons as well.

While availability of capital or economic surplus enabled concentration of relatively capital intensive factories in South Canara, it was dearth of capital and availability of human labour that enabled labour intensive factories to bloom in Malabar. By this I do not mean any kind of economic reductionism, but only underscore that economic factors are decisive/critical in the case of material processes and its location specificities. Besides, we have shown how religious ideology had synergetic relation with economic rationality and also how work was internalised as worship. Moreover, we have also explicated how social relations, especially caste relations, enable certain processes and disable others. In fact, it would not be an overstatement if one goes to the extent of stating that material processes are indistinguishably intertwined with other processes other than the former. But then, in the case of regional distribution of factories and regional/locational concentration of specific type of material process, economic factors do play a lead role.

Notes

1. International Gold Standard is "A monetary system under which the basic unit of currency is defined by a stated quantity of gold and which is usually characterised by the coinage and circulation of gold, unrestricted conversion of money into gold and free export and import of gold for setting of international obligations." Retrieved from www.marriam-webster.com on 20-11-2017.
2. "A monetary standard under which gold does not circulate domestically and international debts are settled primarily in currency of nations that maintain gold and especially gold bullion standard". Retrieved from www.marriam-webster.com on 20-11-2017.
3. For a detailed account of the changes in trading pattern in India after 1914, see: Raghaviah, W.B. opp.cit.
4. The firm Carr, Tagore and Company is considered as the first equal participation between the British and Indian entrepreneurs. This venture undertook a number of activities like Hoogly Steamship Co, See Rajat Ray, opp.cit.
5. During hydrogenation, vegetable oils are reacted with hydrogen gas at about 60°C. A nickel catalyst is used to speed up the reaction. The double bonds are converted to single bonds in the reaction. In this way unsaturated fats can be made into saturated fats – they are hardened.
6. Manure that is made from fish.
7. For a detailed account of the industrial promotion in Thiruvithamur see Ram Mohan, K.T. opp.cit.
8. One example is Bengal Chemical Factory established by the nationalist See: Bipan Chandra. *The Rise and Growth of Economic Nationalism in India. Economic policies of Indian National Leadership* 1880-1905. opp.cit p. 131.
9. This information has been told to author by senior members of the weaving community in Kannur.
10. Rajarajewshwari Weaving Mill grew into a large enterprise with 250 looms and having a large export component.

11. Henkeys Tile Works was taken over by the Custodian of Enemy Property and eventually sold to a British firm.
12. I am thankful to Dr.Ratnakar Sadananda who is from the Basel Missison community of South Canara for this pertinent observation.
13. These banks are Canara Bank, Syndicate Bank, Vijaya Bank, Karnataka Bank and Corporation Bank. All these banks are now in the public sector.

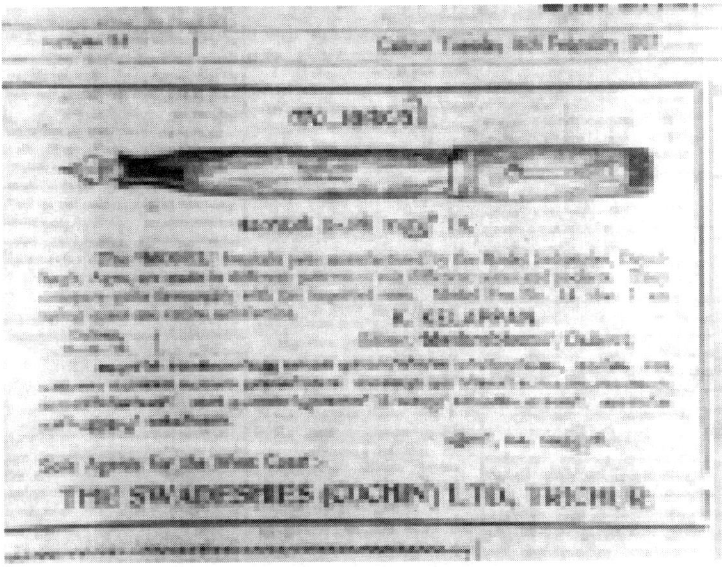

Advertisement of Swareshi products pen (Mathrubhumi 1934)

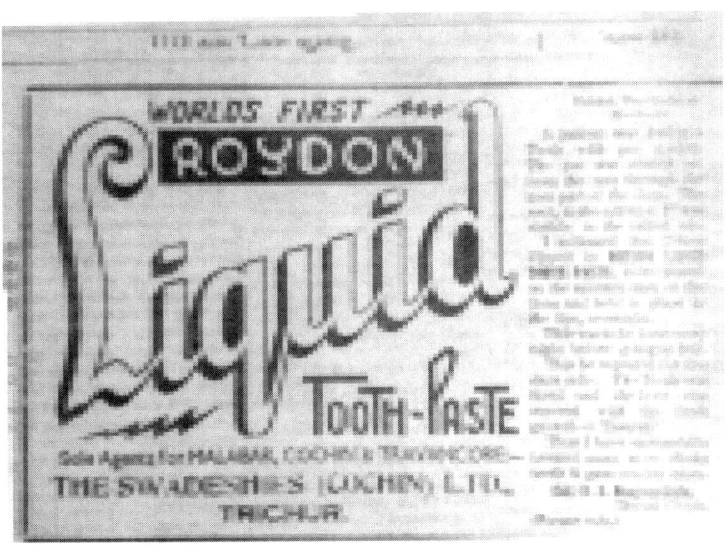

Advertisement of Swareshi products Tooth Paste (Mathrubhumi 1937)

Technology demonstration 1 Pinto Chekku for decoterisation and oil pressing

Technology demonstration - 2 Artesian well

Bibliography

Aaron, S. (1974). *Jeevathasmarnakal* (Malayalam). Kannur: Deshamithran Printing and Publishing.

Agur, C.A. (1903). *Church History of Travancore*. Madras: SPG Press.

Bader, W. (1904). The Beginnings of the Works of Basel Mission in Malabar. *The Harvest Field*, Vol. XV. Mysore: Wesleyan Press.

Bagchi, A. K. (1976). De industrialisation in India in the Nineteenth Century: Some Theoretical Implications. *Journal of Development Studies* Vol. 12 No2.

Bagchi, A. K. (1980). *Private Investment in India 1900-1939*. New Delhi: Orient Longman.

Bagchi, A.K. (1982). *The Political Economy of Underdevelopment.* Cambridge: Cambridge University Press.

Balakrishnan, P.V. (1981). *Matrilineal System in Malabar.* Kannur: Published by the author.

Barboza, D. (1970). *A Description of the Coast of East Africa and Malabar* (Reprint). London: Halukut Society.

Basel Mission. (1856). *Report of the Industrial Commission.* Basel: Basel Mission.

Basel Mission. *Annual Reports of the Basel Evangelical Missionary Society* (Referred in end notes as RBM). Reports published for the years: 1846, 1854, 1856, 1869, 1870, 1871, 1872, 1875, 1876, 1877, 1879, 1881, 1882, 1886, 1887, 1888, 1891, 1893, 1894, 1895, 1896, 1901, 1912, 1913, 1914. Mangalore: Basel Mission Press.

Basler Handels -Gesellschaft 1859-1959 (German), (The Basel Trading Company, official history). Section: Undertaking in India.pp. 250-273. Zurich: Basel Trading Company.

Benjamin, Haggot, Beckhart. (1970). *Banking Systems.* Bombay: Times of India Press.

Bliss, E.M.(Ed). (1890). *Encyclopedia of Missions.* Vol. I. New York.

Boag, G.T. (1931). *The Madras Presidency 1881-1931*. Madras: Government Press.

Buchanan, D. H. (1934). *The Development of Capitalist Enterprises in India.* London: Frank Cass.

Calvin, J. (1939 Reprint). *A Compendium of the Institutes of the Christian Religion.* Board of Christian Education at the Presbyterian Church in the United States of America.

Chadwick, O. (1965). *The Reformation.* London: Holder and Stoughonton.

Chandra, B. (1968). Re-interpretation of nineteenth century economic history. *Indian Economic and Social History Review,* 35-74.

Chandra, B. (1982). *The Rise and Growth of Economic Nationalism in India. Economic policies of Indian National Leadership 1880-1905.* New Delhi: Peoples Publishing House.

Chandra, B. (1989). *India's Struggle for Independence 1857-1947.* New Delhi: Penguin Books.

Chandra, B. (1999) *Essays on Colonialism.* Hyderabad: Orient Longman.

Chirayath, John, Thomas. (1969). *A study of Tile Industry in Kerala.* Trivandrum: Labour and Industrial Bureau.

Chundel, C. (Ed). (1977). *Malayala Patra Charitram* (Malayalam). (History of Newspapers). (Malayalam). Trichur: Centenary Celebration Committee.

Clough, Shepard. B. *Economic Development of Western Civilization.* (1959). New York: McGrew Hill.

Dalton, E. (1963). *The Baker Family in India.* Kottayam: CMS.

Dankar, W. J. (1971). *Profit For the Lord.* Michigan: William B. Eerdmans.

Dasgupta, A. (1967). *Malabar in Asian Trade 1740-1800.* Cambridge: Cambridge University Press.

David, M. D. (1985). Caste Background of Basel Mission Christians. Godwin Shiri (Ed), *Wholeness in Christ.* 164-178. Mangalore: The Karnataka Theological Research Institute.

Desai, M. (1971). Demand for Cotton Textiles in the Nineteenth Century India. *Indian Economic and Social History Review,* Vol. III, 1971.

Dharma Kumar & Tapan Raychaudhury (Eds). (1894). *The Cambridge Economic History of India,* Vol. II. Bombay: Orient Longman.

Dharma Kumar. (1965). *Land and Caste in South India; Agricultural Labour in the Madras Presidency During the Nineteenth Century.* Cambridge: Cambridge University Press.

Dilip Menon, M. (1994). *Caste, Nationalism and Communism in South India. Malabar, 1900-1948.* New Delhi: Cambridge University Press.

Dutt, R. C. (1882 (1960)). *Economic History of India Under Early British Rule.* Nasik: Ministry of Information and Broadcasting, Government of India.

Dutt, R.C. (1990 Reprint). *Economic History of India. Vol. 2, 1902-1904.* New Delhi: Low Priced Publications.

Dykes, J. (1858). *General Manual of Ryotwar Tenure.* Madras: Government of Madras.

Edona, E.J. (1940). *Economic Conditions of Protestant Christians in Malabar with Special Reference to Basel Mission.* Unpublished manuscript.

Eisenstadat. (1967). *The Protestant Ethic and Modernization.* New York: Basic Books.

Elamkulam, Kunjan Pillai, P.N. (1970). *Studies in Kerala History.* Kottayam: National Book Stall.

Ferguson, N. (2009). *The Ascent of Money.* London: Penguin Books.

Ferm, V. (1945). *An Encyclopedia of Religions.* New York: Philosophical Library.

Fieldhouse, D.K. (1981). *Colonialism 1840-1945 An Introduction.* London: Weidenfeld & Nicolson.

Firth.C.B. (1960). *An Introduction to Indian Church History.* Madras: Christian Literature Society.

Fischer, R. (1978). *Die Baseler Missionindustrie In Indien 1850-1913 Rekruiterung und Disziplinierung der Arbeiterschaft (German).* (The Basel Mission Industries in India 1850-1913. Recruiting and Disciplining of the Labour Force). Zurich: Verlag Reihe.

Forrester, B. D. (1980). *Caste and Christianity.* London: Curzon Press.

Frank, Andre Gunder. (1975). *On Capitalism And Underdevelopment.* New York: Oxford University Press.

Frohnmeyer, J. (1893). *Industrial Mission.* Paper presented at the Decennial Missionary Conference, Bombay: Mangalore: Basel Mission Press.

Frykenberg, R.E. (1969). The Ryotwari System and Social Organization in Madras Presidency. Frykenberg (Ed), *Land control and social structure in Indian history.* Madison: University of Wisconcin Press.

Furtado, Sebastian. (1980). *Church Revival- A Study Based on the History and Experience of the Basel Mission Church in South Canara.* Unpublished Bachelor of Divinity thesis. Karnataka Theological Research Institute. Mangalore.

Gadgil, D. (1924 (1942)). *Industrial Evolution of India in Recent Times.* New Delhi: Oxford University Press.

George, Tharian & Tharakan, Michael, P.K. (1986). Penetration of Capital Into Traditional Economy. The case of Tea Plantations in Kerala, 1880-1950. *Studies in History,* Vol. 2, No. 1, New series.

Gopalan Kutty, K. (2007). *Malabar Padanangal.* (Malayalam) (Studies on Malabar). Trivandrum: State Institute of languages.

Government of India. (1911). *Census of India* Vol. XII (Madras), Part I. Madras: Government Press.

Government of India. (1882). *Statistical Atlas of Malabar.* Madras: Government Press.

Government of India. (1920). *Large Industrial Establishments in India.* Calcutta: Government Press.

Government of India. Department of Industries. (1939). *Report of the Department of Industries.* Madras: Government Press.

Government of Madras Presidency. (1892) *Statistical Atlas of Malabar.* Madras: Government Press.

Government of Madras Presidency. (1914). *Supplement to the Statement of Imports and Exports for the Month of January 1914 for Subsidiary Ports of Madras.* Madras: Government Press.

Graeter, B. *Orphanages and Industrial Establishments.* Mangalore: Basel Mission Press.

Habib, Irfan. (1975). Colonisation of the Indian Economy.1757-1900. *Social Scientist,* Vil III, No8. March 1975.

Habib, I. (2006). *Essays in Indian History.* New Delihi: Tulika

Habib, I. (2006). *Indian Economy 1858-1914.* New Delhi: Tulika.

Hardgrave, L. R. Jr. (1968). The Breast Cloth Controversy, Caste Consciousness and Social Change in Travancore. *Indian Economic and Social History Review,* Vol. V No. 2 January 1968.

Heidegger, M. (1977). *The Question Concerning Technology and Other Essays.* New York: Harper and Row.

Hobsbawm, E. (1975). *Age of Capital 1848-1875.* London: Abacus.

Hoffman, H. (1913). *Basel Mission Industries.* Mangalore: Basel Mission Press.

Innes, C. (1908). *Gazateer of Malabar and Anjengo Districts* Vol. I. Madras: Government Press.

Jeffry, Robin (1976). *Decline of the Nayar Dominance: Society and Politics of Travancore 1847-1908.* New Delhi: Vikas.

Jose, N.K. (1979). *Channar Lehala* (Malayalam). Vaikom: Hobby Publications.

Joseph, M.P. (1918). *Principles of Marumakkatayam Law.* Kottayam: CMS.

Kooiman, D. (1884). The Gospel of Coffee: Mission education and employment in nineteenth century Travancore. *Economic and Political Weekly.* Vol. XIX, No. 35, 7th September 1984.

Kurup, K.K.N. (2000). *Land Monopoly and Agrarian System.* Calicut: University of Calicut.

Kurup, K.K.N. (1981). *William Logan, A Study in the Agrarian Relations of Malabar.* Calicut: Sandhya Publications.

Kurup, K.K.N. (1982). *Adhunika Keralam Charithragaveshana Prabhandagal* (Malayalam) (Modern Kerala Research Paper in History). Trivandrum: State Institute of Languages.

Kurup, K.K.N. (1993*). The Legacy of Basel Mission and Hermann Gundert in Malabar.* Calicut: Gundert Anniversery Committee.

Kurup, K.K.N. (2000). *Land Monopoly and Agrarian System in South Kanara with Special Reference to Kasaragod Taluk.* Calicut: University of Calicut.

Leadbeater, S.R. (1993). *Politics of Textiles. Indian Cotton Mill Industry and the Legacy of Swadeshi 1900-1985.* New Delhi: Sage.

Logan, W. (1887). Malabar Manual. Vol. I. Madras: Government Press.

Ludden, D. (1985). Peasant History in South Asia. In *The New Cambridge History of India.* Cambridge: Cambridge University Press.

Malayala Basel Mission Sabhayude Charitra Samshepam. (Malayalam).(1934). (Brief History of Malayala Basel Mission Church). Malayalam. Calicut: Vintage Books.

Margret, F. (2003). *From Contact to Conquest: Transition to British Rule in Malabar.* New Delhi: Oxford University Press.

Martin, H. H. (1988). *Technologies of the Self: A Seminar with Michael Foucault.* Massachusetts: University of Massachusetts.

Marx, K. (1954). *Capital.* Vol. I. Moscow: Progress.

Mathew, K.S. (1979). *Society in Medieval Malabar.* Kottayam: Jaffe Books.

Matsui, Toru. (1968). On the Nineteenth Century Economic History- A Review of Re-interpretation. *Indian Economic and Social History Review.* Vol. V, No. 1, March 1968.

Mehta, S.D. (1953). *Indian Cotton Textile Industry: An Economic Analysis.* Bombay: Textile Association.

Meyer, C.A. (1952*). Land and Society in Malabar.* Bombay: Oxford University Press.

Miller, R. E. (1976). *Mappila Muslims of Kerala: A Study In Islamic Trends.* Madras: Orient Longmans.

Mohan, S. (2015). *Modernity of Slavery.* New Delhi: Oxford University Press.

Morris, D. M. (1968). Towards a Reinterpretation of Nineteenth Century Indian Economic History. *Indian Economic and Social History Review.* Vol. V, No. 2.

Muthanna. (1977). *Karnatka- History, Administration and Culture.* Bangalore: Published by the author.

Namboodiripad, E.M.S. (1967). *Kerala, Yesterday, Today and Tomorrow.* Calcutta: National Book Agency.

Nehru, J. (1956). *Discovery of India.* London: Meridian Books.

Panikkar, G. (1900). *Malabar and its Folk.* New Delhi: Asian Educational Services.

Panikkar, K.N (1990). *Peasant Protests and Revolts in Malabar.* New Delhi: Indian Council of Historical Research, The People's Publishing House.

Pavlov, V.I. (1981). *Historical Premises for India's Transition to Capitalism.* Moscow: Nauka Publishing House.

Pickett, J., Wasckom. (1993). *Christian Mass Movements in India.* New York: Abingdon.

Raghavan, M. (2016). *State Failure And Human Miseries. A Study With Special Focus on Famines in British Malabar.* New Delhi: Kalpaz.

Raghaviah, J. (1990). *Basel Mission Industries in Malabar and South Canara: 1834-1914;A Study of Its Social and Economic Impact.* New Delhi: Gyan Publishing House.

Raghaviah, J. (2011). *Industrial Development of Malabar 1914-1947: Processes and Trajectories* (Unpublished monograph). New Delhi: Indian Council of Social Science Research.

Raghaviah, W.B. (1937). India's Foreign Trade: 1900-1930, And It's Economic Background. Unpublished Ph D thesis submitted to University of Edinburg, U.K.

Ram Mohan, K.T. (1996). *Material Processes and Developmentalism: Interpreting Economic Change in Colonial Tiruvithamkur 1800-1945.*Unpublished Ph D thesis submitted to the University of Kerala.

Ramachandran Nair, A. (1986). *Slavery in Kerala.* New Delhi: Mittal Publications.

Ray, R. (1979*). Industrialisation in India, Growth and conflict in the Private Corporate sector, 1914-47.* New Delhi: Oxford University Press.

Ray, R. (1992). *Entrepreneurship and industry in India, 1800-1947.* New Delhi: Oxford University Press.

Ray, R.K. (1979). *Industrialisation in India, Growth and Conflict in the Private Corporate Sector 1914-1947.* New Delhi: Oxford University Press.

Robson. (1903). The Basel Mission Industries. *The Harvest Field.* No. 14, Mysore: Wesleyan Press.

Roy, T . (2006). *Economic History of India.* New Delhi: Oxford University Press.

Rutherford, T.G. (1933). *Madras District Gazateers, Statistical Appendix for Malabar District.* Madras: Government Press.

Sarkar, S. (1983). *The Colonial Economy. Modern India 1885-1947.* New Delhi: Macmillan.

Schosser, J. (1915). A Short Survey Evangelical Missionary Society of Basel. *Harvest Field,* 373-378.

Shankaran Nambuthiri, K. (2009). *Aryanmarude Kkudiyettaam Keralithil* (Malayalam) (Migration of Aryans to Kerala). II Part Kunnamkulam: Panchangam Press.

Shea, Thomas. W. (1959). Barriers to Development in Traditional Societies, Malabar, A Case Study. *Journal of Economic History,* Vol. XIX, No. 4, December, 1959.

Shiri, G. (2009 (1985)). Caste and Economic Background of Early Basel Mission Christians in South Kanara: A Historical Survey. Shiri G. (Ed). *Wholeness in Christ* (pp. 179-199). Mangalore: The Karnataka Theological Research Institute.

Shirikov, G. (1980*). Industrialisation of India.* New Delhi: Peoples Publishing House.

Sourabh, D. (2010). *After Conversion. Cultural History of Modern India.* New Delhi: Cambridge University Press.

Srinivasan, M. (1977). *A History of Karnataka From Earliest Times to the Present Day.* New Delhi: S. Chand & Co.

Srinivasan, M. (1977). *A History of Karnataka From the Earliest Time to the Present Day.* New Delhi: S.Chand.

Stuart, H. A. (1895). *Madras District Manuals. South Canara* Vol. II. Madras: Government Press.

Sturrock, J. (1984). *Manual of South Canara District.* Vol. I. Madras: Government Press.

Swai, B. (1978). Notes on the Colonial State with Special Reference to Malabar in the 18th and 19th Centuries. *Social Scientist,* Vol. 6, No12, March 1978.

Tawny, R. H. (1975). *Religion And the Rise of Capitalism.* Middlesex: Pelican.

Tayabji, N. (1993). *Colonialism, Chemical Technology and Industry in South India.* Madras: Oxford University Press.

Tharakan, M. (1984). Socio Economic Factors in the Educational Development: Case of Nineteenth Century Travancore. *Economic and political weekly,* Vol. No. 19, No. 45 and 46, 10th and 17th November, 1984.

Tharakan, M. & Issac T.M. (1986). *Sree Narayana Movement in Travancore 1888-1939: A Study of Social Basis and Ideological Reproduction. Trivandrum: Centre For Development Studies,* Working Paper No. 214.

Thomson, G. (1905). *Samuel Hebich of India, the Master Fisher of Man.* Cuttack: Orissa Mission Press.

Thurston, E. (1909). *Castes and Tribes of Southern India.* Madras: Government Press.

Varghese, T.C (1970). *Agrarian Change and Economic Consequences.* Bombay: Allied Publishers.

Walker, Willis. (1976). *A History of Christian Church.* Edinburgh: Clark.

Weber, M. (1976 Reprint). *Protestant Ethic and the Spirit of Capitalism.* London: George Allan & Unwin.

Wigram, R. (1900). *Malabar Law and Custom.* Madras: Higginbotham and Co.

Yesudas, R. N. (1975). *People's Revolt In Travancore.* Trivandrum: Kerala Historical Society.

References

Aaron, S. (1974). *Jeevathasmarnakal (Malayalam).* Cannanore: Deshamithran Printing and Publishing.

Bagchi, A. K. (1976). De-industrialisation in India in the Nineteenth Century: Some Theoretical Implications. *Journal of Development Studies* Vol. 12, No. 2.

Barboza, D. (1970). *A Description of the Coast of East Africa and Malabar (Reprint).* London: Halukut Society.

Basel Mission. (1882). *Report of the Basel Mission.* Mangalore: Basel Mission Press.

Basel Mission. *Annual Reports of the Basel Evangelical Missionary Society* (Hereafter referred as Report of Basel Mission (RBM). Mangalore: Basel Mission Press. Reports referred are noted with the prefix RBM followed by the year of the report. Example: RBM 1854

Basel Trading Company. (1959). *Basler Handels-Gesellschaft 1859-1959* (German), is the unpublished official history of the Basel Trading Company prepared by Union Trading Corporation International, successor company of Mission Trading Company, Basel.

Bliss, E. M. (Ed), (1891. Reprint 2007).*Encyclopedia of Missions Vol. I.* New York: Kessinger Publishing

Chandra, B (1989). *India's Struggle for Independence 1857-1947.* New Delhi: Penguin Books.

Chandra, B. (1968). Reinterpretation of Nineteenth Century Economic History. *Indian Economic and Social History Review,* 35-74.

Chandra, B. (1982). *The Rise and Growth of Economic Nationalism in India. Economic policies of Indian National Leadership 1880-1905.* New Delhi: Peoples Publishing House.

Chundel, Chummar(Ed). (1977). *Malayala Patra Charitram (History of Malayalam Newpapers) (Malayalam).* Trichur: Centenary Celebration Committee.

Dalton, E. (1963). *The Baker Family in India.* Kottayam: CMS Press.

Dankar, W. J. (1971). *Profit for the Lord.* William B. Eerdmans Publishing Company: Michigan.

Dasgupta, A. (1967). *Malabar in Asian Trade 1740-1800.* Cambridge: Cambridge University Press.

David, M. D. (1985). Caste Background of Basel Mission Christians. In G. Shiri (Ed), *Wholeness in Christ* (pp. 164-178). Mangalore: The Karnataka Theological Research Institute.

Dutt, R. C. (1882 (1960)). *Economic History of India Under Early British rule.* Naskik: Ministry of Information and Broadcasting, Government of India.

Dykes, J.W.B. (1858). *General Manual of Ryotwar Tenure.* Madras: Government of Madras.

Ferguson, N. (2009). *The Ascent of Money.* London: Penguin Books.

Firth.C.B. (1960). *An Introduction to Indian Church History.* Madras: Christian Literature Society.

Fischer, R. (1978). *Die Baseler Missinindustrie In Indien 1850-1913 Rekruiterung und Disziplinierung der Arbeiterschaft Arbeiterschaft.* Zurich: Verlag Reihe. (German) (The Basel Mission Industries in India 1850-1913. Recruiting and Disciplining of the Labour Force).

Forrester, B. D. (1980). *Caste and Christianity.* London: Curzon Press.

Frohnmeyer, J. (1893). *Industrial Mission.* Paper presented at the Decennial Missionary Conference, Bombay. Mangalore: Basel Mission Press.

Gadgil, D. (1924 (1942)). *Industrial Evolution of India in Recent Times.* New Delhi: Oxford University Press.

Government of India. (1882). *Statistical Atlas of Malabar.* Madras: Government Press.

Government of Madras Presidency. (1939). *Report of the Department of Industries.* Madras: Government Press.

Graeter, B. *Orphanages and Industrial Establishments.* Mangalore: Basel Mission Press.

Heidegger, M. (1977). *The Question Concerning Technology and Other Essays.* New York: Harper and Row.

Hoffman, H. (1913). *Basel Mission Industries.* Mangalore: Basel Mission Press.

India, G. o. (1911). *Census of India Vol. XII (Madras), Part I.* Madras: Government Press.

Innes, C. (1908). *Gazateer of Malabar and Anjengo Districts Vol. I.* Madras: Government Press.

Issac, T. M. (1986). *Sree Narayana Movement in Travancore 1888-1939. A Study of Social Basis and Ideological Reproduction.* Thiruvananthapuram: Centre For Development Studies. Working Paper No 214.

Kurup, K.K.N. (2000). *Land Monopoly and Agrarian System in South Kanara with Special Reference to Kasaragod Taluk.* Calicut: University of Calicut.

Logan, W. (1882). *Report on Tenancy in Malabar.* Not published.

Logan, W. (1887 (1989)). *Malabar Manual Vol. 1.* Madras: Government Press.

Logan, W. (1887). *Malabar Manual Vol. I.* Madras: Government Press.

Ludden, D. (1985). Peasant History in South Asia. In *The New Cambridge History of India.* Cambridge: Cambridge University Press.

Martin, H. H. (1988). *Technologies of the Self: A Seminar With Michael Foucault.* Massachusetts: University of Massachusetts Press.

Marx, K. *Capital (Reprint 1954) Vol. I.* Moscow: Progress Publishers.

Miller, R. E. (1976). *Mappila Muslims of Kerala: A study In Islamic trends.* Madras: Orient Longmans.

Mohan, S. (2015). *Modernity of Slavery.* New Delhi: Oxford University Press.

Morris, D. M. (1968). Towards a Reinterpretation of Nineteenth Century Indian Economic History. *Indian Economic and Social History Review Vol. V, No2 .*

Nehru, J. (1956). *Discovery of India.* London: Meridian Books.

Panikkar, G. (1983 (1900)). *Malabar And Its Folk.* New Delhi: Asian Educational Services.

Panikkar, K.N. (1990). *Peasant Protests and Revolts in Malabar.* New Delhi: Indian Council of Historical Research, The People's Publishing House.

Ram Mohan, K.T. (1996). *Material Processes and Developmentalism: Interpreting Economic Change in Colonial Thiruvithamur 1800-1945.* Unpublished PhD thesis submitted to University of Kerala, Thiruvananthapuram.

Raghavan, M. (2016). *State Failure and Human Miseries. A Study With Special Focus on Famines in British Malabar.* New Delhi: Kalpaz Publications.

Raghaviah, J. (1990). *Basel Mission Industries in Malabar and South Canara: 1834-1914; A Study of Its Social and Economic Impact.* New Delhi: Gyan Publishing House.

Raghaviah, J. (2011). *Industrial Development of Malabar 1914-1947: Process and Trajectories.* New Delhi: Submitted to Indian Council of Social Science Research.

Raghaviah, W.B. (1937). *India's Foreign Trade 1900-1930 And Its Economic Background.* Unpublished Ph D thesis submitted to the University of Edinburg.

Ray, R. (1979). *Industrialisation in India, Growth and Conflict in the Private Corporate Sector, 1914-47.* New Delhi: Oxford University Press.

Ray, R. (1992). *Entrepreneurship and Industry in India, 1800-1947.* New Delhi: Oxford University Press.

Schosser, J. (1915). A Short Survey of Evangelical Missionary Society of Basel. *Harvest Field,* 373-378.

Shankaran Nambuthiri, K. (2009). *Aryanmarude Kudiyettaam Keralithil (Malayalam) II Part (Migration of Aryans).* Kunnamkulam: Panchangam Press.

Shea, T. W. (1959, December). Barriers to Economic Development in Traditional Societies, Malabar, A Case Study. *Journal of Economic History,* pp. 405-22.

Shiri, G. (2009 (1985)). Caste and economic background of early Basel Mission Christians in South Kanara: a historical survey. In G. (. Shiri, *Wholeness in Christ* (pp. 179-199). Mangalore: The Karnataka Theological Research Institute.

Shirikov, G. (1980). *Industrialisation of India.* New Delhi: People's Publishing House.

Stuart, H. A. (1895). *Madras District Manuals. South Canara* Vol. II. Madras: Government Press.

Sturrock, J. (1906). *Gazateer of South Canara.* Madras : Government Press.

Sturrock. (1896). *Manual of South Canara District.* Madras : Government Press.

Tharakan, M. (1984). Socio Economic Factors in the Educational Development: Case of Nineteenth Century Travancore. *Economic and political weekly,* Vol. No. 19, No. 45 and 46, 10th and 17th November, 1984.

Tawny, R. H. (1975). *Religion And the Rise of Capitalism.* Middlesex: Pelican.

Tayabji, N. (1993). *Colonialism, Chemical Technology and Industry in South India.* Madras: Oxford University Psress.

Varghese, T.C. (1970). *Agrarian Change and Economic Consequences.* Bombay: Allied Publishers.

Weber, M. (1976). *Protestant Ethic And the Rise of Capitalism.* London: George Alan and Unwin.

Wigram, R. (1900). *Malabar Law and Custom.* Madras: Higginbotham and Co.

Yesudas, R. N. (1975). *People's Revolt In Travancore.* Trivandrum: Kerala Historical Society.

Index

A

Abyssinian Twill Cotton, 234
Abyssinian War, 229
Acacia catechu, 125
Afghan War, 229
Africa, 131, 137
African continent, 25
African, 27
Agathi, 76
Agra, 84
Ahmadabad, 127
Alapuzha, 77
Alex Albuquerque Pai, 270, 272
Alfred Chatterton, 255, 256
Alleppy, 77
Amiya Kumar Bagchi, 228, 229, 253
Ananda Rao Kauntinya, 116
Anandapur, 116
Anantapur, 53
Andhra Pradesh, 85
Androth, 76
Anjengo, 76, 231
Arabian Sea, 31, 73, 75, 76, 97, 98
Arabic, 177
Arabs, 78
Arakkal, 76
Architectural Terracotta Ware, 137
Arunachal Pradesh, 224
Aspinwall, 77
Assam, 85, 223, 236
Athineum, 130
Augustine Peter, 148
Australia, 27, 129, 137
Avadh, 84
Ayurveda, 182

B

Balarama Varma, 224
Balaramapuram, 225
Balmatta Hill, 116, 149
Bangalore, 131
Barboza, 134
Barmahal district, 85
Basel German Mission College, 170
Basel Mission Church, 138, 139
Basel Mission factory, 147
Basel Mission Industries temple, 225
Basel Mission Industry, 146
Basel Mission Press, 135
Basel Mission Society, 133
Basel Mission, 137, 161, 162, 171, 173, 176, 194, 197, 233
Basel Missionary, 147
Bay of Bengal, 76

Beethovan, 215
Belthangady, 97
Bengal Presidency, 255
Bengal Province, 148
Bengal, 80, 83, 104, 148, 236
Benjamin Baily, 173, 176
Betgeri, 53
Beypore, 78
Bharathapuzha river, 55
Bhavani, 76
Bhutas, 194
Bible Women, 168
Bible, 175
Bihar, 229
Bijapur, 53
Billava caste, 34, 60, 117, 118
Billava, 60, 173
Billavas, 200
Bipin Chandra, 228, 229, 260
Bohra Muslims, 78
Bohras, 108
Bolma, 117
Bombay (now Mumbai), 127, 244, 268
Bombay Presidency, 53, 74, 98, 184
Borneo, 137
Brahmin, 73, 103
Britain, 52, 149, 229
British Army, 125
British Collector, 149
British Empire, 27, 137
British Government, 121, 149
British Imperial Government, 148
British India, 25, 26
British Indian Empire, 236
British Indian Government, 26, 151
British machine, 231
British Malabar, 82
British Parliament, 52
British rule, 84
Buckingham, 262
Burma (Myanmar), 27, 80, 267
Burma (present Myanmar), 236
Byari, 32, 74

C

C Krishnan Nayar, 269
C. Renz, 174
Calcutta (now Kolkata), 259
Calicut Port, 80
Calicut Tile Factory, 270
Calicut Tile Works, 239
Calicut, 25, 55, 75, 79, 131, 145, 162, 170, 226, 257
Calvin, 47, 49
Calvinism, 46, 48, 50, 67
Calvinist ethos, 202, 203
Calvinist theology, 195
Cameroon, 27, 137, 149
Canada, 44
Canara Bank, 245
Canara Banking Corporation, 245
Canara district, 179
Cannanore, 75, 76
Cape Comorin, 73
Carnatic tradition, 214
Caste system, 32
Catholic Christian community, 272
Catholic Christian, 28, 108, 272
Ceiling Tiles, 137
Central Kerala, 64
Ceylon (now Sri Lanka), 27, 236
Chalia community, 269

Chaliya caste, 123, 269
Chaliya families, 224
Chaliya weavers, 224, 231
Chaliya, 224, 268
Chaliyans, 231
Chaliyas, 79
Chatterton, 259
Chennai, 55
Chennappa Uttangi, 178, 180
Chera Kingdom, 75
Cheruma castes, 60
Cheruma communities, 65
Cheruma, 164
Cheruma/Pulaya caste, 167
Cherumans, 61
Chittoor, 175
Chombala, 126, 212, 213, 215
Choorakkadan Aaron, 265
Christ Jesus, 164
Christanuja Watsa, 180
Christendom, 207
Christian church, 164
Christian convert, 130
Christian culture, 211
Christian Gottlieb Blumhardt, 45
Christian marriage, 210
Christian missionary, 43, 172
Christian religion, 216
Christian Village, 212
Christianity, 31, 43, 59, 116, 163, 200, 203, 210
Christians, 50, 58, 103, 131, 142, 146, 203, 210, 214, 215
Christoff Greiner, 25
Christopher Irion, 174, 215
Church Assembly, 210
Church Missionary Society (CMS), 26, 51, 53, 64, 149, 164
Church of England, 27
Church of South India (CSI), 165
Churches, 46
Clay Flooring Tiles, 137
Cochin State, 76
Cochin, 73, 77
Codacal, 55, 183, 212, 213, 262
Coimbatore area, 79
Coimbatore district, 223
Coimbatore, 76, 224
Colonialism, 273
Commonwealth Trust, 36
Coondapore, 97
Coorg, 53
Count Nikolaus Ludwig Zinzendorf, 44
Culture, 194

D

Dakshina Kannada district, 97
Danish East India Company, 80
Danish mission, 163
Deccan Plateau, 225
Deutsche Christums Gesellschaft (German Christian Society), 45
Devaswam, 86
Devil Worship, 181
Dharwar, 53
Discriminating protection, 254
District Gazeteer, 231
Diwan Sri. Ramaswami lyyer, 258
Dr Gundart, 175
Dr Hermann Gundert, 175
Dr Schneiter, 184

Dr Ambat, 184
Dr Joseph, 184
Dr Liebendorfer, 184
Dr Robert Herman, 185
Dr Wittenberg, 184
Dr D.R. Gadgil, 227
Dr Stokes, 184
Drainage Pipes, 137
Dravidian family, 177
Duarte Barboza, 134
Dutch East India Company, 80
Dutch, 29, 79

E

E.Diaz, 174
East Bengal, 259
East India Company (EIC), 29, 52, 83, 227
Economic Impact, 225
Egypt, 147
Enemy Trading Act, 26, 150
England, 25, 128, 150, 198, 230
Ernad taluk, 92
Eskimos, 44
Eugene Liebendorfer, 183
Europe, 43, 44, 46, 47, 66, 79, 127, 132, 208, 228, 231, 242
European civilization, 43, 194
European Missionaries, 202
European powers, 29, 77
European technology, 195
European, 214, 215
Europeans, 131, 241
Ezhava, 165

F

F. Muller, 174
F.Muller, 176
Ferdinand Kittel, 178, 179
Feroke factories, 138
Feroke River, 270
Feroke, 141, 145, 239, 262
First World War, 25, 26, 30, 35, 36, 128, 137, 148, 150, 153, 252, 253, 261
Flower Pots, 137
Fort Cochin, 76
France, 44, 149
Francis Hamilton Buchanan, 229
Frederick Nicolson, 256
Frederick Ziegler, 178, 180
Freedom Movement, 260, 261
French East India Company, 80
French, 29, 79
Frohnmeyer, 163, 206

G

Gadag Betgeri, 184
Gadgil, 227
Galatians, 164
Galileo Galilei, 197
George Plebst, 135
German missionaries, 25
German national Henkey, 270
German, 66, 208, 215
Germany, 44, 115, 135, 147, 149, 173, 175, 183, 184, 239, 241
Ghana, 137
Girls Orphanage, 213
Gnananiskshepam, 176
Goa, 73
Godfrey Weigle, 178
Gokarnam, 73
Gold Coast (Ghana), 27
Gottleb Prabhakaran Puthanpurakkal, 209

Gottleb, 208
Governor Thomas Munro, 85
Gowda Saraswat Brahman community, 271
Gowda Saraswat Brahmin (GSB), 78, 101, 103, 174
Gowda Saraswat Brahmin lineage, 103
Great War, 150
Gudde, 117
Gujaratis, 78, 108
Guledgud, 53
Gundert, 175
Gurupura, 98

H

Handloom industry, 274
Hanging Wall Tiles, 137
Harvest Festival, 211
Havyek, 101
Hebich, 178
Hermann Gundert, 179
Herrrmann Moegling, 179
Hinduism, 63, 203
Hindustani, 177, 214
Holeya caste, 167
Holeya community, 101
Holy Communion, 210
Hridyaya Darpana, 178
Hubli, 53

I

Illikunnu, 149
Indian Communist Party, 261
Indian Empire, 129
Indian Fiscal Commission, 254
Indian National Congress, 260, 261
Indian Ocean, 75
Industrial Revolution, 122, 198, 202, 228, 230, 237, 242
Iraq, 129
Irfan Habib, 228
Islam, 63
Italian astronomer, 197

J

J. Knobloch, 174
J. Ph. Fabricius, 173
J.M. Fritz, 174
Jaipur, 85
Janmom, 86, 271
Jawaharlal Nehru, 261
Jewish community, 207
Jodhpur, 85
Johan Sebastian, 215
Johannes Frohnmeyer, 170
Johannes Haller, 125
Johannes Lehner, 25
John Calvin, 46
Josef Josenhans, 122
Joseph Muliyil, 177
Jothi Vicharana, 178
Justice Thomas Strange, 90

K

K.K.N. Kurup, 102
Kabini, 76
Kabul War, 179
Kadiki, 117
Kalhatti, 53
Kallai river, 79
Kallu, 200
Kalpeni, 76
Kanakkar, 272
Kanipayyur, 226
Kannada literature, 180
Kannada script, 174
Kannada, 32, 74, 99, 130, 173, 174, 180
Kannur Bank, 268

Kannur district, 224
Kannur factories, 145
Kannur region, 30, 36, 232, 244, 263, 265, 267, 273
Kannur, 75, 126, 128, 133, 146, 147, 148, 212, 226, 232, 235, 238, 245, 265, 269, 274
Kanom tenure, 101, 107, 272
Kanom, 89
Kanyakumari, 73, 163
Kappayya Bhandari, 270
Karkala, 97
Karl Huttinger, 132
Karl Sarasin, 67
Karl, 208
Karnataka State, 74
Karnataka Vidhyavardhaka Sangha, 180
Karnataka, 85, 97, 98, 162
Karnatic Mills, 262
Kasaragod, 97, 100
Katchies, 78
Kathamale, 180
Kavaratti, 76
Kaveri river, 76
Keity valley, 53
Kerala Pazhama, 176
Kerala Soap Institute, 257
Kerala society, 208
Kerala Yuvavu, 175
Kerala, 26, 51, 53, 64, 74, 75, 85, 86, 96, 97, 163, 164, 202, 211, 230, 237
Keralam, 73
Keralopakari, 175
Khalsa, 179
King Zamorin, 75, 85
Kittan, 208
Kittel, 180
Kodungallur, 75
Kolar Gold Mines, 270
Kolathiri, 75
Konkani language, 74
Konkani, 32, 99, 174
Konkanis, 108
Koraga, 99
Kotagiri, 53
Kottayam, 26, 64
Kozhikode, 75, 212
Kraista Sabha Patra, 180
Krishnan, 208
Kristhanuja Watsa, 178
Kuchies, 108
Kudroli factory, 138
Kudroli Tile Factory, 273
Kulakkat, 27, 52
Kumaradhara, 98
Kumbharas, 234
Kurdoli, 145
Kushava community, 234
Kushava potters, 235
Kushava, 134

L

L J. Frohnmeyer, 174
L. Johannes Frohnmeyer, 203
Labrador, 44
Lake Victoria, 137
Lakshadweep islands, 76
Lakshadweep, 97
London Missionary Society (LMS), 26, 51, 149, 164
London Missionary Society, 53, 175
London, 53, 130
Lord Roberts, 125
Loyalty, 195

Lucas Joshua, 130
Luther, 49

M

Macmillan, 130
Madhya Pradesh, 85
Madras (now Chennai), 148, 262
Madras District Manuals, 99
Madras Presidency, 25, 53, 74, 81, 85, 90, 98, 106, 223, 230, 255, 258, 259
Madras Province, 151
Madras University, 130
Mahalwari system, 84
Mahalwari, 83
Mahar, 99
Maharashtra, 85
Mahatma Gandhi, 261
Mahodayapuram, 75
Malabar Christian College, 161, 170, 171
Malabar district, 28, 30, 31, 60, 73, 74, 76, 83, 88, 90, 97, 98, 101, 104, 134, 167, 171, 172, 173, 200, 224, 226, 257, 261, 262, 264, 269, 270, 273
Malabar Handloom Factory, 148, 265
Malabar Marumakkatayam Act, 261
Malabar region, 170, 239
Malabar Tenancy Regulation Act, 261
Malabar, 25, 26, 27, 28, 30, 31, 53, 55, 59, 60, 68, 79, 82, 123, 164, 166, 182, 194, 197, 199, 211, 213, 221, 223, 224, 230, 231, 234, 235, 243, 246, 261, 264, 267, 271, 272
Malappuram region, 262
Malaya, 129
Malayalam, 32, 74, 128, 130, 147, 173, 174, 175, 176, 177, 179, 200, 223
Malayalis, 176
Malayan, 27
Malaysia, 137
Malikhana, 85
Managing Agencies, 255
Mangalore districts, 97
Mangalore region, 30
Mangalore town, 116
Mangalore Well, 270
Mangalore, 36, 53, 55, 74, 77, 97, 125, 131, 132, 133, 135, 145, 149, 170, 180, 186, 226, 232, 239, 240, 262, 265, 270, 273
Mangaluru, 77
Manibar, 75
Manipur, 223
Manjeri, 53
Mappila Muslims, 63
Mappilas (Muslims), 63
Marumakkathayam law, 94
Marwari money, 245
Matheus Jesupriya, 273
Max Muller, 173
Max Weber, 46, 47, 242
Mechanical Establishment, 132, 133, 170, 186, 240
Meghalaya, 223
Melibaria, 75
Mercara, 53, 116, 131
Michel Foucault, 196
Mission Compounds, 212
Mission Trading Company, 132, 133, 134, 150, 151, 242

Mizoram, 224
Moegling, 178
Mogaveera, 99
Mohammedan, 64
Mohammedanism, 64
Mombasa, 137
Moplas, 64
Moravian Mission (Unitas Fractrum), 44
Moravian Mission, 44, 66
Mozart, 215
Mr. Lucas Joshua, 240
Mughal Empire, 83
Mughal governance, 84
Mughal rulers, 84
Muhurtham, 201
Mulagani tenure, 272
Mulaganidar tenure, 272
Mulawarg, 271
Mulewargdars, 272
Mulibar, 75
Mulki, 55, 117, 213
Mumbai, 133, 240
Muslim, 103, 259
Muslims, 28, 63
Mysore rulers, 90
Mysore, 76

N

Nadar community, 165
Nagarcoil, 27
Nagel, 147
Nambudiri caste, 203
Nambuthiri Brahman, 86
Nambuthiri, 208, 226
Nandini, 98
Narayanan, 75, 79
NasirTayabji, 273
National Movement, 259
Natural Philosophy, 197
Navigation, 81
Nayadis, 61
Nayar, 269
Netherlands, 197
Nethravathi river, 11, 135, 270, 271
Netravati, 98
Nichlaus Von Brunn, 45
Nicolson, 259
Nileshwaram, 101
Nilgiri District, 53
Nilgiris, 76
Nirmalan, 209
Non Christians, 142
North Canara district, 53, 97, 184, 225
North Canara, 74
North Karnataka region, 179

O

Olavakkot, 262
Onam festival, 211
Onam, 211, 226
Ootacamand, 131
Oru nazhika dooram, 201

P

Palakkad, 138, 212
Palghat (now Palakkad), 55
Palghat, 55, 141
Panikkar K. N., 63
Panikkar, 61
Parapperi, 213, 215
Parashurama, 73
Paraya communities, 89
Paschimodayam, 176
Patamala, 176
Payyanur, 261
Pazhamchol Mala, 175

Peninsula, 27
Persian, 177
Philosophers, 173
Pietist Movement, 43
Polyphonic music, 215
Portuguese, 29, 177
Pound Sterling, 151
Prakavya Malika, 179
Prof. Morris D Morris, 227
Protestant Christian, 47
Pulaya communities, 89
Pulaya, 164, 165
Pulayas, 165, 203
Punjab, 76
Puritanism, 49
Purna Swaraj, 261
Purshothamdas, 269
Puthiyara, 129, 262
Puthur, 97

R

R.C Dutt, 228
Raghavan, 82
Raghaviah, 232, 235, 270
Raigo Tile Works, 270
Rajarajeshwari Handloom Factory, 232
Rajarajeshwari Textiles, 266
Rajasthan, 85
Rajyasamacharam, 175
Rampur, 76
Red Sea, 75
Refractory Bricks, 137
Reunification under Bismarck, 149
Rhine, 208
Robert Wigram, 94, 95
Roman Catholic Christian community, 271
Roman Catholic Christian, 270
Roman Catholic Christians, 103, 271
Roman law, 89
Romantic Movement, 173
Rudolph Fischer, 59
Russia, 52
Ryotwari system, 84, 85, 89, 90
Ryotwari, 83

S

Salem district, 85
Salt Glazed Stones, 137
Salt Satyagraha, 261
Sambandam relationship, 204
Samuel Aaron, 265, 266
Samuel Hebich, 25, 116
Sanmaranavidya, 175
Schubert, 215
Scottish Company, 77
Second World War, 252
Shakunthalam, 173
Shambhavi, 98
Shankaran Nambuthiri, 226
Shivalli, 101
Shivaram Shetty, 273
Sir Alfred Chatterton, 255
South Africa, 261
South Canara district, 28, 31, 55, 73, 97, 99, 100, 101, 102, 108, 109, 124, 170, 182, 199, 222, 224, 225, 227, 230, 232, 237, 244, 251, 262, 264, 267, 269, 271, 272, 274
South Canara region, 225
South Canara, 25, 26, 27, 28, 30, 31, 32, 34, 53, 68, 74, 80, 83, 86, 133, 134, 166, 174, 180, 185, 194, 197, 199, 200, 211, 221, 223,

226, 230, 234, 235, 243, 245, 264, 270
South Germany, 221
South Kerala, 177
South Mahratta, 53
South Travancore, 27
Spadigam, 209
Sr. Kathe Fritz, 184
Sree Narayana Guru, 166
Sri Anantheshwar temple, 100
Sri Narayana Guru, 166, 268
Srirangapattanam, 29, 53, 98
St. Mathew, 182
St.Martin's Church, 45
Stanes Maylor, 77
Statistical Atlas, 82
Steam engines, 233
Strict church rules, 204
Sukumari, 177
Sumatra, 137
Supriyan, 209
Swadeshi Movement, 30, 35, 36, 148, 149, 259, 260
Swadeshi Mundu, 128, 244, 260
Swadeshi Paper, 260
Swadeshi Pen, 260
Swadeshi Soap, 260
Swiss city, 44
Switzerland, 25, 67, 115, 150, 221, 241
Swizz banking, 67
Swizz Government, 151
Syndicate Bank, 245
Syrian Christians, 26
Syrian Church, 165

T

T .Raychaudhuri, 228, 229
Taliparamba village, 224
Tamil Nadu, 27, 85, 127, 164, 175, 270
Tannur, 64
Tayabji, 255
Technical Enquiries, 255
Technology, 196
Tellicherry (now Thalasseri), 55
Tellicherry Fort, 80
Tellicherry, 126, 149, 226
Terracotta Vases, 137
Tharagambadi, 173
Tharavadu, 209
Thiruvithamkoor (Travancore), 73
Thiruvithamkoor kingdom, 225
Thiruvithamkoor State, 224
Thirvananthapuram, 225
Thiyya caste, 60, 166, 200
Thiyya community, 164, 268, 274
Thiyya, 60, 268
Thiyya/Billava castes, 166
Thiyyan, 65
Thiyyas, 165
Thomas Christian, 148, 265
Thomas Issac, 96
Thomas Strange, 149
Thulu, 74
Tipu Sultan, 29, 53, 98
Tirunelveli, 175
Tiya caste, 208
Tiya, 65
Toru Matsui, 228, 229
Towel Mission, 52
Traditional Chaliya weavers, 230
Traditional Hindu society, 169, 177
Traditional Indian music, 214

Traditional technology, 236
Tranquebar Mission, 163
Travancore, 76
Tuebingin University, 175
Tulu, 130, 174
Tuluvas, 181

U

Uchilla, 117
Udagamandalam, 131
Udipi district, 97
Udipi, 55, 97
Udipiall, 117
Ulia, 208
Uttangi, 180

V

Vadakara, 55, 213
Valarthachan, 174
Vaniyamkulam, 55, 183, 184, 212
Vasco de Gama, 78, 79
Veerashaiva Dharma, 180
Veerashaiva religion, 179
Velichappadu/Theyyam, 200
Vengalam vayal, 118
Verumpattom, 89
Vijaya Bank, 245
Vijayanagara empire, 99
Vishakapatanam, 83
Vishu, 226
Volbrecht Nagel, 147
Vritanda Patrika, 179

W

W. G. Wuerth, 179
Wargdar, 100
Wayanad hills, 77
Wayanad region, 77
Wayanad, 77
Webster's Shikari, 234
West Africa, 149
West Bengal, 259
Western Ghats, 31, 76, 97, 98
Wilhelmina Sukumari Maliekkal, 209
Wilhelmina, 208
William Carey, 172
William Goodacre, 77
William Logan, 92, 93

Y

Yesudas, 51

Z

Zamindari system, 83, 84
Zamindari, 83
Zwingli, 49